THE WEB

The Past, Present *and* Future
of the World Wide Web *by*
its Inventor

TIM BERNERS-LEE

with Mark Fischetti

TEXERE

LONDON · NEW YORK

To Nancy

First published in Great Britain in 1999 by Orion Business

This edition published by
TEXERE Publishing Limited
71-77 Leadenhall Street
London EC3A 3DE
Tel: +44 (0)20 7204 3644
Fax: +44 (0)20 7208 6701
www.texerepublishing.com

A subsidiary of
TEXERE LLC
55 East 52nd Street
New York, NY 10055
Tel: +1 (212) 317 5106
Fax: +1 (212) 317 5178

A CIP catalogue record for this book
is available from the British Library

ISBN 1-58799-018-0

Printed and bound in Great Britain by
Butler & Tanner Ltd, Frome and London

Contents

Acknowledgements

A book is quite a project. I had thought about one from time to time, but did not take it on until Michael Dertouzos introduced me to Mark Fischetti as someone who, unlike me, could actually make it happen without stopping everything for a year. And so began the telling of the story, past, present and future. Without Mark this book would never have been more than an idea and some bits of unordered web pages. I owe great thanks to Mark for applying his ability to find the thread running through my incoherent ramblings and then a way to express it simply.

Mark and I together owe thanks to everyone else involved in this process: to Michael for the idea of doing it and the encouragement, to Ike Williams for organising it, and to Liz Perle at Harper San Francisco for her excruciating honesty and insistence that the book be what it could be. William Patrick played a great role in that step, helping us get it to a form with which we were all happier. We all have to thank Lisa Zuniga and the production team for turning the bits into a book. If you are reading this on paper, then the miracle of coordination must have been pulled off despite all my missed deadlines.

Many of these people mentioned have suffered the shock of meeting my stubbornness at wanting to call the shots over working methods and ways of transferring data. I apologise ... this time: Next time, we'll do it all online!

The book owes its existence indirectly to everyone who has

been involved in making the dream of the Web come true. One of the compromises that is part of a book is that some occasions and activities turn out to be appropriate for showing what life was like and what the principles behind it were. Others, while just as important, don't turn up as examples in the narrative. So the index of the book doesn't serve as a hall of fame, as plenty of people have necessarily been left out or, perhaps even more strangely, it was only practical to describe one particular part of their many contributions. All the consortium team (W3T), present and alumni (listed on the www.w3.org site), are priceless people – working with them is great.

I would like to thank permanently, irrespective of this book, everyone who has taken time out to move the Web onward for the common good. For everyone who has helped, there have also been the managers and family who actively or passively provided encouragement. For me, the managers were Peggie Rimmer and Mike Sendall at CERN, whose wisdom and support have been very special to me.

To thank my immediate family here would suggest I were only thanking them for helping with the book, and for putting up with my strange behaviour during book crises. The support you three have given me is more than that – it is a sense of perspective and reality and fun that underlies everything we do, of which the Web and this has been one, though a notable, part.

Tim Berners-Lee
Cambridge, Massachusetts

Foreword

Weaving the Web is a unique story about a unique innovation, by a unique inventor.

Amid the barrage of information about the World Wide Web, one story stands out – that of the creation and ongoing evolution of this incredible new thing that is surging to encompass the world and become an important and permanent part of our history. This story is unique because it is written by Tim Berners-Lee, who created the Web and is now steering it along exciting future directions. No one else can claim that. And no one else can write this – the true story of the Web.

Tim's innovation is also unique. It has already provided us with a gigantic Information Marketplace, where individuals and organisations buy, sell, and freely exchange information and information services among one another. The press, radio and television never got close; all they can do is spray the same information out from one source towards many destinations. Nor can the letter or the telephone approach the Web's power, because even though those media enable one-on-one exchanges, they are slow and devoid of the computer's ability to display, search, automate and mediate. Remarkably – compared with Gutenberg's press, Bell's telephone, and Marconi's radio – and well before reaching its ultimate form, Berners-Lee's Web has already established its uniqueness.

Thousands of computer scientists had been staring for two

decades at the same two things – hypertext and computer networks. But only Tim conceived of how to put those two elements together to create the Web. What kind of different thinking led him to do that? No doubt the same thinking I see driving him today as he and the World Wide Web Consortium team that he directs strive to define tomorrow's Web. While the rest of the world is happily mouthing the mantra of electronic commerce, he is thinking of the Web as a medium that would codify, in its gigantic distributed information links, human knowledge and understanding.

When I first met Tim, I was surprised by another unique trait of his. As technologists and entrepreneurs were launching or merging companies to exploit the Web, they seemed fixated on one question: 'How can I make the Web mine?' Meanwhile, Tim was asking, 'How can I make the Web yours?' As he and I began planning his arrival at the MIT Laboratory for Computer Science and the launching of the World Wide Web Consortium, his consistent aim was to ensure that the Web would move forward, flourish and remain whole, despite the yanks and pulls of all the companies that seemed bent on controlling it. Six years later, Tim's compass is pointed in exactly the same direction. He has repeatedly said no to all kinds of seductive opportunities if they threatened, in the least, the Web's independence and wholeness, and he remains altruistic and steadfast to his dream. I am convinced that he does so not only from a desire to ensure the Web's future, but also from a wellspring of human decency that I find even more impressive than his technical prowess.

When I first suggested to Tim that he write this book, and having just finished one myself, I was envisioning a series of books from the MIT Laboratory for Computer Science (LCS) in which we would discuss in everyday language our innovations and their social impact. Many people in the world believe that technology is dehumanising us. At LCS, we believe that technology is an inseparable child of humanity and that for true progress to occur, the two must walk hand in hand, with neither one acting as servant to the other. I thought it would be important and interesting for the world to hear from the people who create our future rather than from some sideline futurologists – especially when those innovators are willing to expose the technical forces and societal dreams that drove them to their creations. Tim has risen to this challenge admirably, exposing his deep beliefs about how the Web could evolve and shape our society in ways that are fresh and differ markedly from the common wisdom.

In *Weaving the Web,* Tim Berners-Lee goes beyond laying out the compelling story of the Web: He opens a rare window into the way a unique person invents and nurtures a unique approach that alters the course of humanity.

Michael L. Dertouzos

Michael L. Dertouzos is the director of the MIT Laboratory for Computer Science and the author of the book *What Will Be.*

Enquire Within upon Everything

When I first began tinkering with a software program that eventually gave rise to the idea of the World Wide Web, I named it Enquire, short for *Enquire Within upon Everything*, a musty old book of Victorian advice I noticed as a child in my parents' house outside London. With its title suggestive of magic, the book served as a portal to a world of information, everything from how to remove clothing stains to tips on investing money. Not a perfect analogy for the Web, but a primitive starting point.

What that first bit of Enquire code led me to was something much larger, a vision encompassing the decentralised, organic growth of ideas, technology, and society. The vision I have for the Web is about anything being potentially connected with anything. It is a vision that provides us with new freedom, and allows us to grow faster than we ever could when we were fettered by the hierarchical classification systems into which we bound ourselves. It leaves the entirety of our previous ways of working as just one tool among many. It leaves our previous fears for the future as one set among many. And it brings the workings of society closer to the workings of our minds.

Unlike *Enquire Within upon Everything,* the Web that I have tried to foster is not merely a vein of information to be mined, nor is it just a reference or research tool. Despite the fact that the ubiquitous *www* and *.com* now fuel electronic commerce and stock markets all over the world, this is a large, but just one, part of the Web. Buying books from Amazon.com and stocks from E-trade is not all there is to the Web. Neither is the Web some idealised space where we must remove our shoes, eat only fallen fruit, and eschew commercialisation.

The irony is that in all its various guises – commerce, research, and surfing – the Web is already so much a part of our lives that familiarity has clouded our perception of the Web itself. To understand the Web in the broadest and deepest sense, to fully partake of the vision that I and my colleagues share, one must understand how the Web came to be.

The story of how the Web was created has been told in various books and magazines. Many accounts I've read have been distorted or just plain wrong. The Web resulted from many influences on my mind, half-formed thoughts, disparate conversations and seemingly disconnected experiments. I pieced it together as I pursued my regular work and personal life. I articulated the vision, wrote the first Web programs, and came up with the now pervasive acronyms URL (then UDI), HTTP, HTML, and, of course, World Wide Web. But many other people, most of them unknown, contributed essential ingredients, in much the same almost random fashion. A group of individuals holding a common dream and working together at a distance brought about a great change.

My telling of the real story will show how the Web's evolution and its essence are inextricably linked. Only by understanding

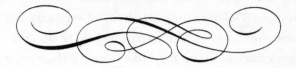

Enquire Within upon Everything

When I first began tinkering with a software program that eventually gave rise to the idea of the World Wide Web, I named it Enquire, short for *Enquire Within upon Everything*, a musty old book of Victorian advice I noticed as a child in my parents' house outside London. With its title suggestive of magic, the book served as a portal to a world of information, everything from how to remove clothing stains to tips on investing money. Not a perfect analogy for the Web, but a primitive starting point.

What that first bit of Enquire code led me to was something much larger, a vision encompassing the decentralised, organic growth of ideas, technology, and society. The vision I have for the Web is about anything being potentially connected with anything. It is a vision that provides us with new freedom, and allows us to grow faster than we ever could when we were fettered by the hierarchical classification systems into which we bound ourselves. It leaves the entirety of our previous ways of working as just one tool among many. It leaves our previous fears for the future as one set among many. And it brings the workings of society closer to the workings of our minds.

Unlike *Enquire Within upon Everything,* the Web that I have tried to foster is not merely a vein of information to be mined, nor is it just a reference or research tool. Despite the fact that the ubiquitous *www* and *.com* now fuel electronic commerce and stock markets all over the world, this is a large, but just one, part of the Web. Buying books from Amazon.com and stocks from E-trade is not all there is to the Web. Neither is the Web some idealised space where we must remove our shoes, eat only fallen fruit, and eschew commercialisation.

The irony is that in all its various guises – commerce, research, and surfing – the Web is already so much a part of our lives that familiarity has clouded our perception of the Web itself. To understand the Web in the broadest and deepest sense, to fully partake of the vision that I and my colleagues share, one must understand how the Web came to be.

The story of how the Web was created has been told in various books and magazines. Many accounts I've read have been distorted or just plain wrong. The Web resulted from many influences on my mind, half-formed thoughts, disparate conversations and seemingly disconnected experiments. I pieced it together as I pursued my regular work and personal life. I articulated the vision, wrote the first Web programs, and came up with the now pervasive acronyms URL (then UDI), HTTP, HTML, and, of course, World Wide Web. But many other people, most of them unknown, contributed essential ingredients, in much the same almost random fashion. A group of individuals holding a common dream and working together at a distance brought about a great change.

My telling of the real story will show how the Web's evolution and its essence are inextricably linked. Only by understanding the Web at this deeper level will people ever truly grasp what its full potential can be.

Journalists have always asked me what the crucial idea was, or what the singular event was, that allowed the Web to exist one day when it hadn't the day before. They are frustrated when I tell them there was no 'Eureka!' moment. It was not like the legendary apple falling on Newton's head to demonstrate the concept of gravity. Inventing the World Wide Web involved my growing realisation that there was a power in arranging ideas in an unconstrained, weblike way. And that awareness came to me through precisely that kind of process. The Web arose as the answer to an open challenge, through the swirling together of influences, ideas and realisations from many sides, until, by the wondrous offices of the human mind, a new concept jelled. It was a process of accretion, not the linear solving of one well-defined problem after another.

I am the son of mathematicians. My mother and father were part of the team that programmed the world's first commercial, stored-program computer, the Manchester University 'Mark I', which was sold by Ferranti Ltd. in the early 1950s. They were full of excitement over the idea that, in principle, a person could program a computer to do most anything. They also knew, however, that computers were good at logical organising and processing, but not random associations. A computer typically keeps information in rigid hierarchies and matrices, whereas the human mind has the special ability to link random bits of data. When I smell coffee, strong and stale, I may find myself again in a small room over a corner coffeehouse in Oxford. My brain makes a link, and instantly transports me there.

One day when I came home from high school, I found my

father working on a speech for Basil de Ferranti. He was reading books on the brain, looking for clues about how to make a computer intuitive, able to complete connections as the brain did. We discussed the point; then my father went on to his speech and I went on to my homework. But the idea stayed with me that computers could become much more powerful if they could be programmed to link otherwise unconnected information.

This challenge stayed on my mind throughout my studies at Queen's College at Oxford University, where I graduated in 1976 with a degree in physics. It remained in the background when I built my own computer with an early microprocessor, an old television and a soldering iron, as well as during the few years I spent as a software engineer with Plessey Telecommunications and with D.G. Nash Ltd.

Then, in 1980, I took a brief software consulting job with CERN,* the famous European Particle Physics Laboratory in Geneva. That's where I wrote Enquire, my first weblike program. I wrote it in my spare time and for my personal use, and for no loftier reason than to help me remember the connections among the various people, computers and projects at the lab. Still, the larger vision had taken firm root in my consciousness.

Suppose all the information stored on computers everywhere were linked, I thought. *Suppose I could program my computer to create a space in which anything could be linked to anything.* All the bits of information in every computer at CERN, and on

---

* The name CERN derives from the name of the international council (Conseil Européen pour la Recherche Nucléaire), which originally started the lab. The council no longer exists, and 'Nuclear' no longer describes the physics done there, so, while the name CERN has stuck, it is not regarded as an acronym.

the planet, would be available to me and to anyone else. There would be a single, global information space.

Once a bit of information in that space was labelled with an address, I could tell my computer to get it. By being able to reference anything with equal ease, a computer could represent associations between things that might seem unrelated but somehow did, in fact, share a relationship. A web of information would form.

Computers might not find the solutions to our problems, but they would be able to do the bulk of the legwork required, assisting our human minds in intuitively finding ways through the maze. The added excitement was that computers also could follow and analyse the tentative connective relationships that defined much of our society's workings, unveiling entirely new ways to see our world. A system able to do that would be a fantastic thing for managers, for social scientists and, ultimately, for everyone.

Unbeknownst to me at that early stage in my thinking, several people had hit upon similar concepts, which were never implemented. Vannevar Bush, one-time dean of engineering at MIT, became head of the US Office of Scientific Research and Development during World War II and oversaw development of the first atomic bomb. In a 1945 article in the *Atlantic Monthly* titled 'As We May Think', he wrote about a photo-electro-mechanical machine called the Memex, which could, by a process of binary coding, photocells, and instant photography, make and follow cross-references among microfilm documents.

Ted Nelson, a professional visionary, wrote in 1965 of 'Literary Machines', computers that would enable people to write and publish in a new, nonlinear format, which he called *hypertext*. Hypertext was 'nonsequential' text, in which a reader was not constrained to read in any particular order, but could follow links and delve into the original document from a short quotation. Ted described a futuristic project, Xanadu, in which all the world's information could be published in hypertext. For example, if you were reading this book in hypertext, you would be able to follow a link from my reference to Xanadu to further details of that project. In Ted's vision, every quotation would have been a link back to its source, allowing original authors to be compensated by a very small amount each time the quotation was read. He had the dream of a utopian society in which all information could be shared among people who communicated as equals. He struggled for years to find funding for his project, but success eluded him.

Doug Engelbart, a researcher at Stanford University, demonstrated a collaborative workspace called NLS (oN Line System) in the 1960s. Doug's vision was for people to use hypertext as a tool for group work. In order to help himself steer his computer's cursor across the screen and select hypertext links with ease, Doug invented a wooden block with sensors and a ball underneath, and called it a *mouse*. In a now-famous video, which I didn't see until 1994, Doug demonstrated using electronic mail and hypertext links with great agility with his homemade mouse in his right hand and a five-key piano-chord keyboard in his left hand. The idea was that a person could interface with the machine in a very close, natural way. Unfortunately, just like Bush and Nelson, Doug was too far ahead of his time. The personal computer revolution, which would make Engelbart's 'mouse' as familiar as the pencil, would not come along for another fifteen years. With that revolution, the idea of hypertext would percolate into software design.

Of course, the next great development in the quest for global connectivity was the Internet, a general communications infrastructure that links computers together, on top of which the Web rides. The advances by Donald Davis, by Paul Barran and by Vint Cerf, Bob Kahn and colleagues had already happened in the 1970s, but were only just becoming pervasive.

I happened to come along with time, and the right interest and inclination, after hypertext and the Internet had come of age. The task left to me was to marry them together.

CHAPTER 2

Tangles, Links and Webs

The research centre for particle physics known as CERN straddles the French–Swiss border near the city of Geneva. Nestled under the limestone escarpments of the Jura mountains, ten minutes from the ski slopes, with Lac Leman below and Mont Blanc above, it offered unique research opportunities, and the area offered a very pleasant place to live.

Engineers and scientists arrived at CERN from all over the world to investigate the most fundamental properties of matter. Using enormous machines, they would accelerate tiny nuclear particles through a series of tubes that, though only a few inches wide, ran for several kilometres within a mammoth circular underground tunnel. Researcheres would rev up the particles to extremely high energies, then allow them to collide. For an unimaginably brief instant, new particles might be made, then lost. The trick was to record the high-energy debris from the cataclysm as it careered into one of two detectors inside the tunnel, each the size of a house, jammed full of electronics.

Research on this scale was so expensive that it had to involve collaborations among many nations. Visiting scientists would run their experiments at CERN, then go back to their home institutions to study their data. Though it was a central facility, CERN was really an extended community of people who had relatively little common authority. The scientists brought a wide variety of computers, software and procedures with them, and, although they came from different cultures and spoke different languages, they managed to find a way to work together because of their shared interest in particle physics and their desire to see a huge project succeed. It was a tremendously creative environment.

In 1980, CERN was in the process of replacing the control system for two of its particle accelerators. The work was getting behind, and CERN needed help. I had, by chance, been consulting elsewhere in Switzerland when my friend and colleague Kevin Rogers called from England to suggest we apply.

Upon our arrival to be interviewed, Kevin and I were given a tour, and soon found ourselves on a catwalk, looking out and over what looked like a huge, chaotic factory floor. This vast experimental hall was filled with smaller experiments, obscured by the concrete-block walls between them, hastily built to cut down radiation. Continuing along the catwalk, we came to the control room. Inside were racks and racks of computing hardware, with no lighting except for the glow of the many indicator lamps and dials. It was an electronic engineer's paradise, with columns of oscilloscopes and power supplies and sequencing equipment, most of it built specially for or by CERN.

At this time, a computer was still a sort of shrine to which scientists and engineers made pilgrimage. Most people at CERN did not have computer terminals in their offices; they had to come to a central facility, such as the terminal room next to the control room, to actually program a computer system. Kevin and I would soon join a team of people who would ultimately bring about the demise of that control room. Alas, the racks of glowing electronics would be slowly dismantled and replaced by a boring oval of computer consoles, run by much more powerful software.

The big challenge for contract programmers was to try to understand the systems, both human and computer, that ran this fantastic playground. Much of the crucial information existed only in people's heads. We learned the most in conversations at coffee at tables strategically placed at the intersection of two corridors. I would be introduced to people plucked out of the flow of unknown faces, and I would have to remember who they were and which piece of equipment or software they had designed. The weblike structure of CERN made the job even harder. Of the ten thousand people in the CERN phone book, only five thousand or so were at CERN at any given time, and only three thousand or so were actually salaried staff. Many of the others had a desk, and visited from their home institutions only every now and again.

To house contractors who suddenly arrived in a panic to help advance some project or other, management had erected portable cabins on the top of a grassy hill on the grounds. Groups of us would discuss our ideas at lunch overlooking the Swiss vineyards, or as we walked down the long flight of concrete steps from the hill to the experiment hall and terminal room to do the programming. I filled in the odd moments when I wasn't officially working on the Proton Synchrotron Booster by tinkering with my play program, the one I called Enquire. Once I had a rough version, I began to use it to keep track of who had written which program, which program ran on which machine, who was part of which project. Informal discussions at CERN would invariably be accompanied by diagrams of circles and arrows scribbled on napkins and envelopes, because it was a natural way to show relationships between people and equipment. I wrote a four-page manual for Enquire that talked about circles and arrows, and how useful it was to use their equivalent in a computer program.

In Enquire, I could type in a page of information about a person, a device or a program. Each page was a 'node' in the program, a little like an index card. The only way to create a new node was to make a link from an old node. The links from and to a node would show up as a numbered list at the bottom of each page, much like the list of references at the end of an academic paper. The only way of finding information was browsing from the start page.

I liked Enquire and made good use of it because it stored information without using structures like matrices or trees. The human mind uses these organising structures all the time, but can also break out of them and make intuitive leaps across the boundaries – those coveted random associations. Once I discovered such connections, Enquire could at least store them. As I expanded Enquire, I kept a vigilant focus on maintaining the connections I was making. The program was such that I could enter a new piece of knowledge only if I linked it to an existing one. For every link, I had to describe what the relationship was. For example, if a page about Joe was linked to a page about a program, I had to state whether Joe made the program, used it or whatever. Once told that Joe used a program, Enquire would also know, when displaying information about the program, that it was used by Joe. The links worked both ways.

Enquire ran on the group's software development computer. It did not run across a network, and certainly not the Internet, which would not be used at CERN for years to come. Enquire had two types of links: an 'internal' link from one page (node) to another in a file, and an 'external' link that could jump between files. The distinction was critical. An internal link would appear on both nodes. An external link went in only one direction. This was important because, if many people who were making such a link to one page could impose a return link, that one page would have thousands of links on it that the page's owner might not want to bother to store. Furthermore, if an external link went in both directions, then changing both files would involve storing the same information in two places, which is almost always asking for trouble: the files would inevitably get out of step.

Eventually, I compiled a database of people and a database of software modules, but then my consulting time was up. When I left CERN, I didn't take the Enquire source code with me. I had written it in the programming language Pascal, which was common, but it ran on the proprietary Norsk Data SYNTRAN-III operating system, which was pretty obscure. I gave the eight-inch floppy disk to a systems manager, and explained that it was a program for keeping track of information. I said he was welcome to use it if he wanted. The program was later given to a student, who said he liked the way it was written – written as a Pascal program should be written. The few people who saw it thought it was a nice idea, but no one used it. Eventually, the disk was lost, and with it the original Enquire.

When I left CERN I rejoined a former colleague, John Poole. Two years earlier, Kevin and I had been working with John, trying to upgrade the then-boring dot-matrix printers with the then-revolutionary microprocessor so they could print fancy graphics. The three of us would sit in the front room of John's house, his golden Labrador nestled under one of the desks, and try to perfect the design. We had succeeded in just a few months, but John hadn't had the money to go on paying us a salary, and wouldn't until he'd sold the product. That's when we had started looking for contract work and ended up at CERN.

After I had been at CERN for six months, John called. 'Why don't you come back?' he said. 'I've sold the product, we've got a contract. Now we need some software support for it.' John had incorporated as Image Computer Systems, and Kevin and I returned to help.

We rewrote all the motor controls to optimise the movement of the print head so it was fast. It could also print Arabic, draw three-dimensional pictures, and give the effect of preprinted stationery while using less expensive paper. We wrote our own markup language in which documents were prepared, and the printer could also handle input codes of much more expensive typesetting machines. We could change not only fonts but almost any aspect of the printer's behaviour.

The business went well, but the technology we were working with was limited to what we could put into printers. I felt I needed a change from living in Britain, and I remembered that CERN had a fellowship programme. In the spring of 1983 I decided to apply, arriving eventually in September 1984. As a gift upon my departure from Image, John gave me a Compaq personal computer. It was touted as one of the first 'portable' computers, but it looked more like a sewing machine, more 'luggable' than portable. With my new PC, and the freshness that comes with change, I wrote in my spare time another play program, called Tangle. I wanted to continue to explore the ideas about connections that were evolving in my head.

In an extreme view, the world can be seen as only connections, nothing else. We think of a dictionary as the repository of meaning, but it defines words only in terms of other words. I liked the idea that a piece of information is really defined only by what it's related to, and how it's related. There really is little else to meaning. The structure is everything. There are billions of neurons in our brains, but what are neurons? Just cells. The brain has no knowledge until connections are made between neurons. All that we know, all that we are, comes from the way our neurons are connected.

Computers store information as sequences of characters, so meaning for them is certainly in the connections among characters. In Tangle, if a certain sequence of characters recurred, it would create a node that represented the sequence. Whenever the same sequence occurred again, instead of repeating it, Tangle just put a reference to the original node. As more phrases were stored as nodes, and more pointers pointed to them, a series of connections formed.

The philosophy was: what matters is in the connections. It isn't the letters, it's the way they're strung together into words. It isn't the words, it's the way they're strung together into phrases. It isn't the phrases, it's the way they're strung together into a document. I imagined putting in an encyclopedia this way, then asking Tangle a question. The question would be broken down into nodes, which would then refer to wherever the same nodes appeared in the encyclopedia. The resulting tangle would contain all the relevant answers.

I tested Tangle by putting in the phrase 'How much wood would a woodchuck chuck?' The machine thought for a bit and encoded my phrase in what was a very complex, tangled data structure. But when I asked it to regurgitate what it had encoded, it would follow through all the nodes and output again, 'How much wood would a woodchuck chuck?' I was feeling pretty confident, so I tried it on 'How much wood would a woodchuck chuck if a woodchuck could chuck wood?' It thought for a while, encoded it, and when I asked it to decode, it replied: 'How much wood would a woodchuck chuck if a woodchuck chuck wood chuck chuck chuck wood wood chuck chuck chuck …' and it went on for ever. The mess it had made was so horrendously difficult to debug that I never touched it again. That was the end of Tangle – but not the end of my desire to represent the connective aspect of information.

I had always stayed on the boundary of hardware and software, which was an important and exciting place to be, especially as software more and more took over hardware functions. When I applied for my fellowship to CERN, I specified that I wanted a job that would allow me to work on both, and suggested three places there where I could do that. I ended up being hired to work with 'data acquisition and control', the group responsible for capturing and processing the results of experiments. Peggie Rimmer, who hired me, would also teach me, as it turned out, a lot about writing standards, which was to come in useful later on. I was in a position to see more of CERN this time, to appreciate more of its complexity. Although attached to a central computing division, my group worked with the individual experiment groups, each of which was a diverse mixture of scientists from all over the world.

By 1984, CERN had grown. A new accelerator, the Large Electron Positron accelerator, was being built. Its tunnel, twenty-seven kilometres in circumference, ran from a hundred metres under CERN to, at its farthest point, three hundred metres beneath the foothills of the Jura mountains, dwarfing other accelerators. The computing diversity had increased too. A newer generation of computers, operating systems and programming languages was being used, as were a variety of networking protocols to link the many computers that sustained the big experiments. Machines from IBM, Digital Equipment Corp. (DEC), Control Data – we had them all, as well as the new choice of PC or Mac in personal computers and different word processors.

People brought their machines and customs with them, and everyone else just had to do their best to accommodate them. Then teams went back home and, scattered as they were across time zones and languages, still had to collaborate. In all this connected diversity, CERN was a microcosm of the rest of the world, though several years ahead in time.

I wrote a general 'remote procedure call' (RPC) program to facilitate communication between all the computers and networks. With RPC, a programmer could write a program on one sort of computer but let it call procedures on other computers, even if they ran on different operating systems or computer languages. The RPC tools would work over whatever network or cable there happened to be available in a given case.

I began to re-create Enquire on the Compaq. I wrote the program so that it would run on both the luggable Compaq and the VAX minicomputer made by DEC that I was using at CERN.

I didn't do such a good job the second time around, though: I just programmed in the internal links, and never got around to writing the code for the external links. This meant that each web was limited to the notes that would fit in one file: no link could connect those closed worlds. The debilitating nature of this restriction was an important lesson.

It was clear to me that there was a need for something like Enquire at CERN. In addition to keeping track of relationships between all the people, experiments and machines, I wanted to access different kinds of information, such as a researcher's technical papers, the manuals for different software modules, minutes of meetings, hastily scribbled notes and so on. Furthermore, I found myself answering the same questions asked frequently of me by different people. It would be so much easier if everyone could just read my database.

What I was looking for fell under the general category of *documentation systems* – software that allows documents to be stored and later retrieved. This was a dubious arena, however. I had seen numerous developers arrive at CERN to tout systems that 'helped' people organise information. They'd say, 'To use this system all you have to do is divide all your documents into four categories' or 'You just have to save your data as a WordWonderful document' or whatever. I saw one protagonist after the next shot down in flames by indignant researchers because the developers were forcing them to reorganise their work to fit the system. I would have to create a system with common rules that would be acceptable to everyone. This meant as close as possible to no rules at all.

This notion seemed impossible until I realised that the diversity of different computer systems and networks could be a rich resource – something to be represented, not a problem to be eradicated. The model I chose for my minimalist system was hypertext.

My vision was to somehow combine Enquire's external links with hypertext and the interconnection schemes I had developed for RPC. An Enquire program capable of external hypertext links was the difference between imprisonment and freedom, dark and light. New webs could be made to bind different computers together, and all new systems would be able to break out and reference others. Plus, anyone browsing could instantly add a new node connected by a new link.

The system had to have one other fundamental property: it had to be completely decentralised. That would be the only way a new person somewhere could start to use it without asking for access from anyone else. And that would be the only way the system could scale, so that as more people used it, it wouldn't get bogged down. This was good Internet-style engineering, but most systems still depended on some central node to which everything had to be connected – and whose capacity eventually limited the growth of the system as a whole. I wanted the act of adding a new link to be trivial; if it was, then a web of links could spread evenly across the globe.

So long as I didn't introduce some central link database, everything would scale nicely. There would be no special nodes, no special links. Any node would be able to link to any other node. This would give the system the flexibility that was needed, and be the key to a universal system. The abstract document space it implied could contain every single item of information accessible over networks – and all the structure and linkages between them.

Hypertext would be most powerful if it could conceivably point to absolutely anything. Every node, document – whatever it was called – would be fundamentally equivalent in some way. Each would have an address by which it could be referenced. They would all exist together in the same space – the information space.

By late 1988 I was plotting to somehow get a hypertext system going. I talked to my boss, Mike Sendall. He said it sounded like a reasonable idea, but that I should write up a proposal. A proposal? I had no idea what went into a 'proposal' at CERN. I thought, however, that I'd never get the go-ahead to develop a hypertext documentation system unless it was approved as a formal project. I thought hard about how to get the excitement of this idea into a form that would convince people at CERN.

Although Enquire provided a way to link documents and databases, and hypertext provided a common format in which to display them, there was still the problem of getting different computers with different operating systems to communicate with each other. Ben Segal, one of my mentors in the RPC project, had worked in the States and had seen the Internet. He had since become a lone evangelist for using it at CERN. He went around pointing out how Unix and the Internet were binding universities and labs together all over America, but he met a lot of resistance. The Internet was nearly invisible in Europe because people there were pursuing a separate set of network protocols being designed and promoted by the International Standards Organisation (ISO). Whether because of the 'not invented here' feeling, or for honest technical reasons, the Europeans were

trying to design their own international network by committee.

I was intrigued with the Internet, though. The Internet is a very general communications infrastructure that links computers together. Before the Internet, computers were connected using dedicated cables from one to another. A software program on one computer would communicate over the cable with a software program on another computer, and send information such as a file or a program. This was originally done so that the very expensive early computers in a lab or company could be used from different sites. Clearly, though, one computer could not be linked to more than a few others, because it would need tens or hundreds of cables running from it.

The solution was to communicate indirectly over a network. The Internet is a network of networks. Its essence, though, is a set of standardised *protocols* – conventions by which computers send data to each other. The data are transmitted over various carriers, such as telephone lines, cable TV wires and satellite channels. The data can be text, an e-mail message, a sound, an image, a software program – whatever. When a computer is ready to send its data, it uses special software to break the data into packets that will conform to two Internet protocols that govern how the packets will be shipped: IP (Internet Protocol) and TCP (Transmission Control Protocol). The software labels each packet with a unique number. It sends the packets out over the phone or cable wire, and the receiving computer uses its own Internet software to put them back together according to the labels.

The Internet was up and running by the 1970s, but transferring information was too much of a hassle for a noncomputer expert. One would run one program to connect to another computer, and then in conversation (in a different language) with

the other computer, run a different program to access the information. Even when data had been transferred back to one's own computer, decoding it might be impossible.

Then electronic mail was invented. E-mail allowed messages to be sent from one person to another, but it did not form a space in which information could permanently exist and be referred to. Messages were transient. (When the World Wide Web arrived, riding on top of the Internet, it would give information a place to persist.)

CERN's lateness in adopting the Internet was surprising, because the laboratory had been very much on the leading edge of networking and telecommunications. It had developed CERNnet, its own home-brewed network, for lack of commercial networks. It had its own e-mail systems. And it was at the forefront of gatewaying between different proprietary mail and file systems.

I was interested in the Internet because it could perhaps provide a bridge between different computer operating systems and networks. CERN was a technological melting pot. Many physicists were used to Digital's VAX/VMS operating system and the DECnet communications protocols. Others preferred the growing rival operating system, Unix, which used Internet protocols. Every time a new experiment got started there would be battles over whether to use VAX/VMS and DECnet, or Unix and TCP/IP. I was beginning to favour TCP/IP myself, because TCP was starting to become available for the VMS, too. It didn't initially come from Digital, but from Wollongong University in Australia.

Using TCP/IP would mean that the Unix world, which already used TCP/IP, would be satisfied, and those in the VAX world could get into the Unix world, too. Finally, there was a way for

both contenders to communicate with each other, by picking up a piece of TCP/IP software from Wollongong. I became so convinced about TCP/IP's significance that I added code to the RPC system so that it could communicate using TCP/IP, and created an addressing system for it that identified each remote service in the RPC system. That's when the Internet came into my life.

For the proposal, I also had to think out what was needed to scale up Enquire into a global system. I would have to sell this project as a documentation system – a perceived need at CERN – and not as a hypertext system, which just sounded too precious. But if this system was going to go up as a way of accessing information across a network, it would be in competition with other documentation systems at CERN. Having seen prior systems shot down, I knew the key would be to emphasise that it would let each person retain his own organisational style and software on his computer.

The system needed a simple way for people to represent links in their documents, and to navigate across links. There was a model in online 'help' programs: if there was an instruction or tool on the screen that a user didn't understand, he just clicked on it and more information would appear. This approach was called *hot buttons*, a derivative of Ted Nelson's hypertext that had subsequently been used by Apple Computer's 'Hypercard' and later in some way by many point-and-click help systems. I decided that on my system, if someone wanted to put a hypertext link into a piece of text, the words noting the link would be highlighted in some way on the screen. If a viewer clicked on a highlighted word, the system would take him to that link.

∞

The pieces were starting to fall into place. TCP/IP would be the network protocol of choice. For 'marketing' purposes, I would propose the system as one that would work over DECnet, with the added benefit that someone could communicate over the Internet, too. That left one hole: for people to communicate and share documents, they had to have a simple, but common, addressing scheme so they'd know how to address their files and others would know how to request files. I adapted the simple RPC addressing scheme.

In presenting my argument to an experiment group, I would note that they typically have different kinds of documented information – a 'help' program, a telephone book, a conference information system, a remote library system – and they would be looking for ways to create a consistent master system. They would have three choices: (1) design yet another documentation scheme that is supposedly better than all the ones that have been attempted before it; (2) use one of the existing schemes and make do with its limitations; or (3) realise that all these remote systems have something in common. I would tell them, 'We can create a common base for communication while allowing each system to maintain its individuality. That's what this proposal is about, and global hypertext is what will allow you to do it. All you have to do is make up an address for each document or screen in your system and the rest is easy.'

In March 1989 I took the leap to write a proposal. I wanted to explain that generality was the essence of a web of information. On the other hand, I felt I had to make the system seem to be something that could happen only at CERN. I was excited about escaping from the straitjacket of hierarchical documentation systems, but I didn't want the people responsible for any hierarchical system to throw rocks at me. I had to show how this system could integrate very disparate things, so I provided an example of an Internet newsgroup message, and a page from my old Enquire program.

I was brash enough to look forward to having a web of data that could be processed by machine. I said:

> An intriguing possibility, given a large hypertext database with typed links, is that it allows some degree of automatic analysis. [...] Imagine making a large three-dimensional model, with people represented by little spheres, and strings between people who have something in common at work.
>
> Now imagine picking up the structure and shaking it, until you make some sense of the tangle: perhaps you see tightly knit groups in some places, and in some places weak areas of communication spanned by only a few people. Perhaps a linked information system will allow us to see the real structure of the organisation in which we work.

Little did I know that PhD theses would later be done on such topics.

For all the decisions about which technical points to include in the proposal or exclude, and which social advantages of the system to emphasise, I was rather light on the project management details:

> I imagine that two people for six to twelve months would be sufficient for this phase of the project. A second phase would almost certainly involve some programming in order to set up a real system at CERN on many machines. An important part of this, discussed below, is the integration of a hypertext system with existing data, so as to provide a universal system, and to achieve critical usefulness at an early stage.

By the end of March 1989 I had given the proposal to Mike Sendall; to his boss, David Williams; and to a few others. I gave it to people at a central committee that oversaw the co-ordination of computers at CERN. But there was no forum from which I could command a response. Nothing happened.

While I waited for some kind of feedback, I tested the idea in conversation, and reactions varied. CERN people moved through a number of overlapping loyalties, perhaps one to CERN, one to an experiment, to an idea, to a way of doing things, to their original institute ... not to mention the set of Macintosh users or IBM/PC users. Another reason for the lacklustre response was that CERN was a physics lab. There were committees to decide on appropriate experiments, because that was the stock-in-trade, but information technology was very much a means to an end, with less structure to address it. The situation was worse for very general ideas such as global hypertext. Even the RPC project, also an exercise in generality, had little formal support from within CERN, but it had enough support among different groups that I could keep it going.

In the meantime, I got more involved with the Internet, and read up on hypertext. That's when I became more convinced than ever that I was on the right track. By early 1990 I still had received no reactions to the proposal. I reformatted it and put a new date on it: May 1990. I gave it to David Williams again, and again it got shelved.

During this time I was talking to Mike Sendall about buying a new kind of personal computer called the NeXT. NeXT Inc. had recently been started by Steve Jobs, who had founded Apple Computer and brought the first intuitive point-and-click, folders interface to personal computers. Ben Segal, our Unix and Internet evangelist, had mentioned that the NeXT machine had a lot of intriguing features that might help us. I asked Mike to let me buy one (bringing Ben with me for weight), and he agreed. He also said, 'Once you get the machine, why not try programming your hypertext thing on it?' I thought I saw a twinkle in his eye.

By buying a NeXT, we could justify my working on my long-delayed hypertext project as an experiment in using the NeXT operating system and development environment. I immediately began to think of a name for my nascent project. I was looking for words that would suggest its new kind of structure. Mesh, or Information Mesh, was one idea (used in the diagram in the proposal), but it sounded a little too much like *mess*. I thought of Mine of Information, or MOI, but *moi* in French means 'me', and that was too egocentric. An alternative was The Information Mine, but that acronym, TIM, was even more egocentric! Besides, the idea of a mine wasn't quite right, because it didn't encompass the idea of something global, or of hypertext, and it represented only getting information out – not putting it in.

I was also looking for a characteristic acronym. I decided that I would start every program involved in this system with 'HT', for hypertext. Then another name came up as a simple way of representing global hypertext. This name was used in mathematics as one way to denote a collection of nodes and links in which any node can be linked to any other. The name reflected the distributed nature of the people and computers that the system could link. It offered the promise of a potentially global system.

Friends at CERN gave me a hard time, saying it would never take off – especially since it yielded an acronym that was nine syllables long when spoken. Nonetheless, I decided to forge ahead. I would call my system the 'World Wide Web'.

CHAPTER 3

info.cern.ch

While it seemed to be uphill work convincing anyone at CERN that global hypertext was exciting, one person was an immediate convert: Robert Cailliau.

Though now the Electronics and Computing for Physics division, by coincidence Robert had in 1980 been in the same Proton Synchotron division as I, and had in fact written the text-formatting program I had used to print the Enquire manual. A Flemish-speaking Belgian, Robert had had the lifelong frustration of people insisting on addressing him in French. After taking an engineering degree at the University of Ghent he picked up a master's at the University of Michigan, an experience that left him with an accent in English that is impossible to identify. Indeed, it became a parlour game for newcomers at CERN to try to guess exactly where he was from.

A dapper dresser who methodically schedules haircuts according to the solstice and equinox, Robert is fastidious in all things. He is the kind of engineer who can be driven mad by the incompatibility of power plugs. No wonder, then, that he would be attracted to a solution to computer incompatibility, especially coming with a simple user interface. In the marriage of hypertext and the Internet, Robert was best man.

Robert's real gift was enthusiasm, translated into a genius for spreading the gospel. While I sat down to begin to write the Web's code, Robert, whose office was a several-minute walk away, put his energy into making the WWW project happen at CERN. He rewrote a new proposal in terms he felt would have more effect. A CERN veteran since 1973, he lobbied among his wide network of friends throughout the organisation. He looked for student helpers, money, machines, and office space.

By the time Mike Sendall approved my purchase of the NeXT machine, I had already gone to the hypertext industry looking for products onto which we could piggyback the Web. At CERN there was a 'Buy, don't build' credo about acquiring new technology. There were several commercial hypertext editors, and I thought we could just add some Internet code so the hypertext documents could be sent over the Internet. I thought the companies engaged in the then fringe field of hypertext products would immediately grasp the possibilities of the Web. Unfortunately, their reaction was quite the opposite. 'Nope,' they said. 'Too complicated.'

Undaunted, in September 1990 Robert and I went to the European Conference on Hypertext Technology (ECHT) at Versailles to pitch the idea. The conference exhibition was small, but there were a number of products on display, such as a multimedia training manual for repairing a car.

I approached Ian Ritchie and the folks from Owl Ltd, which had a product called Guide. In Peter Brown's original Guide work at the University of Southampton, when a user clicked on a hypertext link, the new document would be inserted right there

in place. The version now commercialised by Owl looked aston-
ishingly like what I had envisioned for a Web browser – the
program that would open and display documents, and prefer-
ably let people edit them, too. All that was missing was the
Internet. *They've already done the difficult bit!* I thought, so I
tried to persuade them to add an Internet connection. They were
friendly enough, but they, too, were unconvinced.

I got the same response from others at the conference. It
seemed that explaining the vision of the Web to people was
exceedingly difficult without a Web browser in hand. People had
to be able to grasp the Web in full, which meant imagining a
whole world populated with Web sites and browsers. They had
to sense the abstract information space that the Web could bring
into being. It was a lot to ask.

The hypertext community may also have been slightly demor-
alised. Their small conference was not getting any bigger, and
no one was sure where the field was headed. The lack of commercial successes had perhaps left a certain cynicism about bright
new ideas that could change the world.

Another possibility I saw was called Dynatext, and was from
Electronic Book Technology, a company in Rhode Island started
by Andy Van Dam, the Brown University researcher who had
coined the term *electronic book*. I thought the company's software could be turned into a Web browser/editor rather easily.
However, like many hypertext products at the time, it was built
around the idea that a book had to be 'compiled' (like a computer program) to convert it from the form in which it was
written to a form in which it could be displayed efficiently.
Accustomed to this cumbersome multistep process, the EBT
people could not take me seriously when I suggested that the

original coded language could be sent across the Web and displayed instantly on the screen.

They also insisted on a central link database to ensure that there were no broken links. Their vision was limited to sending text that was fixed and consistent – in this case, whole books. I was looking at a living world of hypertext, in which all the pages would be constantly changing. It was a huge philosophical gap. Letting go of that need for consistency was a crucial design step that would allow the Web to scale. But it simply wasn't the way things were done.

Despite the 'Buy, don't build' credo, I came to the conclusion that I was going to have to create the Web on my own. In October 1990 I began writing code for the Web on my new computer. The NeXT interface was beautiful, smooth, and consistent. It had great flexibility, and other features that would not be seen on PCs till later, such as voice e-mail, and a built-in synthesizer. It also had software to create a hypertext program. Its failure to take over the industry, despite all these advantages, became for me a cautionary tale. NeXT required users to accept all these innovations at once – too much.

My first objective was to write the Web *client* – the program that would allow the creation, browsing and editing of hypertext pages. It would look basically like a word processor, and the tools on the NeXT's system, called NeXTStep, were ideal for the task. I could create an application, menus and windows easily, just dragging and dropping them into place with a mouse. The meat of it was creating the actual hypertext window. Here I had some coding to do, but I had a starting place, and soon had a fully functional word processor complete with multiple fonts, paragraph and character formatting, even a spellchecker! No delay of gratification here. Already I could see what the system would look like.

I still had to find a way to turn text into hypertext, though. This required being able to distinguish text that was a link from text that wasn't. I delved into the files that defined the internal workings of the text editor, and happily found a spare thirty-two-bit piece of memory, which the developers of NeXT had graciously left open for future use by tinkerers like me. I was able to use the spare space as a pointer from each span of text to the address for any hypertext link. With this, hypertext was easy. I was then able to rapidly write the code for the Hypertext Transfer Protocol (HTTP), the language computers would use to communicate over the Internet, and the Universal Resource Identifier (URI), the scheme for document addresses.

By mid-November I had a client program – a point-and-click browser/editor – which I just called *WorldWideWeb*. By December it was working with the Hypertext Markup Language (HTML) I had written, which describes how to format pages containing hypertext links. The browser would decode URIs, and let me read, write, or edit Web pages in HTML. It could browse the Web using HTTP, though it could save documents only into the local computer system, not over the Internet.

I also wrote the first Web *server* – the software that holds Web pages on a portion of a computer and allows others to access them. Like the first client, the server actually ran on my desktop NeXT machine. Though the server was formally known as nxoc01.cern.ch (NeXT, Online Controls, 1), I registered an alias for it – 'info.cern.ch.' – with the CERN computer system folks. That way, the server would not be tied by its address to my NeXT machine; if I ever moved its contents to another machine, all the hypertext links pointing to it could find it. I started the first global hypertext Web page, on the info.cern.ch server, with my own notes, specifications of HTTP, URI, and HTML, and all the project-related information.

At this point Robert bought his own NeXT machine and we revelled in being able to put our ideas into practice: communication through shared hypertext.

At long last I could demonstrate what the Web would look like. But it worked on only one platform, and an uncommon one at that – the NeXT. The HTTP server was also fairly crude. There was a long way to go, and we needed help. Ben Segal, who had a knack for adjusting staffing levels behind the scenes, spotted a young intern named Nicola Pellow. A maths student from England, Nicola was working for a colleague in a neighbouring building but didn't have enough to do.

A big incentive for putting a document on the Web was that anyone else in the world could find it. But who would bother to install a client if there wasn't exciting information already on the Web? Getting out of this chicken-and-egg situation was the task before us. We wanted to be able to say that if something was on the Web, then anyone could have access to it – not just anyone with a NeXT!

When I gave talks, I showed a diagram with machines of all types connected to the Internet, from mainframes with simple character-orientated terminals through PCs, Macs and more. To make this possible, I urged Nicola to give the Web the best browser she could, but to assume as little as possible, so this interface could work on any kind of computer. The least common denominator we could assume among all different types of computers was that they all had some sort of keyboard input device, and they all could produce ASCII (plain text) characters. The browser would have to be so basic that it could even work on a paper Teletype. We therefore called it a *line-mode* browser, because Teletype machines and the earliest computer terminals operated by displaying text one line at a time.

Meanwhile, I took one quick step that would demonstrate the concept of the Web as a universal, all-encompassing space. I programmed the browser so it could follow links not only to files on HTTP servers, but also to Internet news articles and newsgroups. These were not transmitted in the Web's HTTP protocol, but in an Internet protocol called FTP (file transfer protocol). With this move, Internet newsgroups and articles were suddenly available as hypertext pages. In one fell swoop, a huge amount of the information that was already on the Internet was available on the Web.

The *WorldWideWeb* browser/editor was working on my machine and Robert's, communicating over the Internet with the info.cern.ch server by Christmas Day 1990.

As significant an event as this was, I wasn't that keyed up about it, only because my wife and I were expecting our first child, due Christmas Eve. As fate would have it, she waited a few extra days. We drove to the hospital during a New Year's Eve storm and our daughter was born the next day. As amazing as it would be to see the Web develop, it would never compare to seeing the development of our child.

∞

As the new year unfolded, Robert and I encouraged people in the Computing and Networking division to try the system. They didn't seem to see how it would be useful. This created a great tension among us about how to deploy our limited resources. Should we be evangelising the Web? Should we develop it further on the NeXT? Should we reprogram it for the Mac or the PC or Unix, because even though the NeXT was an efficient machine, few other people had them? After all, what good was a 'worldwide' web if there were only a few users? Should we tailor the Web to the high-energy physics community, so they'd have a tool that was theirs and would support it, since CERN was paying our salaries? Or should we generalise the Web and really address the global community, at the risk of being personally disenfranchised by CERN?

Trading in the NeXT for some ordinary computer would have been like trading in a favourite sports car for some truck. More important, the Web was already written for it. If we switched to developing the Web for the much more widely used PC, acceptance might be quicker, but the point was to get people to try what we already had. If we stopped progress and went back to redoing things for the PC, we might never get it done. I decided to stick with the NeXT.

As for the application, my gut told me I had to pursue my larger vision of creating a global system. My head reminded me, however, that to attract resources I also needed a good, visible reason to be doing this at CERN. I was not employed by CERN to create the Web. At any moment some higher-up could have questioned how I was spending my time, and while it was unusual to stop people at CERN from following their own ideas, my informal project could have been ended. However, it was too

soon to try to sell the Web as the ultimate documentation system that would allow all of CERN's documents, within and between projects, to be linked and accessible, especially given the history of so many failed documentation systems. Small but quantifiable steps seemed in order. Our first target, humble beginning that it was, would be the CERN telephone book.

The phone book existed as a database on CERN's ageing mainframe. Bernd Pollermann, who maintained it and all sorts of other central information, was charged with somehow providing all this material to each and every user on his or her favourite system. I managed to persuade Bernd that the Web was just what he needed to make life a great deal simpler. If he created a server, I told him, we would get the browsers on to everyone's desktop. He went for it.

I got my simple server to run on the mainframe, then chopped it in two, so that the essential HTTP-related Internet functions were done by my code (written in C language) and Bernd was left to write the rest of the server in his favourite language, 'REXX.' To make all the documents available, he just had to learn to write HTML, which took him only a few afternoons. Soon the entire world of his search engines, databases and catalogues was available as hypertext.

That brought us back to the search for a browser. We started porting Nicola's line-mode client on to all sorts of machines, from mainframes through Unix workstations to plain DOS for the PC. These were not great showcases for what the Web should look like, but we established that no matter what machine someone was on, he would have access to the Web. This was a big step, but it was achieved at some sacrifice in that we decided not to take the time to develop the line-mode browser as an editor.

Simply being able to read documents was good enough to bootstrap the process. It justified Bernd's time in getting his servers up. But it left people thinking of the Web as a medium in which a few published and most browsed. My vision was a system in which sharing what you knew or thought should be as easy as learning what someone else knew.

Mundane as it was, this first presentation of the Web was, in a curious way, a killer application. Many people had workstations, with one window permanently logged on to the mainframe just to be able look up phone numbers. We showed our new system around CERN and people accepted it, though most of them didn't understand why a simple ad hoc program for getting phone numbers wouldn't have done just as well.

Of course, we didn't want our brainchild with all its tremendous potential to be locked in at this rather pedestrian level. To broaden the Web's horizons, I set about giving talks and conducting demonstrations. So that people could see something 'out there on the Web' other than the phone book, and to practise what we preached, Robert and I continued to document the project in hypertext on info.cern.ch.

What we had accomplished so far was based on a few key principles learned through hard experience. The idea of universality was key: the basic revelation was that one information space could include them all, giving huge power and consistency. Many of the technical decisions arose from that. The need to encode the name or address of every information object in one URI string was apparent. The need to make all documents in some way 'equal' was also essential. The system should not constrain the user; a person should be able to link with equal ease to any document wherever it happened to be stored.

This was a greater revelation than it seemed, because hypertext systems had been limited works. They existed as databases on a floppy disk or a CD-ROM, with internal links between their files. For the Web, the external link is what would allow it to actually become 'worldwide'. The important design element would be to ensure that when two groups had started to use the Web completely independently at different institutions, a person in one group could create a link to a document from the other with only a small incremental effort, and without having to merge the two document databases or even have access to the other system. If everyone on the Web could do this, then a single hypertext link could lead to an enormous, unbounded world.

CHAPTER 4

Protocols: Simple Rules
for Global Systems

Incompatibility between computers had always been a huge pain in everyone's side, at CERN and anywhere else where they were used. CERN had all these big computers from different manufacturers, and various personal computers, too. The real world of high-energy physics was one of incompatible networks, disk formats, data formats, and character-encoding schemes, which made any attempt to transfer information between computers generally impossible. The computers simply could not communicate with each other. The Web's existence would mark the end of an era of frustration.

As if that weren't advantage enough, the Web would also provide a powerful management tool. If people's ideas, interactions and work patterns could be tracked by using the Web, then computer analysis could help us see patterns in our work, and facilitate our working together through the typical problems that beset any large organisation.

One of the beautiful things about physics is its ongoing quest to find simple rules that describe the behaviour of very small, simple objects. Once found, these rules can often be scaled up to describe the behaviour of monumental systems in the real world. For example, by understanding how two molecules of a gas

interact when they collide, scientists using suitable mathematics can deduce how billions of billions of gas molecules – say, the earth's atmosphere – will change. This allows them to analyse global weather patterns, and thus predict the weather. If the rules governing hypertext links between servers and browsers stayed simple, then our web of a few documents could grow to a global web.

The art was to define the few basic, common rules of 'protocol' that would allow one computer to talk to another, in such a way that when all computers everywhere did it, the system would thrive, not break down. For the Web, those elements were, in decreasing order of importance, universal resource identifiers (URIs), the Hypertext Transfer Protocol (HTTP) and the Hypertext Markup Language (HTML).

What was often difficult for people to understand about the design was that there was nothing else beyond URIs, HTTP and HTML. There was no central computer 'controlling' the Web, no single network on which these protocols worked, not even an organisation anywhere that 'ran' the Web. The Web was not a physical 'thing' that existed in a certain 'place.' It was a 'space' in which information could exist.

I told people that the Web was like a market economy. In a market economy, anybody can trade with anybody, and they don't have to go to a market square to do it. What they do need, however, are a few practices everyone has to agree to, such as the currency used for trade, and the rules of fair trading. The equivalent of rules for fair trading, on the Web, are the rules about what a URI means as an address, and the language the computers use – HTTP – whose rules define things like which one speaks first, and how they speak in turn. When two computers agree they can talk, they then have to find a common way to represent their data so they can share it. If they use the same software for documents or graphics, they can share directly. If not, they can both translate to HTML.

The fundamental principle behind the Web was that once someone somewhere made available a document, database, graphic, sound, video or screen at some stage in an interactive dialogue, it should be accessible (subject to authorisation, of course) by anyone, with any type of computer, in any country. And it should be possible to make a reference – a link – to that thing, so that others could find it. This was a philosophical change from the approach of previous computer systems. People were used to going to find information, but they rarely made references to other computers, and when they did they typically had to quote a long and complex series of instructions to get it. Furthermore, for global hypertext, people had to move from thinking about instructions to thinking in terms of a simple identifier string – a URI – that contained all the essential details in a compact way.

Getting people to put data on the Web often was a question of getting them to change perspective, from thinking of the user's access to it not as interaction with, say, an online library system, but as navigation through a set of virtual pages in some abstract space. In this concept, users could bookmark any place and return to it, and could make links into any place from another document. This would give a feeling of persistence, of an ongoing existence, to each page. It would also allow people to use the mental machinery they naturally have for remembering places and routes. By being able to reference anything with equal ease, the Web could also represent associations between things that might seem unrelated but for some reason did actually share a relationship. This is something the brain can do easily, spontaneously. If a visitor came to my office at CERN, and I had a fresh cutting of lilac in the corner exuding its wonderful, pungent scent, his brain would register a strong association between the office and lilac. He might walk by a lilac bush a day later in a park and suddenly be reminded of my office. A single click: lilac ... office.

The research community had used links between paper documents for ages: tables of contents, indexes, bibliographies and reference sections are hypertext links. On the Web, however, research ideas in hypertext links can be followed up in seconds, rather than weeks of making phone calls and waiting for deliveries in the mail. And suddenly, scientists could escape from the sequential organisation of each paper and bibliography, to pick and choose a path of references that served their own interest.

But the Web was to be much more than a tool for scientists. For an international hypertext system to be worthwhile, of course, many people would have to post information. The physicist would not find much on quarks, nor the art student on Van Gogh, if many people and organisations did not make their information available in the first place. Not only that, but much information – from phone numbers to current ideas and today's menu – is constantly changing, and is only as good as it is uptodate. That meant that anyone (authorised) should be able to publish and correct information, and anyone (authorised) should be able to read it. There could be no central control. To publish information, it would be put on any server, a computer that shared its resources with other computers, and the person operating it defined who could contribute, modify and access material on it. Information was read, written or edited by a client, a computer program, such as a browser/editor, that asked for access to a server.

Several protocols already existed for transferring data over the Internet, notably NNTP for Network News and FTP for files. But these did not do the negotiating I needed, among other things. I therefore defined HTTP, a protocol simple enough to be able to get a Web page fast enough for hypertext browsing. The target was a fetch of about one-tenth of a second, so there was no time for a conversation. It had to be 'Get this document' and 'Here it is!'

Of course if I had insisted everyone use HTTP, this would also have been against the principle of minimal constraint. If the Web were to be universal, it should be as unconstraining as possible. Unlike the NeXT computer, the Web would come as a set of ideas that could be adopted individually in combination with existing or future parts. Though HTTP was going to be faster, who was I to say that people should give up the huge archives of data accessible from FTP servers?

The key to resolving this was the design of the URI. It is the most fundamental innovation of the Web, because it is the one specification that every Web program, client or server, anywhere uses when any link is followed. Once a document had a URI, it could be posted on a server and found by a browser.

Hidden behind a highlighted word that denotes a hypertext link is the destination document's URI, which tells the browser where to go to find the document. A URI address has distinct parts, a bit like the five-digit zip code used by the US postal system. The first three numbers in a zip code designate a certain geographic region – a town, or part of a city or county. The next two numbers define a very specific part of that region – say, a few square blocks in a city. This gets the mail to a local post office. Carriers from there use the street name or box number to finish the routing.

Slashes are used in a URI address to delineate its parts. The first few letters in the URI tells the browser which protocol to use to look up the document, whether HTTP or FTP or one of a small set of others. In the address http://www.foobar.com/doc1, the *www.foobar.com* identifies the actual computer server where these documents exist. The *doc1* is a specific document on the www.foobar.com server (there might be hundreds, each with a different name after the single slash). The letters before the double slash signify the communications protocol this server uses.

The big difference between the URI and postal schemes, however, is that while there is some big table somewhere of all zip codes, the last part of the URI means whatever the given server wants it to mean. It doesn't have to be a file name. It can be a table name or an account name or the coordinates of a map or whatever. The client never tries to figure out what it means: it just asks for it. This important fact enabled a huge diversity of types of information systems to exist on the Web. And it allowed the Web to immediately pick up all the NNTP and FTP content from the Internet.

At the same time that I was developing the Web, several other Internet-based information systems were surfacing. Brewster Kahle at Thinking Machines had architected their latest powerful parallel processor. Now he saw a market for the big machines as search engines and designed the Wide Area Information Servers (WAIS) protocol to access them to form a system like the Web but without links – only search engines.

Clifford Newman at the Information Sciences Institute proposed his *Prospero*-distributed file system as an Internet-based information system, and Mark McCahill and colleagues at the University of Minnesota were developing a campus-wide information system called *gopher*, named for the university's mascot. To emphasise that all information systems could be incorporated into the Web, I defined two new URI prefixes that could appear before the double slash – 'gopher:' and 'wais:' – that would give access to those spaces. Both systems took off much more quickly than the Web and I was quite concerned at the time that they would suffocate it.

HTTP had a feature called *format negotiation* that allowed a client to say what sorts of data format it could handle, and allow the server to return a document in any one of them. I expected all kinds of data formats to exist on the Web. I also felt there had to be one common, basic lingua franca that any computer would be required to understand. This was to be a simple hypertext language that would be able to provide basic hypertext navigation, menus, and simple documentation such as help files, the minutes of meetings and mail messages – in short, 95 per cent of daily life for most people. Hence HTML, the Hypertext Markup Language.

I expected HTML to be the basic warp and weft of the Web, but documents of all types – video, computer-aided design, sound, animation and executable programs – to be the coloured threads that would contain much of the content. It would turn out that

HTML would become amazingly popular for the content as well.

HTML is a simple way to represent hypertext. Once the URI of a document tells a browser to talk HTTP to the server, then client and server have to agree on the format of the data they will share, so that it can be broken into packets both will understand. If they both knew WordPerfect files, for example, they could swap WordPerfect documents directly. If not, they could both try to translate to HTML as a default and send documents that way. There were some basic design rules that guided HTML, and some pragmatic, even political, choices. A philosophical rule was that HTML should convey the structure of a hypertext document, but not details of its presentation. This was the only way to get it to display reasonably on any of a very wide variety of different screens and sizes of paper. Since I knew it would be difficult to encourage the whole world to use a new global information system, I wanted to bring on board every group I could. There was a family of markup languages, the standard generalised markup language (SGML), already preferred by some of the world's documentation community and at the time considered the only potential document standard among the hypertext community. I developed HTML to look like a member of that family.

Designing HTML to be based on SGML highlighted one of the themes of the development of the Web: the constant interplay between the diplomatically astute decision and the technically clean thing to do. SGML used a simple system for denoting instructions, or 'tags', which was to put a word between angle brackets (such as *<h1>* to denote the main heading of a page), yet it also had many obscure and strange features that were not well understood. Nonetheless, at the time, the Web needed support and understanding from every community that could become involved, and in many ways the SGML community provided valuable input.

SGML was a diplomatic choice at CERN as well. SGML was being used on CERN's IBM machines with a particular set of tags that were enclosed in angle brackets, so HTML used the same tags wherever possible. I did clean up the language a certain amount, but it was still recognisable. I chose this direction so that when a CERN employee saw the angle brackets of HTML, he or she would feel, *Yes, I can do that.* In fact, HTML was even easier to use than CERN's version of SGML. The people promoting the SGML system at CERN could possibly be powerful figures in the choice of CERN's future directions and I wanted them to feel happy about the Web.

I never intended HTML source code (the stuff with the angle brackets) to be seen by users. A browser/editor would let a user simply view or edit the language of a page of hypertext, as if he were using a word processor. The idea of asking people to write the angle brackets by hand was to me, and I assumed to many, as unacceptable as asking one to prepare a Microsoft Word document by writing out its binary-coded format. But the human readability of HTML was an unexpected boon. To my surprise, people quickly became familiar with the tags and started writing their own HTML documents directly.

As the technical pieces slowly fell into place, Robert and I were still faced with a number of political issues that gave us more than a twinge of anxiety. First of all, the Web was still not a formal project. At any moment some manager of the Computing and Networking division could have asked me to stop the work, as it wasn't part of any project, and it could have been considered inappropriate for CERN.

For eight months Robert, Nicola and I refined the basic pieces of the Web and tried to promote what we were creating. We drafted a work plan for the Electronics and Computing for Physics division, where Robert was, to try to get funding from them, but no one responded. Accordingly, while developing the technology and trying to promote it to our colleagues, we still had to maintain a somewhat low profile.

The other problem we faced was simply the climate at CERN. There was a constant background of people promoting ideas for new software systems. There was competition among systems created within the experiment groups themselves – software for running a physics experiment, but also for everything from handling electronic mail and organising documents to running the Coke machine. There was competition over which network to use, among them DECnet, the Internet and whatever home-brewed thing could be justified. With so many creative engineers and physicists in one place, innovations were constant. At the same time, CERN obviously couldn't tolerate everybody creating unique software for every function.

Robert and I had to distinguish our idea as novel, and one that would allow CERN to leap forward. Rather than parade in with our new system for cosmic sharing of information, we decided to try to persuade people that we were offering them a way to extend their existing documentation system. This was a concrete and potentially promising notion. We could later get them to sign on to the dream of global hypertext. Our argument was that everyone could continue to store data in any form they like, and manage it any way they like. The Web would simply help people send and access information between each other, regardless of the operating system or formats their computers use. The only thing they'd have to do was follow the same simple URI addressing scheme. They didn't 'have to' use HTTP or HTML, but those tools were there if they ran into an incompatibility problem.

As we made these points, we also noted that using HTML was easy, since it was so much like SGML. I may have promoted this angle too much, however. Although SGML had been adopted as a standard by the ISO, it was not well defined as a computer language. I also got a strong push back from many people who insisted that it would be too slow. I had to explain that the only reason SGML was slow was the way it had historically been implemented. Still, I often had to demonstrate the World Wide Web program reading an HTML file and putting it on the screen in a fraction of a second before people were convinced.

Some people were intrigued, but many never accepted my argument. Rather than enter into useless debate, I simply forged ahead with HTML and showed the Web as much as possible. Robert and I held a few colloquia open to anyone in our divisions. We also told people about it at coffee. Occasionally, a group of people getting ready to do an experiment would call to say they were discussing their documentation system, and ask if I could come over and give them my thoughts about it. I'd meet a group of maybe twenty and show them the Web, and perhaps they wouldn't use it then, but the next time through they'd know about it and a new server would quietly come into being.

Meanwhile, Robert and I kept putting information on the info.cern.ch server, constantly upgrading the basic guide to newcomers on how to get onto the Web, with specifications and pointers to available software.

I continued to try to get other organisations to turn their hypertext systems into Web clients. I found out about a powerful SGML tool called Grif, developed by a research group at the French lab INRIA, which ran on Unix machines and PCs. A company by the same name, Grif, had since been spun off in nearby Grenoble, and I was hopeful its leaders would entertain the idea of developing a Web browser that could also edit. They had a beautiful and sophisticated hypertext editor; it would do graphics, it would do text in multiple fonts, it would display the SGML structure and the formatted document in two separate windows, and allow changes to be made in either. It was a perfect match. The only thing missing was that it didn't run on the Internet. Same story.

I tried to persuade the people at Grif to add the software needed for sending and receiving files over the Internet, so their editor could become a Web browser, too. I told them I would give them the software outright; they would just have to hook it in. But they said the only way they would do that was if we could get the European Commission to fund the development. They didn't want to risk taking the time. I was extremely frustrated. There was a growing group of people who were excited about the possibilities of the World Wide Web, and here we had the technology for a true hypertext browser/editor mostly developed, and we couldn't bridge the gap. Getting Commission funding would have put eighteen months into the loop immediately. This mind-set, I thought, was disappointingly different from the more American entrepreneurial attitude of developing something in the garage for fun and worrying about funding it when it worked!

In March 1991, I released the *WorldWideWeb* program to a limited number of CERN people who had NeXT computers. This would at least allow them to write their own hypertext and make the Web information that Robert and I were putting on info.cern.ch available to them.

Word spread within the high-energy physics community, furthered by the cross-pollinating influence of travel. In May 1991 Paul Kunz arrived for a visit from the Stanford Linear Accelerator (SLAC) in Palo Alto. Like me, he was an early NeXT enthusiast, and he had come to CERN to work on some common NeXT programs. Since he had the right computer, he was in a position to use the Web directly, and he loved it.

When Paul returned to SLAC he shared the Web with Louise Addis, the librarian who oversaw all the material produced by SLAC. She saw it as a godsend for their rather sophisticated but mainframe-bound library system, and a way to make SLAC's substantial internal catalogue of online documents available to physicists worldwide. Louise persuaded a colleague who developed tools for her to write the appropriate program, and under Louise's encouragement SLAC started the first Web server outside of CERN.

Seeing that the high-energy physics people at SLAC were so enthusiastic about the Web, we got more aggressive about promoting it within CERN. In May, Mike Sendall got us an appearance before the C5 committee, which was continually looking at computing and communications, to explain how useful the Web could be, so management would continue to justify the work. Robert and I wrote a paper, too, 'Hypertext at CERN', which tried to demonstrate the importance of what we were doing.

What we hoped for was that someone would say, 'Wow! This is going to be the cornerstone of high-energy physics communications! It will bind the entire community together in the next ten years. Here are four programmers to work on the project and here's your liaison with Management Information Systems. Anything else you need, you just tell us.' But it didn't happen.

In June we held talks and demonstrations within CERN, and wrote about the Web in the CERN newsletter. Because I still had no more staff, it was taking longer than I had hoped to get the functionality of the NeXT version on to PCs and Macs and Unix machines.

I was still hoping that by spreading the word we could attract the attention of more programmers. Since those programmers were unlikely to be high-energy physicists, in August I released three things – the *WorldWideWeb* for NeXT, the line-mode browser, and the basic server for any machine – outside CERN by making them all available on the Internet. I posted a notice on several Internet newsgroups, chief among them alt.hypertext, which was for hypertext enthusiasts. Unfortunately, there was still not much a user could see unless he had a NeXT.

Putting the Web out on alt.hypertext was a watershed event. It exposed the Web to a very critical academic community. I began to get e-mail from people who tried to install the software. They would give me bug reports, and 'wouldn't it be nice if …' reports. And there would be the occasional 'Hey, I've just set up a server, and it's dead cool. Here's the address.'

With each new message I would enter in info.cern.ch a hypertext link to the new web site, so others visiting the CERN site could link to that address as well. From then on, interested people on the Internet provided the feedback, stimulation, ideas, source-code contributions and moral support that would have been hard to find locally. The people of the Internet built the Web, in true grassroots fashion.

For several months it was mainly the hypertext community that was picking up the Web, and the NeXT community because they were interested in software that worked on the platform. As time went on, enough online people agreed there should be a newsgroup to share information about the Web, so we started one named comp.infosystems.www. Unlike alt.hypertext, this was a mainstream newsgroup, created after a global vote of approval.

Another small but effective step to increase the Web's exposure was taken when I opened a public telnet server on info.cern.ch. Telnet was an existing protocol, also running over the Internet, that allowed someone using one computer to open up an interactive command-line session on another computer. Anyone who used a telnet program to log into info.cern.ch would be connected directly to the line-mode browser. This approach had the disadvantage that the user would see the Web as a text-only read-only system. But it opened the Web to millions of people who could not install a Web browser on their own machine. It meant that someone putting up a Web server could say to 'telnet to info.cern.ch then type "go www.foobar.com" ,' which was a whole lot easier than requiring them to install a Web browser. The initial home page seen by users of this public service would include links to instructions for downloading their own browser. Years later we would have to close down the service, since the machine couldn't support the load, but by then it would have done its job.

The most valuable thing happening was that people who saw the Web, and realised the sense of unbound opportunity, began installing the server and posting information. Then they added links to related sites that they found were complementary, or simply interesting. The Web began to be picked up by people around the world. The messages from systems managers began to stream in: 'Hey, I thought you'd be interested. I just put up a Web server.'

Nicola had to leave the effort in August 1991, since her internship ended and she had to return to college. True to form, Ben Segal found yet another gem to replace her. Jean-François Groff was full of enthusiasm for the whole idea of the Web, and for NeXT. He came to CERN from France through a 'co-operant' programme that allowed the brightest young people, instead of spending a year in military service, to work for eighteen months at a foreign organisation as a volunteer.

By this time we had reached another awkward decision point about the code. Much of the code on the NeXT was in the language objective-C. I wanted people to use it widely, but objective-C compilers were rare. The common language for portable code was still C, so if I wanted to make it possible for more people around the Internet to develop Web software, it made sense to convert to C. Should I now, in the interest of practical expediency, convert all my objective-C code back into the less powerful C, or should I keep to the most powerful development platform I had?

The deciding factor was that Nicola's line-mode browser was written in C. I decided to make the sacrifice and, while keeping the object-orientated style of my design, downgraded all the common code that I could export from *WorldWideWeb* on the

NeXT into the more common C language.

This was a pile of work, but it opened up new possibilities and also allowed a certain cleaning up as I went along. Jean-François arrived at just the right time. For weeks we sat back to back in my office spewing out code, negotiating the interfaces between each other's module in remarks over our shoulders.

'Can you give me a method to find the last element?'

'OK. Call it "lastElement"?'

'Fine. Parameters?'

'List, element type. You got it.'

'Thanks!'

We rolled out the Web-specific code and also had to duplicate some of the tools from the NeXTStep tool kit. The result, since a collection of bits of code for general use is called a library, we called 'libwww'.

Unfortunately, CERN's policy with co-operants like Jean-François was that they had to leave when their time was up. They saw a danger in the staff abusing the programme as a recruitment stream, and forbade the employment of any of these people in any way in the future. When Jean-François came to the end of his term, we tried everything we could to allow him to continue to work on the Web, but it was quite impossible. He left and started a company in Geneva, infodesign.ch, probably the very first Web design consultancy.

Meanwhile, I had begun to keep logs of the number of times pages on the first Web server, info.cern.ch at CERN, were accessed. In July and August 1991 there were from ten to one hundred 'hits' (pages viewed) a day.

This was slow progress, but encouraging. I've compared the effort to launch the Web to that required to launch a bobsleigh:

everyone has to push hard for a seemingly long time, but sooner or later the sleigh is off on its own momentum and everyone jumps in.

In October we installed 'gateways' to two popular Internet services. A gateway was a little program, like that opening up Bernd's mainframe server, that made another world available as part of the Web. One gateway went to the online help system for Digital's VAX/VMS operating system. Another was to Brewster Khale's WAIS for databases. This was all done to add incentive for any particular individual to install a browser. VMS targeted the physics community, and WAIS the Internet community. I also started an online mailing list, www-talk@info.cern.ch, for technical discussions as a forum for the growing community.

Always trying to balance the effort we put into getting involvement from different groups, Robert and I decided we now had to promote the Web hard within the hypertext community. A big conference, Hypertext '91, was coming up in December in San Antonio. Most of the important people in the field would be there, including Doug Engelbart, who had created the mouse and a collaborative hypertext system way back in the 1960s. Though it was difficult to find the time, we cobbled together a paper for it, but didn't do a very good job. It was rejected – in part because it wasn't finished, and didn't make enough references to work in the field. At least one of the reviewers, too, felt that the proposed system violated the architectural principles that hypertext systems had worked on up till then.

We were able to persuade the conference planners to let us set up a demonstration, however. Robert and I flew to San Antonio with my NeXT computer and a modem. We couldn't get direct Internet access in the hotel. In fact, the hypertext community was so separated from the Internet community that we couldn't get any kind of connectivity at all. How could we demonstrate the Web if we couldn't dial up info.cern.ch? Robert found a way. He persuaded the hotel manager to string a phone line into the hall alongside the main meeting room. That would allow us to hook up the modem. Now we needed Internet access. During our cab ride from the airport, Robert had asked the driver what the nearest university was and found out that it was the University of Texas in San Antonio. So Robert called the school and found some people who understood about the Internet and maybe the Web, and they agreed to let us use their dial-in service so we could call the computer back at CERN.

The next challenge was to get the Swiss modem we had brought to work with the American electrical system. We bought a power adapter that would take 110 volts (rather than the Swiss 220 volts). Of course it didn't have the right little plug to connect to the modem. We had to take the modem apart, borrow a soldering gun from the hotel (Robert was rightly proud of this feat!), and wire it up directly. Robert got everything connected, and it worked.

We didn't have real Internet connectivity, just a dial-in Unix login, so we could show only the graphic World Wide Web program working on local data. Nonetheless, we could demonstrate the line-mode browser working live. We were the only people at the entire conference doing any kind of connectivity. The wall of the demo room held project titles above each booth, and only one of them had any reference to the World Wide Web – ours.

At the same conference two years later, on the equivalent wall, every project on display would have something to do with the Web.

CHAPTER 5

Going Global

As the Web slowly spread around the world, I started to be concerned that people who were putting up servers would not use HTTP, HTML and URIs in a consistent way. If they didn't, they might unintentionally introduced roadblocks that would render links impotent.

After I returned to CERN from San Antonio, I wrote several more Web pages about the Web's specifications. I would update them when good ideas came back from other users on the www-talk mailing list. While this was a start, I wanted to open the Web technology to wider review. Since everything to date had taken place on the Internet, and much of it involved Internet protocols, I felt that the place to get a process going was the Internet Engineering Task Force (IETF), an international forum of people who chiefly corresponded over e-mailing lists, but who also met physically three times a year. The IETF operates on a great principle of open participation. Anyone who is interested in any working group can contribute.

As a good software engineer, I wanted to standardise separately each of the three specifications central to the Web: the

URI addressing scheme, the HTTP protocol by which computers talked to each other, and the HTML format for hypertext documents. The most fundamental of these was the URI spec.

The next meeting of the IETF was in March 1992 in San Diego, and I went to see how things worked, and how to start a working group. The answer came from Joyce Reynolds, who oversaw one area within the IETF. She said I had to first hold a 'birds-of-a-feather' session to discuss whether there should be a working group. If there was consensus, people at the session could draw up a charter for a working group to begin at the next IETF meeting. The working group could edit a specification and take it through to a standard. The subsequent meeting would be held in July in Boston.

IETF meetings were characterised by people in T-shirts and jeans, and at times no footwear. They would meet in different small rooms and talk excitedly. The networking, of course, was paramount. Compared with Geneva in March, it was a pleasure for me to sit with folks outdoors in sunny, warm San Diego.

One day over coffee I was seated at a white metal table out in the open air, chatting with Larry Massinter from Xerox PARC and Karen Sollins, who had been a student of Dave Clark, the professor at MIT's Laboratory for Computer Science who was very involved with the design of the TCP protocol that had made possible practical use of the Internet. Karen had stayed on at MIT to pursue a project called the Infomesh, to create ways computers could exchange hints to each other about where to find documents they were both interested in.

Larry and Karen asked me what I was doing next. I told them I was considering going on sabbatical. I had been at CERN seven years, and while there was no concept of a sabbatical at CERN,

I felt I needed a break and some new perspective. I needed to think about where to take myself and the Web. After I returned to CERN, both Larry and Karen called independently with offers to come and visit them if I did take leave. I could join Karen as a visiting researcher at MIT, and join Larry as a visitor at Xerox PARC.

Both invitations were appealing, because both institutions were highly respected and either could give me a much-needed view of what was happening in the United States rather than Europe, and in information technology rather than physics.

Encouraged by the enthusiasm of people like Larry and Karen, Robert and I released notes about the Web on more Internet newsgroups. But we were frustrated by the fact that the Web's use within CERN itself was very low. We trod a fine line between dedicating our time to supporting users within CERN at the risk of neglecting the outside world, and pursuing the goal of global interactivity at the risk of being bawled out for not sticking to CERN business.

By now the Web consisted of a small number of servers, with info.cern.ch the most interconnected with the rest. It carried a list of servers, which to a degree could co-ordinate people who were putting information on the Web. When the list became larger, it needed to be organised, so I arranged it in two lists, by geography and by subject matter. As more servers arrived, it was exciting to see how the subjects filled out. Arthur Secret, another student, joined me for a time and set up the lists into what we called the Virtual Library, with a tree structure that allowed people to find things.

Part of the reason the Web was not being used much within CERN – or spreading faster outside CERN, for that matter –

was the lack of point-and-click clients (browsers) for anything other than the NeXT. At conferences on networking, hypertext and software, Robert and I would point out that for the Web to grow, we really needed clients for the PC, Macintosh and Unix. At CERN, I was under pressure to make a client for the X Window system used by most Unix workstations, but I had no resources. We were so busy trying to keep the Web going that there was no way we could develop browsers ourselves, so we energetically suggested to everyone everywhere that the creation of browsers would make useful projects for software students at universities.

Our strategy paid off when Robert visited Helsinki University of Technology. Several students there decided to make their combined master's project a Web browser. Because the department was 'OTH,' they decided to call the browser Erwise (OTH + Erwise = 'Otherwise').

By the time it was finished in April 1992, Erwise was quite advanced. It was written for use on a Unix machine running X-Windows. I went to Finland to encourage the students to continue the project after they finished their degrees, and to extend the browser to an editor, but they had remarkably little ongoing enthusiasm for the Web; they had already decided that when they graduated they were going to go on to what they saw as more tantalising or lucrative software projects. No one else around the institute wanted to pick up the project, either. Certainly I couldn't continue it; all the code was documented in Finnish!

Another graphical point-and-click browser came at almost the same time, however. Pei Wei, a very inventive student at UC Berkeley, had created an interpretive computer language called

Viola, for Unix computers. He had been working on it a long time, and it had powerful functionality for displaying things on the screen. To demonstrate the power of Viola, Pei decided to write a Web browser, ViolaWWW. It was quite advanced: it could display HTML with graphics, do animations and download small, embedded applications (later known as *applets*) off the Internet. It was ahead of its time, and though Pei would be given little credit, ViolaWWW set an early standard, and also had many of the attributes that would come out several years later in the much-hyped program HotJava, which would take the Web community by storm.

Pei released a test version of his browser on the Web in May 1992. The only detracting feature was that it was hard for a user to install on his computer. One had to first install Viola, and then ViolaWWW as a Viola application. This took time and was complicated. But finally, people working on Unix machines – and there were lots of them at corporations and universities around the world – could access the Web.

Although browsers were starting to spread, no one working on them tried to include writing and editing functions. There seemed to be a perception that creating a browser had a strong potential for payback, since it would make information from around the world available to anyone who used it. Putting as much effort into the collaborative side of the Web didn't seem to promise that millionfold multiplier. As soon as developers got their client working as a browser and released it to the world, very few bothered to continue to develop it as an editor.

Without a hypertext editor, people would not have the tools to really use the Web as an intimate collaborative medium. Browsers would let them find and share information, but they could not work together intuitively. Part of the reason, I guessed, was that collaboration required much more of a social change in how people worked. And part of it was that editors were more difficult to write.

For these reasons, the Web, which I designed to be a medium for all sorts of information, from the very local to the very global, grew decidedly in the direction of the very global, and as a publication medium but less of a collaboration medium.

There were some pockets of strong internal use. CERN, eventually, was one. Within Digital Equipment there were a hundred Web servers early on that were not available from the outside. These internal servers were not well publicised, so journalists could not see them. Years later the media would suddenly 'discover' the 'rise' of these internal Web networks and invent the term *intranet*, with the notion that they were used largely for internal corporate communications. It seemed somewhat ironic to me, since this had been happening all along, and was a principle driving the need for the Web in the first place.

With Erwise and Viola on board, Robert set out to design a browser for his favourite computer, the Macintosh. Robert was a purist, rather than a pragmatist like me. In the Mac he found the realisation of his highest ideals of how computers should be: simple and intuitive to use. But Robert's idealism was sometimes a tough match for the practical need to get a project done. As mentioned earlier, I had found a little extra space in the text-editor code on the NeXT machine, where I could store the URI addressing information defining each hypertext link. This proved essential to being able to make the Web server in a simple way.

The designers of the Macintosh text editor had a similar structure, but without the extra space. However, they had set aside thirty-two bits for storing the text colour, and used only twenty-four of them. I suggested we use the spare eight bits, and steal a few more from those used for colour, which would not cause any change in the colours that would be noticeable to users.

Robert was appalled – appalled at the idea of using a field intended for the colour for another purpose, appalled at stuffing the hypertext data into the cracks of the colour data. The program was held up for some time while I tried to persuade Robert that taking this admittedly less elegant but simple route would allow him to get on with the rest of the project and actually get the Web browser running. In the end, he accepted my kludge, but in fact had little time to pursue the program. Later on one summer, Nicola Pellow returned for a few weeks and picked it up, and at one point it was basically working. We named it Samba.

Every team benefits from a variety of styles, and my collaboration with Robert was no exception. Robert's insistence on quality of presentation would carry us though many papers, demonstrations and presentations. All along, Robert tirelessly trawled for more resources. He ended up getting the students Henrik Frystyk Nielsen and Ari Luotonen to join the team. Henrik, an affable blond Dane, took responsibility for the code library and the line-mode browser. Ari, a wild dark Finn who had worked on the Erwise project, took on the server. Each made his mark and put more time and energy into the products than I could have, in some cases turning them upside down to rewrite them into something better. This effort supported a dramatically growing number of Web sites, and 'productised' our work so users would find it easy to install and use.

As the browsers appeared, so did new servers, with ever-increasing frequency. Occasionally, one new server would demonstrate to the community what could be done in a whole new way, and pour fresh energy into the young field. One that impressed me was a server of information about Rome during the Renaissance. The Vatican had lent a (physical) exhibit to America's Library of Congress. Some of the material in it had been photographed, scanned into a computer and made available in the form of image files on an FTP Internet server. Then in Europe, Frans van Hoesl, who was aware of the Web, created a hypertext world of this material on a Web site. The site took the form of a virtual museum; a browser chose a wing to visit, then a corridor, then a room.

On my first visit, I wandered to a music room. There were a number of thumbnail pictures, and under one was an explanation of the events that caused the composer Carpentras to present a decorated manuscript of his *Lamentations of Jeremiah* to Pope Clement VII. I clicked, and was glad I had a twenty-one-inch colour screen: suddenly it was filled with a beautifully illuminated score, which I could gaze at probably more easily and in more detail than I could have done had I gone to the original exhibit at the Library of Congress. This use of the Web to bring distant people to great resources, and the navigational idiom used to make the virtual museum, both caught on and inspired many excellent Web sites. It was also a great example of how a combination of effort from around the world could lead to fantastic things.

Another classic of its time was a server by Steve Putz at Xerox PARC. He had a database of geographical information that would generate a virtual map on the fly in response to a user's clicks to zoom and pan. It would prove to be the first of many map Web servers to come.

Seeing such sites, scientists and government groups, who had an obligation to make their data available, were realising it would be easier to put the information up on the Web than to answer repeated requests for it. Typically, when another scientist requested their data, they had had to write a custom program to translate their information into a format that the person could use. Now they could just put it on the Web and ask anyone who wanted it to go get a browser. And people did. The acceptability of the Web was increasing. The excuses for not having a browser were wearing thinner. The bobsleigh was starting to glide.

As June 1992 approached, I increasingly felt the need for a sabbatical. David Williams, head of my division at CERN, had seen this coming and was ready with an offer I couldn't refuse. He explained that I could go away for a year and have my job when I returned. However, during that year I would lose my CERN salary and benefits, which were quite good, and I would have to pay all my travel expenses. As an alternative, David said I could go away for an extended business trip for three months and he would pay me a per diem rate for this 'extended duty travel', on top of my ongoing salary and benefits. Not surprisingly, I chose the second option. My wife and I planned a three-month mixture of work and vacation. I would visit MIT's Laboratory for Computer Science (LCS) in Cambridge, Massachusetts, and also attend the IETF meeting in neighbouring Boston. Then we would vacation in New Hampshire, and end up in the San Francisco area where I would visit Xerox PARC.

The summer turned out to be a great opportunity for me to take a snapshot of the state of the Web's penetration and acceptance in the States.

People at LCS had installed Viola, and MIT was well into the Web. The name 'www.mit.edu' was taken very early on by a student computing club, so 'web.mit.edu' would become and remain the name of MIT's main server. At LCS, I described the ideas behind the Web to a select group of individuals in the fifth-floor auditorium. Some of the researchers and administrators wondered a bit why I was there. I was trying to see how this creation, which was really a matter of engineering, fit in from the point of view of the research community, what the Web could learn from researchers in the field, and why it hadn't happened before.

At the IETF meeting I held my birds-of-a-feather session to investigate forming a working group to standardise the URI spec, as Joyce Reynolds had suggested. We met in a small room at the Hyatt Hotel. I presented the idea of a *universal document identifier* – my initial name for it – and said I was interested in its being adopted as an Internet standard. A number of things went less than smoothly. The open discussion was great. I felt very much in the minority. There was another minority who seemed to resent me as an intruding newcomer.

Even though I was asking for only a piece of the Web to be standardised, there was a strong reaction against the 'arrogance' of calling something a universal document identifier. How could I be so presumptuous as to define my creation as 'universal'? If I wanted the UDI addresses to be standardised, then the name '*uniform* document identifiers' would certainly suffice. I sensed an immediate and strong force among the people there. They were trying to confine the Web to some kind of tidy box: nothing could be universal. Others viewed the IETF as a place where something universal might be created, but that something was not going to be the Web. Those tensions would continue through that IETF meeting and subsequent ones. Some people wanted to integrate the Web with other information systems, which directly begged the point, because the Web was defined to be the integration of all information systems.

I tried to explain at the session how important it was that the Web be seen as universal, but there was only so much time, and I decided not to waste my breath. I thought, *What's in a name?* If it went through the standards process and these people agreed, and all I needed was to call it *uniform*, as long as I got the right spec that was fine by me. I was willing to compromise so I could get to the technical details. So *universal* became *uniform*, and *document* became *resource*.

As it turns out, it had been important to nail down the name, because behind the name was the fundamental philosophical underpinnings of what the Web was trying to be. Ultimately, the group did decide to form a uniform-resource-identifier working group. However, they decided that *identifier* wasn't a good label for what the Web used. They wanted to emphasise that people could change the URIs when moving documents, and so they should be treated as some sort of transitive address. *Locator* was chosen instead, like a branding, a warning mark on the technology. I wanted to stick with *identifier,* because, though in practice many URIs did change, the object was to make them as persistent as possible. We argued, but at the IETF the universal resource identifier became URL, the *uniform resource locator.* In years ahead the IETF community would use the URL acronym, allowing the use of the term *URI* for what was either a URL or something more persistent. I use the general term *URI* to emphasise the importance of universality, and of the persistence of information.

Progress in the URI working group was slow, partly due to the number of endless philosophical rat holes down which technical conversations would disappear. When years later the URI working group had to meet twelve times and still failed to agree on a nine-page document, John Klensin, the then IETF Applications Area director, was to angrily disband it. Sometimes there was a core philosophy being argued, and from my point of view that was not up for compromise. Sometimes there was a basically arbitrary decision (like which punctuation characters to use) that I had already made, and changing it would only mean that millions of Web browsers and existing links would have to be changed. After months of rather uncontrolled arguing in the IETF, it seemed that they had to take either all of the Web, or none of it. In the end I wrote a specification on how URIs were used on the Web, and issued it to the IETF community as an informational 'Request for Comment 1630'. While hurried and with a few mistakes, it was a foothold for future progress. The whole affair would also have gone more smoothly had I been more forceful about the points on which I was prepared to negotiate and those on which I was not.

My stay at LCS had been more inspiring, and the same was true when I went to Xerox PARC. Being security-conscious, PARC had many experimental servers available internally, protected behind a firewall built into their system that prevented outsiders from illegally gaining electronic access. There was a special way of getting a connection from inside to outside. They were not using Viola because it had to be compiled with special code to make this connection, so the first thing I did on arrival was to do that.

I also visited other important actors in the Web world while in the San Francisco area. When going to PARC I would bike in every day past SLAC. I stopped in to see Paul Kunz and Louise Addis, early promoters and implementers of the Web. I also got together with Pei Wei, who was still at UC Berkeley. Although Viola was attracting some attention, the difficulty in installing it limited its appeal. I met Pei at a café outside San Francisco to try to persuade him to make installation easier, and to give editing power to his browser as well – still my ideal. But Pei's interest was always in Viola as a computer language; he saw the Web as just one application of it. I tried to encourage but not push. After all, Viola was broadening the Web's reach tremendously. Part of my reason to meet him was simply to say, in person, 'Thank you, well done.'

Pei's unassuming demeanour and lack of arrogance about his ideas were remarkable given his product, which was great. When I congratulated him and told him that further development would make Viola the flagship of Web browsers, Pei smiled, but he would reserve his program as his own research tool. He would go on to join O'Reilly Associates in Sebastopol, California, run by Dale Dougherty, one of the early Web champions, which was creating various Internet products. He used Viola to demonstrate what online products could look like using different styles.

Because the installation process was a little too complex, Viola was destined to be eclipsed by other browsers to come. Indeed, there was already competition between Web browsers. While Erwise and ViolaWWW competed as browsers for the X Window system on Unix, Tony Johnson at SLAC entered the fray. A physicist, he had developed another browser for X called Midas, partly because he liked to see a program written well, and partly because in his project he wanted to use the Web to disseminate his information, and wanted a browser he could control. He used a nice conceptual model, the programming was very clean, and it allowed him, for example, to import images in a very flexible way.

I met Tony in his office at SLAC. Although he gave presentations around SLAC about Midas, and used it himself, he was as reluctant as Pei or the Erwise group to join in my effort at CERN, even though it would probably provide extra resources. Tony was and is first and foremost a physicist, and he didn't like the idea of supporting Midas for a group any wider than that of his colleagues.

The month I was spending in California was coming to a close, and soon my family and I would have to return to Geneva. But I could not go back without making one more stop, which I knew would be perhaps the greatest treat of the summer. Ted Nelson, who had conceived Xanadu twenty-five years earlier, lived close by, and I had to meet him.

Different people had tackled different aspects of the social implications of hypertext. For Ted, hypertext was the opposite of copyright. The whole idea of Xanadu was driven by his feeling that anybody should be able to publish information, and if someone wanted to use that information, the creator ought to be automatically recompensed. One of the reasons Xanadu never took off was Ted's insistence on a pricing mechanism, and the difficulty of creating one that was consistent across the whole world. In theory this would be possible on the Web with certain extensions, and a system of 'micropayments' – small debentures against a person's bank account – would allow automatic payments in very small quantities. I was not keen on the idea of having only one business model for paying for information. But I was keen on meeting Ted.

We had corresponded only a few times via e-mail, and the fledgling relationship we had was a strange one for me at least, because for a long time I owed Ted money. I had first heard of Ted in 1988 when reading about hypertext. His main book at the time was *Literary Machines*, published by the Mindful Press, which Ted operated as a one-man publishing house. Some time later I got around to sending him an order for the book with a cheque written out in US dollars drawn on my Swiss bank account. Swiss chequs were very international, with a space for the amount and a space for the currency type, but I didn't realise American banks didn't accept them. He sent the book, but I didn't succeed in paying, since he didn't take credit cards and I didn't have US cheques.

And so it had stayed. I called him up from PARC and found that he lived on a houseboat in Sausalito, across the Golden Gate Bridge from San Francisco. It was the place closest to where things were happening that was sufficiently eccentric for him to live. Xanadu had been picked up by Autodesk, and Ted had some dignitary position with the company. But the day I was scheduled to meet him for lunch was a sad one. That very morning Autodesk had decided Xanadu was an impractical project after all. They were dropping it, leaving the project homeless.

Ted kindly bought me an Indian lunch anyway, and then we went back to his office, which seemed to be an attic in a pyramid building on the Sausalito shore. It was full of copies of his books. I gave him the money I owed and he promptly gave me a second book, autographed. We talked about all manner of things, but not a lot about Autodesk.

After lunch Ted walked me to my car in the car park. I took out my 35-mm camera from the trunk to capture the moment. I asked Ted, with some embarrassment, if he would mind posing for my scrapbook. He replied, 'Certainly, not at all. I understand completely.' He then produced from his knapsack a video camera to shoot some video footage of me. Before he did, though, he held the camera at arm's length, pointed it at his head, and shot a little bit of himself explaining that this was Tim Berners-Lee he would be filming, and what the significance was. Ted explained to me that it was his objective to lead the most interesting life he could, and to record as much as possible of that life for other people. To which end he amassed a huge number of video clips, which were indexed with an image of his own head; that way, he could skip through, and whenever he saw his head he could listen for a description of the next clip to come.

The summer of 1992 had been a thrilling time for me. The Web was being seen and used in many more places, and more people were developing browsers for it. I looked over the logs showing the traffic that the first Web server, info.cern.ch, had been getting over the last twelve months. The curve showing the number of daily hits was a dramatic exponential, doubling every three to four months. After one year, the load had grown by a factor of ten.

CHAPTER 6

Browsing

By January 1993 the number of known servers was increasing faster, up to about fifty. The Erwise, Viola and Midas browsers were generally available for use on the X Window system. Samba was working, though not complete, for the Mac. But to me it was clear there was growing competition among the browsers, even if it was on a small scale. Many of the people developing browsers were students, and they were driven to add features to their version before someone else added similar features. They held open discussions about these things on the www-talk mailing list, preserving the open social processes that had characterised Internet software development. But there was still an honourable one-upmanship, too.

One of the few commercial developers to join the contest was Dave Raggett at Hewlett-Packard in Bristol, England. He created a browser called Arena. HP had a convention that an employee could engage in related, useful but not official work for 10 per cent of his or her job time. Dave spent his '10 per cent time', plus a lot of evenings and weekends, on Arena. He was convinced that hypertext Web pages could be much more exciting, like magazine pages rather than textbook pages, and that HTML could be used to position not just text on a page, but pictures, tables and other features. He used Arena to demonstrate all these things, and to experiment with different ways of reading and interpreting both valid and incorrectly written HTML pages.

Meanwhile, the University of Kansas had, independently of the Web, written a hypertext browser, Lynx, that worked with 80 x 24 character terminals. More sophisticated than our line-mode browser, Lynx was a 'screen mode' browser, allowing scrolling backwards and forwards through a document. It had, like Gopher, been designed as a campus-wide information system, and the team joked that Lynxes ate Gophers. Lou Montulli, a student, adapted it to the Web and released a Web browser, Lynx 2.0, in March 1993.

Developing browsers had become a good vehicle for students and engineers to show off their programming skills. David Thompson, a manager at the National Center for Super-computing Applications (NCSA) at the University of Illinois at Urbana-Champaign, wanted students to take a crack at it. He downloaded Viola, got it running and demonstrated its use with the CERN server to the rest of NCSA's Software Design Group.

Marc Andreessen, a student, and Eric Bina, a staff member, decided to create a browser for X. Eric was somewhat like Pei Wei, quietly programming the HTML code and making the thing work. Marc maintained a near-constant presence on the newsgroups discussing the Web, listening for features people were asking for, what would make browsers easier to use. He would program these into the nascent browser and keep publishing new releases so others could try it. He listened intently to critiques, almost as if he were attending to 'customer relations'. Nourished, it was said, by large quantities of espresso, he would fix bugs and add little features late at night in reaction to user feedback.

This was in total contrast to any of the other student developers. Marc was not so much interested in just making the program work as in having his browser used by as many people as possible. That was, of course, what the Web needed.

The resulting browser was called Mosaic. In February 1993 NCSA made the first version available over the Web. I tried it at CERN. It was easy to download and install, and required very little learning before I had point-and-click access to the Web. Because of these traits, Mosaic was soon picked up more rapidly than the other browsers. Mosaic was much more of a product.

It troubled me in a way that NCSA was always talking about Mosaic, often with hardly a mention of the World Wide Web. Perhaps it was just pure enthusiasm.

I was scheduled to give a presentation to the Fermi National Accelerator Laboratory (Fermilab) in Chicago in March, which had put up a server as SLAC had done. I decided I would visit NCSA as well, since it was only a few hours' drive away.

While in Chicago I met Tom Bruce, a stage manager turned systems administrator turned programmer who had recently cofounded the Legal Information Institute at Cornell University, to provide online legal information and law findings. He thought the Web was just what the institute needed to distribute this information to the legal community. He had realised that most lawyers used IBM PCs or compatibles, which ran the Windows operating system, and would need a browser. So he had written Cello, a point-and-click browser for Windows. It was at alpha release (an early test version) in March, and he had come to

Chicago to give a talk to the legal community about it. For the first time, people could see the Web in its multicolour, multifont glory on the world's most widespread computing platform.

I found Tom in an auditorium just after he had finished his talk. His laptop computer was still on, with its screen projected on to a big movie screen at the head of the room. There he demonstrated Cello to me, the two of us sitting alone in this big room looking up at this big image of the Web. He had multiple fonts, colours and user-selectable styles. He used a dotted line around text denoting a hypertext link, which fitted with Windows conventions. I found out in talking with him afterwards that he had worked professionally with lighting and audiovisual equipment in the theatre. I had done the same thing in an amateur way. We shared an enthusiasm for the vocation, and hit it off.

I asked Tom, and Ruth Pordes, my host at Fermilab and a source of honest wisdom, to come with me to meet Marc Andreessen and the folks at NCSA. Ruth drove us down across the seemingly interminable cornfields. As someone who had been living in Geneva, I was struck by a remarkable lack of mountains.

The three of us found the Software Development Group, though it was not in the imposing brick and green-glass buildings that housed most of NCSA, but in an annexe to the oil-chemistry building. We met Eric, Marc and the group's leader, Joseph Hardin, in a basement meeting room.

All my earlier meetings with browser developers had been meetings of minds, with a pooling of enthusiasm. But this meeting had a strange tension to it. It was becoming clear to me in the days before I went to Chicago that the people at NCSA were attempting to portray themselves as the centre of Web development, and to basically rename the Web as Mosaic. At NCSA, something wasn't 'on the Web', it was 'on Mosaic'. Marc seemed to sense my discomfort at this.

I dismissed this as a subject of conversation, however, and made my now-standard case for making the Mosaic browser an editor, too. Marc and Eric explained that they had looked at that option and concluded that it was just impossible. It couldn't be done. This was news to me, since I had already done it with the World Wide Web on the NeXT – though admittedly for a simpler version of HTML.

Still, I was amazed by this near universal disdain for creating an editor. Maybe it was too daunting. Or maybe it was just a balance between competing demands on developers' time. But it was also true that most were more excited about putting fancy display features into the browsers – multimedia, different colours and fonts – which took much less work and created much more buzz among users. And Marc, more than anyone, appeared interested in responding to users' wants.

I sensed other tensions as well. There was a huge difference in style among the three men, and each seemed to be thinking separately rather than as a team. Eric, the staffer, was quiet. Marc, the student, gave the appearance that he thought of this meeting as a poker game. Hardin was very academic, the consummate professor in a tweed jacket. He was interested in the social implications of the Web as well as the technology, and in sociological studies of the Web. For him Mosaic was a sequel to a project NCSA already had, a multimedia hypertext system called Collage.

To add to my consternation, the NCSA public-relations department was also pushing Mosaic. It wasn't long before the *New York Times* ran an article picturing Hardin and Larry Smarr, the head of NCSA (not Marc and Eric!), sitting side by side at terminals running the Mosaic browser. Once again, the focus was on Mosaic, as if it were the Web. There was little mention of other browsers, or even the rest of the world's effort to create servers. The media, which didn't take the time to investigate deeper, started to portray Mosaic as if it were equivalent to the Web.

I returned to CERN uneasy about the decidedly peremptory undertones behind NCSA's promotion of Mosaic. NCSA quickly started other projects to get Mosaic on to PCs running Windows, and on to Macintoshes.

The rise of different browsers made me think once again about standardisation. The IETF route didn't seem to be working. I thought that perhaps a different model would. I got more enthused about the idea during a seminar at Newcastle University in my native England, organised by International Computers Ltd. We were bused through the rainy evening from the seminar to dinner. On the way back I sat next to David Gifford, who happened to be a professor at MIT's LCS. I told him I was thinking of setting up some kind of body to oversee the evolution of the Web. I wondered what kind of structure might work, and where to base it. He said I should talk to Michael Dertouzos about it. He explained that Michael was the director of LCS, and said he thought Michael might be interested in doing something. I expressed happy surprise, noted 'mld@hq.lcs.mit.edu', and promptly e-mailed him when I got back to CERN.

I was further motivated by another Internet phenomenon that had recently taken place. The gopher information system at the University of Minnesota had started at about the same time as the Web. It was originally created as an online help system for the university's computing department and spread to become a campuswide information system that also allowed people to share documents over the Internet. Instead of using hypertext and links, it presented users with menus, taking them eventually to documents normally in plain text. I had found that some people, when they saw the Web, thought hypertext was confusing, or worried that somehow they would get lost in hyperspace when following a link. Of course, this could happen in gopherspace too, but computer users were familiar with menus, so the program didn't seem as foreign.

It was just about this time, spring 1993, that the University of Minnesota decided it would ask for a licence fee from certain classes of users who wanted to use gopher. Since the gopher software was being picked up so widely, the university was going to charge an annual fee. The browser, and the act of browsing, would be free, and the server software would remain free to non-profit and educational institutions. But any other users, notably companies, would have to pay to use gopher server software.

This was an act of treason in the academic community and the Internet community. Even if the university never charged anyone a dime, the fact that the school had announced it was reserving the right to charge people for the use of the gopher protocols meant it had crossed the line. To use the technology was too risky.

Industry dropped gopher like a hot potato. Developers knew they couldn't do anything that could possibly be said to be related to the gopher protocol without asking all their lawyers first about negotiating rights. Even if a company wrote its own gopher client or server, the university could later sue for infringement of some intellectual property right. It was considered dangerous as an engineer to have even read the specification or seen any of the code, because anything that person did in the future could possibly be said to have been in some way inspired by the private gopher technology.

At the March 1993 IETF meeting in Columbus, Ohio, held after the announcement, I was accosted in the corridors: 'OK, this is what happened to gopher. Is CERN going to do the same thing with the WWW?' I listened carefully to people's concerns and to what they said they would or would not find acceptable. I also sweated anxiously behind my calm exterior.

During the preceding year I had been trying to get CERN to release the intellectual property rights to the Web code under the General Public License (GPL) so that others could use it. The GPL was developed by Richard Stallman for his Free Software Foundation, and while it allowed things to be distributed and used freely, there were strings attached, such that any modifications also had to be released under the same GPL. In the fallout of the gopher debacle, there were already rumours that large companies like IBM would not allow the Web on the premises if there was any kind of licensing issue, because that would be too constraining. And that included the GPL.

CERN had not yet made up its mind. I returned from Columbus and swiftly switched my request, from getting a GPL to having the Web technology put in the general public domain, with no strings attached.

On 30 April Robert and I received a declaration, with a CERN stamp, signed by one of the directors, saying that CERN agreed to allow anybody to use the Web protocol and code free of charge, to create a server or a browser, to give it away or sell it, without any royalty or other constraint. Whew!

CHAPTER 7

Changes

My experience at NCSA, and the near disaster over licensing, made me more convinced than ever that some kind of body was needed to oversee the Web's development. The Web's fast growth added to my feeling. The Web was starting to change phase. Some people were still sending me e-mail about putting up new servers. But others were not; they just started them. CERN and I were beginning to blend into the background hum. Web activity was increasing at a relentlessly steady, exponential rate. It being midsummer, I once again graphed the number of people who were accessing the CERN server, info.cern.ch. It was now taking ten thousand hits a day. The rate was incredible, still doubling every three or four months, growing by a factor of ten every year, from one hundred hits a day in the summer of 1991, to one thousand in the summer of 1992, to ten thousand in the summer of 1993.

I no longer had to push the bobsleigh. It was time to jump in and steer.

I did not want to form a standards body per se, but some kind of organisation that could help developers of servers and browsers reach consensus on how the Web should operate. With Mosaic picking up the ball and running single-handedly for the goal line, and more and more gopher users considering the Web, evidence was mounting that 'the Web' could splinter into various factions – some commercial, some academic; some free, some not. This would defeat the very purpose of the Web: to be a single, universal, accessible hypertext medium for sharing information.

I talked to people at CERN about starting some kind of consortium. I also swapped e-mails with Michael Dertouzos at MIT's Laboratory for Computer Science. Michael seemed very receptive to the idea. A frequent visitor to Europe and his native Greece, he arranged to meet me in Zurich on 1 February 1994.

I took the train from Geneva to Zurich not knowing quite what Michael wanted, nor what I did. We met at a pleasant café in the old town, and over some characteristic Zurich-style veal and *Rösti*, we ended up sketching plans for the top levels of a consortium. We both returned to our homes to mull over our ideas.

It seemed more than a bit serendipitous that the first WWW Wizards Workshop was scheduled to be held only a month or so later ... in Cambridge, Massachusetts, just a few blocks from MIT. It had been set up by Dale Dougherty of O'Reilly Associates, who again quietly managed to gather the flock.

O'Reilly had just published Ed Kroll's book *Whole Earth Internet Catalog*, which was really the first book that made all this Internet stuff accessible to the public. When I had proof-read it, on the train in Chicago going to meet Tom Bruce, the World Wide Web occupied just one chapter; the rest was about how to use all the various Internet protocols such as FTP and telnet and so on. But the traffic on the Web was increasing fast, and NCSA had just released working versions of the Mosaic browser for Unix, Windows and the Mac. Dale was wondering himself where the Web was going, and felt he could find out, and perhaps also help people make it go somewhat sensibly, by getting everyone together.

About twenty-five of the early Web developers gathered at O'Reilly's offices in Cambridge. There was Lou Montulli, who had adapted Lynx for the Web, and his boss; a group from NCSA including Eric Bina, Marc Andreessen, Chris Wilson, who was porting Mosaic to the PC, and Alex Totic, who was porting it to the Mac; Tom Bruce, author of Cello; Steve Putz from Xerox PARC, of map server fame; Pei Wei, author of Viola; and others. The focus of the meeting was on defining the most important things to do next for the Web development community. In his friendly, encouraging way, Dale got us all talking. I brought up the general idea for a Web consortium. We discussed what it could be like, whether it should be a consortium or an organisation or a club. At one point I put the words *Club Web* up on the whiteboard... Well, it was an option. I led a brainstorming session to list the needs for the next few months, covering the walls on all sides with ideas grouped to make some kind of sense.

The event was quite a bonding occasion for some members of the community. Even for hard-core devotees of the Internet it's fun to meet face to face someone you have communicated with only by e-mail. During the meeting several people commented on how surprised they were that Marc, who had been so vocal on the Internet, was so quiet in person. A few of us were taking photos, and Marc was the only one who basically refused to be photographed. I managed to sneak a picture of him with a telephoto lens, but for all his physical size and lack of hesitation to come out blaring on the www-talk newsgroup, he and the others from NCSA were remarkably self-conscious and quiet.

I returned to CERN with a clearer vision that a consortium was needed. Then one day the phone in my office rang. It was reception saying there were four people from Digital Equipment Corporation to see me. Now, CERN was not a place where people just turned up at reception. It is international, it's huge, people have to come from a long way, they need an escort to find their way around. But suddenly this group of people in suits was here. I quickly commandeered an available conference room. There were three men and one woman: Alan Kotok, the senior consultant; Steve Fink, a marketing man; Brian Reed, DEC's Internet guru at the time; and Gail Grant, from the company's Silicon Valley operations.

Alan had been pushing DEC in the direction of the Web ever since he had been shown a Web browser, and management had asked Steve to put together a team to assess the future of the Internet for DEC. Steve explained that they would be largely redesigning DEC as a result of the Web. While they saw this as a huge opportunity, they were concerned about where the Web was headed, worried that the Web was perhaps defined by nothing more than specifications stored on some disk sitting around somewhere at CERN. They wanted to know what CERN's attitude was about the future path of the Web, and whether they could rest assured that it would remain stable yet evolve.

I asked them what their requirements were, what they felt was important. They felt strongly that there should be a neutral body acting as convener. They were not interested in taking over the Web, or having some proprietary control of it. But they really wanted a body of oversight to which they could become attached. They wondered if CERN would do this.

For me this was a listening meeting. It was important input into the decision about what to do next. I told them I had talked with MIT about perhaps running a group. It might be modelled after the X Consortium, which MIT had organised to take Bob Scheifler's X Window system from his initial design to a platform used by almost all Unix workstations. It seemed to strike them as an exceptional idea.

By October there were more than two hundred known HTTP servers, and certainly a lot more hidden ones. The European Commission, the Fraunhofer Gesellschaft and CERN started the first Web-based project of the European Union, called Webcore, for disseminating technological information throughout the former Soviet bloc countries in Europe. Then in December the media became aware, with articles in major publications about the Web and Mosaic, and everything was being run together.

Meanwhile, the community of developers was growing. It would be obviously exciting to hold a World Wide Web conference to bring them together on a larger scale than the Wizards Workshop had done. I had already talked to Robert about it, and now the need was more pressing. He got the go-ahead from CERN management to organise the first International WWW Conference and hold it at CERN. Robert was excited and checked the schedule of availability for the auditorium and three meeting rooms. There were only two dates open within the next several months. He booked one of them immediately. He came back and said, 'You don't have to do anything. I'll do everything. But this is the date it has to be held.'

I said, 'Well, Robert, that's fine, except that it's the date that my wife and I are expecting our second child.' He realised there were things that could be moved and things that couldn't be. He sighed and went back to see if the other date was still available. It was, but the date, at the end of May, was earlier than the first one, and it left us with short notice to get it all together.

Robert went about quickly co-ordinating all the bits and pieces needed for a conference, including speakers. One of the first people he called was Joseph Hardin at NCSA. But Hardin's response to Robert was: 'Oh, well, we were thinking of holding a conference, and May is basically when we were going to do it, in Chicago. Would you mind cancelling your conference so we can go ahead with ours?'

Robert debated with himself for only a moment. There was honour and pride at stake here, but also the future direction of the Web. The conference was the way to tell everyone that no one should control it, and that a consortium could help parties agree on how to work together while also actually withstanding any effort by any institution or company to 'control' things. Feeling that perhaps NCSA was again trying to beat us to the punch, Robert told Hardin, 'Well, if you had planned your conference so long ago then you certainly would have told us about it by now. So, sorry, we intend to go forward with ours.' He pointed out that we had already booked the space and had passed the point of no return. NCSA decided to hold a second WWW conference in Chicago in November.

As 1994 unfolded, more signs emerged that the general public was beginning to embrace the Web. Merit Inc., which ran the Internet backbone for the National Science Foundation, measured the relative use of different protocols over the Internet. In

March 1993, Web connections had accounted for 0.1 per cent of Internet traffic. This had risen to 1 per cent by September, and 2.5 per cent by December. Such growth was unprecedented in Internet circles.

In January, O'Reilly had announced a product dubbed 'Internet in a Box', which would bring the Internet and Web into homes. It was already possible for anyone to download, free, all the browsers, TCP/IP, and software needed to get on the Internet and Web, but a user had to know a lot about how to configure them and make them work together, which was complicated. Neither the Internet nor the Web had initially been set up for home or individual business use: they were meant for universities, researchers and larger organisations. O'Reilly's product put it all together. All a user had to do was install it on his computer, and pay phone charges for his connection to the Internet.

Soon thereafter, however, many Internet service providers started to spring up – local companies that would give access to the Internet via a local telephone call. They provided all the software a subscriber required. This made Internet in a Box unneeded. And it was a strong indicator of the rapid commercialisation of 'the Net'.

A short month later Navisoft Inc. released a browser/editor for the PC and the Mac, which was remarkably reminiscent of my original World Wide Web client. Navipress, as it was called, allowed a person to browse documents and edit them at the same time. There was no need to download something explicitly, edit it with a different mode, then upload it again – finally, a browser that also functioned as an editor. I was very glad to hear of it. Usually when we had talked about the principles of the Web, most people just didn't get it. But Dave Long and the people at

Navisoft had got it, miraculously, just by reading everything we had written on info.cern.ch and by following the discussions of the Web community. Navipress was a true browser and editor, which produced clean HTML.

I talked again with Michael Dertouzos about forming a consortium. In February he invited me to MIT's LCS to see if we could work out details we'd both be happy with. He took me to lunch at the Hyatt, which I understood was his usual place for serious discussion. The doorman knew him so well he had a cordoned-off space waiting for Michael's BMW at any time. Michael had helped put together other high-level organisations that included academic, industry and government people, and was assuming that a similar model would hold for a Web consortium. But when he asked me where I wanted such an organisation to reside, I hesitantly mentioned I didn't want it to be based just at MIT: I wanted it to be international. I didn't want to defect from Europe to the States. I thought there should be a base in Europe and a base in the States.

To my delight, this made perfect sense to Michael. He was happy to have LCS be part of what he called a two-legged beast. Of Greek descent, Michael had made many transatlantic connections over the years, and had always been interested in fostering joint efforts between the Old World and the New. I had hit not a snag, but one of Michael's hot buttons. We returned to LCS with joint enthusiasm and warmth.

Michael later introduced me to his associate director, Al Vezza, who had helped Bob Scheifler set up the X Consortium and run it from LCS for years. Al took me into his office and asked me blunt questions about the business end of a consortium, questions to which I had no answers, questions about the organisation structure and the business model. Fortunately, Al had answers. He had set up these kinds of things for the X Consortium, and was happy to do the same again. The X Consortium plan had been so well defined that Al ended up persuading me to follow a similar model. CERN clearly had first option to be the European host. Michael, Al and I had pretty much assumed that CERN would sign on. I returned to Geneva and began a series of talks about CERN assuming this new role.

As the talks ensued, Marc Andreessen, who had left NCSA to join Enterprise Integration Technology (EIT), had met businessman Jim Clark. Together they founded Mosaic Communications Corp. The two rapidly hired Lou Montulli of Lynx fame, hired away the core Mosaic development team from NCSA, and set out to commercialise their browser. They'd soon relocate to Mountain View, California, and in April 1994 would rename themselves Netscape.

Despite the news articles hailing it as the first step of an Internet revolution, Netscape's start was very natural. The Mosaic team, unlike any of the other browser teams, had always operated much more like a product development team than a research team. They were much more aware of Mosaic's branding, of customer relations, marketing and delivery. NCSA deliberately adapted Mosaic for multiple platforms so it would reach a large audience. Unlike CERN, NCSA never doubted for a moment that creating commercial products was an appropriate activity. Leveraging Marc's skills, NCSA pushed Mosaic hard, from being a great idea seen in Viola to a must-have product that was going to be on every desktop. Andreessen and Clark set out aggressively to conquer the entire market. To do so they used an unprecedented marketing policy: they released their product for free, so it would be picked up widely and quickly; all someone had to do was download it from the Internet. They also seemed to follow the unprecedented financial policy of not having a business plan at first: they decided not to bother to figure out what the plan would be until the product was world-famous and omnipotent.

The arrival of Web software and services as a commercial product was a very important step for the Web. Many people would not really want to use the Web unless they could be sure they could buy the products they needed from a company with all the usual divisions, including customer support. Robert and I had spent so much time trying to persuade companies to take on the Web as a product. At last, it had happened.

People began to ask me whether I was planning to start a company. Behind that question, maybe they were wondering if I felt the rug had been swept out from beneath my feet by Marc Andreessen and Jim Clark. Of course, I had several options apart from starting a consortium. I had actually thought about starting a company with the working name Websoft, to do much the same as Netscape. (The name was later taken by a real company.) But at this point, starting a company was by no means a guarantee of future riches. It was a financial risk like any startup, and a considerable one in this case, since there was not even a clear market yet.

Furthermore, my primary mission was to make sure that the Web I had created continued to evolve. There were still many things that could have gone wrong. It could have faded away, been replaced by a different system, have fragmented, or changed its nature so that it ceased to exist as a universal medium. I remembered what Phil Gross, chairman of the IETF, had once said about gopher when it was still rising in popularity: 'Things can get picked up quickly on the Internet, but they can be dropped quickly, too.' My motivation was to make sure that the Web became what I'd originally intended it to be – a universal medium for sharing information. Starting a company would not have done much to further this goal, and it would have risked the prompting of competition, which could have turned the Web into a bunch of proprietary products. Theoretically, it would have been possible to have licensed the technology out, but the swift demise of gopher reasoned against that.

I also realised that by following the consortium route I could keep a neutral viewpoint, affording me a much clearer picture of the very dramatic, evolving scene than a corporate position would allow. I wanted to see the Web proliferate, not sink my life's hours into worrying over a product release. While leading a consortium would limit my public opinions due to confidentiality and the requirement of having to be neutral, I'd be free to really think about what was best for the world, as opposed to what would be best for one commercial interest. I'd also be free to wield a persuasive influence over the Web's future technical directions.

I suppose I could, as an alternative, have pursued an academic career, gone to a university somewhere as an assistant professor. But I'd never taken a PhD, and so even at CERN, the grade I had on entry, and the grade I was stuck with throughout my career, was one notch down. I would have had to spend a good amount of time getting a PhD, which would have been in a relatively narrow area. I certainly didn't have the time. And narrowing my view would have meant jumping off the bobsleigh I had managed to push into motion.

A more tempting option was to join the research group of a large benevolent company, which would have allowed me to pursue research that was interesting to me, but also participate in the industry movement to get Web products into the marketplace and into people's real lives. I did talk to several companies and visited a few labs to evaluate this possibility, but there didn't seem to be a good match.

Starting a consortium, therefore, represented the best way for me to see the full span of the Web community as it spread into more and more areas. My decision not to turn the Web into my own commercial venture was not any great act of altruism or disdain for money, of which I would later be accused.

While the press was making a big deal about Mosaic Communications, the first World Wide Web conference was now fast approaching. Robert turned his full attention to pulling off an auspicious event.

The conference began at CERN on 25 May, and would last three days. It was a tremendous gathering. The auditorium held perhaps three hundred people. We limited registration to three hundred, but ended up with three hundred fifty after admitting members of the press, and others who just appeared – testimony to how the Web had grown.

The student volunteers, whom Robert had rounded up to help run the conference, were manning the registration area. Robert and I, of course, were running around trying to get the last-minute things together. But when I went to go into the conference area, I was very effectively bounced by the students, because the conference wasn't open yet. It took me a long time to get across to them the fact that I was actually involved with the organisation that was holding the conference.

As he had promised, Robert had set everything up, and, except for the last-minute rushing, I didn't have to do anything but attend and speak. The environment in the meeting rooms was exciting yet close. There were people from all walks of life brought together by their enthusiasm for the Web. Talks given in the small auditorium were packed. Because it was the first such conference, many people who had been interacting only by e-mail were meeting each other face to face for the first time. And for the first time people who were developing the Web were brought together with all sorts of people who were using it in all sorts of ways. The connections were electric. For example, there was Børre Ludvigsen, who had a home server that allowed people to visit his house, look at a cutaway model of it, see where the computers were in it and browse his bookshelves. He had put his server on a special phone line provided by the Norwegian phone company as part of an experiment. He was talking with people who actually thought they could adapt his approach for health-care applications. The excitement, congeniality and grassroots fervour for furthering the Web inspired the reporters there, overdoing it a little, to dub the meeting the 'Woodstock of the Web'.

In the span of one session in one of the meeting rooms, the agenda was laid down for HTML for the next few years – how to incorporate tables, maths, and the handling of graphics and photographic images. Although anything on an Internet FTP server was available on the Web, HTTP had completely taken off as a more efficient alternative, but it needed a lot more optimisation to keep up with ever-increasing demands to frequently fetch Web pages from a server in rapid succession, and pick up all the graphics embedded in a page. In a birds-of-a-feather session, Dave Raggett proposed a 'Virtual Reality Markup Language', an idea Mark Pesce picked up and ran with to start the whole community doing 3D on the Web and to define VRML.

The only time I felt a bit uneasy was when I gave the closing speech. I talked about several technical points, which was fine. I announced the upcoming consortium, which was fine. But then I finished by pointing out that, like scientists, people in the Web development community had to be ethically and morally aware of what they were doing. I thought this might be construed as a bit out of line by the geek side, but the people present were the ones now creating the Web, and therefore were the only ones who could be sure that what the systems produced would be appropriate to a reasonable and fair society. Despite my trepidation, I was warmly received, and I felt very happy about having made the point. The conference marked the first time that the people who were changing the world with the Web had got together to set a direction about accountability and responsibility, and how we were actually going to use the new medium. It was an important direction to set at this juncture.

I went home feeling very pleased. Exciting though all this was, in my personal life it was dwarfed by the arrival of our second child in June. Family life continued and for a while it seemed MIT had stalled in preparations for the WWW Consortium. Then Al Vezza began calling me at home in the evening to discuss details. The conversations seemed even more odd because of the cultural disconnect. Our little prefab house was in a small French village a few miles from the border with Switzerland. The view from our front yard stretched straight across Geneva to Mont Blanc. From the back garden, where we often ate dinner, was a view of the Jura mountains, cows grazing on the few intervening fields. Given the time difference with Massachusetts, that's often where I was when Al called. I would be wearing shorts, sitting out in the sunshine. Al, who was certainly wearing a grey suit, would be seated in an air-conditioned concrete office building in Cambridge. It was sometimes hard to connect across this gulf.

One evening in early July our phone rang. It was Al, and he was serious. He wanted to know if there was a way he could fax me right then and there. He said he had just got the go-ahead from MIT to form the consortium. LCS was prepared to hire me as a full-time staff member. He had a letter to that effect, and wanted to know when I would start.

It was just ten days before we were due to leave on our vacation. We had not specifically planned any dates after that, since the process of getting the details right at MIT seemed at times to have no end in sight. As it appeared that MIT had now got its ducks in a row, however, there was no reason to wait. 1 September seemed like a good starting date. It would be only ten days after we'd come back from our holiday, but we wanted to start in the States at the beginning of the school year.

Al's next call was on 14 July, Bastille Day. As usual, our village was celebrating with fireworks, lit from a field just across the road from our house. I found that I could not be totally serious with Al, and wondered if he would understand. There we were, watching the fireworks over our little town in the French countryside, across the lake from the Alps. The conversation was almost inaudible with the explosions.

My wife and I were packing our bags for the holiday. Although we assumed we could come back to sort out our affairs, we decided that if there was a question about whether to bring something or not, we should bring it. And so we left, with a young daughter, an infant son and a cavalcade of friends going down to the airport with sixteen cases and boxes. My family never came back. I returned for ten days to sell, with the help of friends, the cars and the house.

Meanwhile, encouraged by George Metakides in Brussels, MIT and CERN inked an agreement to start the World Wide Web Consortium. It was announced in Boston by Martin Bangemann, one of the European Commission's commissioners, who was charged with developing the EC's plan for a Global Information Society. There was a press release. The Associated Press ran a story about it. Reports followed in the *Wall Street Journal*, the *Boston Globe* and other major papers. Mike Sendal and Robert Cailliau had been joined by François Fluckiger, who was to lead the consortium team at CERN. It still wasn't clear how the consortium would fit in there, since this was new. It was clear that MIT was very much in control, moving faster, with more experience and relevant contacts. Some people in Europe expressed concern that Web technology would move west, leaving Europe behind. I knew I had to move to the centre of gravity of the Internet, which was the United States. The American government could congratulate itself on successful research funding that led to the Internet, and Europe could congratulate itself on taxpayer money well spent on CERN.

I left Geneva, off to MIT. Off to America. Off to the World Wide Web Consortium. And off to a new role as facilitator of the Web's evolution.

CHAPTER 8

Consortium

When I arrived at MIT's Laboratory for Computer Science, I camped out in a corridor with two doors and no windows close to the offices of Michael Dertouzos and Al Vezza. Though an office of my own would have been nice, this arrangement actually worked out beautifully because it allowed us to work together very readily – and them to keep an eye on me.

I hadn't had time to get a car yet, so I was commuting by bus from our temporary home. Trudging to work in citified Cambridge was a far cry from rural France, but it was autumn, and the bus ride gave me time to revel in New England's autumnal colours. It also gave me time to think about my new role.

Although I knew I would be forced to introduce some structure, I wanted the consortium to operate in a way that reflected a weblike existence. The Web would not be an isolated tool used by people in their lives, or even a mirror of real life: it would be part of the very fabric of the web of life we all help weave.

The Web scene was beginning to fill with a colourful mix of different types of people, organisations and concerns. The consortium would, too. It would be its own web, and sustain the greater Web, which would help sustain the web of life.

I wanted the consortium to run on an open process like the IETF's, but one that was quicker and more efficient, because we would have to move fast. I also wanted an atmosphere that would allow individuals, representing their companies or organisations, to voice their personal ideas and find ways to reach common understanding. There would always be people who would disagree, and they would be levers for progress. We would get ever closer to true consensus, perhaps never completely achieving it, but delighting in every advance.

This freewheeling design might create tension between my being a manager and leaving the consortium as a very flat space of peer respect and joint decision-making. It might create tension among consortium members, who would have to take leads on issues but always conform to a democratic process. It struck me that these tensions would make the consortium a proving ground for the relative merits of weblike and treelike societal structures. I was eager to start the experiment.

The WWW conferences continued half-yearly at Darmstadt, Boston and Paris, and the academic institutes hosting them founded the International World Wide Web Conference Committee as a nonprofit organisation, to continue the series, with Robert as president. On the business side, Netscape was working furiously to release the first commercial version of its browser by the end of the year. Bill Gates and Microsoft, who had shrugged off the Internet and the Web, were realising they might be missing a good party. Gates assigned people to develop a browser. Microsoft was also investigating the development of an online service that might compete with America Online, CompuServe and Prodigy.

The timing of who was developing which technology, and who was working with whom, would determine the course of events for years to come. In April 1994, Gates had decided that the next version of Microsoft's operating system, Windows 95, should include software for accessing the Internet. The decision came only a few weeks after Clark and Andreessen formed Mosaic Communications. Gates wrote a memo to Microsoft employees saying the Internet would constitute a new and important part of the company's strategy. If Gates had made the decision two months earlier, would he have hired the same NCSA people that Mosaic had just grabbed?

The Web was becoming a business. Rather than develop its own Web code, Microsoft licensed browser code from a small NCSA spin-off called Spyglass. The cost was $2 million – more money than any of us involved from the early days would ever have dreamed of.

In November the major marketing campaigns began. At Comdex, the twice-yearly computer trade show, Microsoft announced with great fanfare that its online service, the Microsoft Network (or MSN), would be launched and that software to access and use it would be part of Windows 95. At the same conference, Jim Clark announced publicly that Mosaic Communications was changing its name to Netscape. NCSA had been annoyed about Clark and Andreessen using its software name, Mosaic, as a product name, too, and when the two had hired away NCSA's people, NCSA took offence. An out-of-court settlement was reached, costing the upstart company close to $3 million in expenses and other fees, and requiring it to find a new name. Netscape was it.

∞

Al and I were having our own debates over a name for the nascent organisation, arriving at the World Wide Web Consortium, or W3C for short. Some of the icons still have a trace of a 'W3O' (Organisation), which held for a while.

While I worked up a technical agenda, Al energetically signed up members. The Digital Equipment people who had surprised me with their visit at CERN were among the first on Al's list of calls. They joined, and people at other companies – from upstart Netscape to stalwarts like Hewlett-Packard and IBM – quickly followed.

Membership was open to any organisation: commercial, educational or governmental, whether for-profit or not-for-profit. The annual fee for full membership was fifty thousand dollars; for affiliate membership it was five thousand dollars. There was no difference in benefits, but to qualify for affiliate status an organisation had to be not-for-profit or governmental, or an independent company with revenues less than fifty million dollars. Netscape joined for the full fifty thousand dollars despite qualifying as an affiliate; it insisted that it join as a big company on principle. Members had to commit to a three-year term of membership, after which they could renew annually. In return, members were free to attend any meeting, and sit on any working group or other ensemble we would put together. They would also get exclusive access to in-depth information on all activities under way, whether they were directly involved or not.

Though we didn't have the motto at the time, the consortium's purpose was to 'lead the Web to its full potential', primarily by developing common protocols to enhance the interoperability and evolution of the Web. To do this, we would stay ahead of a significant wave of applications, services and social changes, by fulfilling a unique combination of roles traditionally ascribed to quite different organisations.

Like the IETF, W3C would develop open technical specifications. Unlike the IETF, W3C would have a small full-time staff to help design and develop the code where necessary. Like industrial consortia, W3C would represent the power and authority of millions of developers, researchers and users. And, like its member research institutions, it would leverage the most recent advances in information technology.

The consortium would also take great pains to remain a 'vendor-neutral' forum for its members. A small, core staff housed at the Laboratory for Computer Science and sites in Europe and Asia would produce specifications and sample code, which members – and anyone else, for that matter – could pick up and use for any purpose, including commercial products, at no charge. Consortium funding from dues (and, initially, public research money) would underwrite these efforts.

There also would be the Advisory Committee, comprising one official representative from each member organisation, who would serve as the primary liaison between that organisation and W3C. The committee's role would be to offer advice on the overall progress and direction of the consortium. I would be the consortium's director; Al would be chairman.

Most of the organisations that were signing up were companies interested primarily in advancing the technology for their own benefit. The competitive nature of the group would drive the developments, and always bring everyone to the table for the next issue. Yet members also knew that collaboration was the most efficient way for everyone to grab a share of a rapidly growing pie.

Although the consortium was seen as primarily an industry group, the US and European governments were supportive. In fact, the US Defense Advanced Research Projects Agency provided seed money, in part because we would be building bridges between academic research and industry. Martin Bangemann, the European Commission commissioner, held a meeting of the European governments, which decided to support CERN's coordination of Europe's part of the consortium.

Not surprisingly, one of my first steps at MIT was to set up a Web server. I took a copy of all the existing Web documentation and specifications from the info.cern.ch server at CERN. The new web address was http://www.w3.org. CERN would maintain info.cern.ch as a forwarding address.

No sooner had I arrived at MIT than I was off to Edinburgh, Scotland, for the next European Conference on Hypermedia Technology. It was run by Ian Ritchie of Owl, whom I had tried to persuade four years earlier to develop a Web browser as part of Owl's hypertext product, Guide. It was here that I saw Doug Engelbart show the video of his original NLS system. Despite the Web's rise, the SGML community was still criticising HTML as an inferior subset, and proposing that the Web rapidly adopt all of SGML. Others felt that HTML should be disconnected from the ungainly SGML world and kept clean and simple.

Dale Dougherty of O'Reilly Associates, who had gathered the early Web creators at the first Wizards workshop and other meetings, saw a third alternative. After one session at the conference, a bunch of us adjourned to a local pub. As we were sitting around on stools nursing our beer glasses, Dale started telling everyone that, in essence, the SGML community was passé and that HTML would end up stronger. He felt we didn't have to accept the SGML world wholesale, or ignore it. Quietly, with a smile, Dale began saying, 'We can change it.' He kept repeating the phrase, like a mantra. 'We can change it.'

Right then and there, fixing SGML was put on the agenda. For the HTML community, the controversy quickly became a huge turn-on. It got them going. And many in the documentation community, also fed up with aspects of SGML, sympathised.

Compared with all the drama taking place in the forming of Web companies, this controversy may have seemed like an esoteric technical point. But the Jim Clarks and Bill Gateses would have no big business decisions to make unless specific decisions like the relationship of HTML to SGML were sorted out. Businesspeople and marketers who thought they were 'driving' the Web would have had nothing to drive.

In October 1994, Netscape released the first version of its browser, dubbed Mozilla. It was a 'beta' or test version, released so people on the Net would try it and send suggestions for improvements. As he had with Mosaic, Andreessen pumped out messages about Mozilla over the newsgroups, and users snapped it up.

Meanwhile, Ari Luotonen, the Finnish student from the Erwise project whom Robert had brought to CERN, was productizing CERN's HTTP code. He made it easy to install, with documentation on how to use it. When his term as a CERN student came to an end, he joined Netscape to work on its server software. The other student at CERN, Henrik Frystyk Nielsen, joined us at the consortium. He would be one of the people who would do the core work on the next upgrade of the hypertext protocol, HTTP 1.1.

As members signed up for the consortium, they advised us about what they wanted to address first. One of the top priorities was network security. Information, such as credit-card numbers, sent over the Web needed to be safeguarded. Netscape was particularly interested because it had a deal looming with mammoth MCI to distribute Netscape's browser on MCI's new Internet service, due to begin in January. Netscape's software, called Secure Sockets Layer (SSL), would protect credit-card purchases on MCI's planned online shopping mall. Seeing SSL as a competitive advantage and feeling that W3C was not yet really up and running, Netscape decided not to wait, and developed the software fairly independently. This was one of the first programs that allowed electronic commerce (e-commerce) to gain credibility.

With so much new, autumn passed quickly. Suddenly it was December 1994. In three short days, huge events took place that would for ever alter the Web's future: the consortium members met for the first time; Netscape released the commercial version of its browser; and CERN decided after all not to be a W3C host site. That bobsleigh I had been pushing from the starting gate for so long was now cruising downhill.

On 14 December at LCS the World Wide Web Consortium held the first meeting of its Advisory Committee. The meeting was very friendly and quite small, with only about twenty-five people. Competitors in the marketplace, the representatives came together with concerns over the potential fragmentation of HTML. This was seen as a huge threat to the entire community. There were so many proposed extensions for HTML that a

standard really was needed. We wrestled over terms – whether the consortium should actually set a 'standard' or stop just short of that by issuing a formal 'recommendation'. We chose the latter to indicate that getting 'rough consensus and running code' – the Internet maxim for agreeing on a workable program and getting it out there to be tried – was the level at which we would work. We also had to move fast, and didn't want to be dragged down by the sort of long international voting process that typified the setting of an actual standard. It was becoming clear to me that running the consortium would always be a balancing act, between taking the time to stay as open as possible and advancing at the speed demanded by the onrush of the technology.

We also decided that if we were going to develop open, common protocols and stay ahead of applications, we would have to support an ongoing effort, primarily by the staff, to create a set of Web tools we could use ourselves to demonstrate new ideas and experiment with proposed specifications. Initially, that meant adopting a browser and server that were a bit ahead of their time. We agreed to use Dave Raggett's Arena browser and the CERN server as our test beds. Certainly, we would make these and any other tools freely available for use by anyone. All people had to do was access the public part of the W3C Web site and download a program.

Indeed, the true art for the consortium would be in finding the minimum agreements, or protocols, everybody would need in order to make the Web work across the Internet. This process did not put the consortium in a position of control: it was just providing a place for people to come and reach consensus. In these early days, before we developed more formal processes, if a member didn't want to be part of a given initiative, the member's representative wouldn't come to that meeting. And if people couldn't agree after serious effort, we'd eventually drop the topic.

Whether inspired by free-market desires or humanistic ideals, we all felt that control was the wrong perspective. I made it clear that I had designed the Web so there should be no centralised place where someone would have to 'register' a new server, or get approval of its contents. Anybody could build a server and put anything on it. Philosophically, if the Web was to be a universal resource, it had to be able to grow in an unlimited way. Technically, if there was any centralised point of control, it would rapidly become a bottleneck that restricted the Web's growth, and the Web would never scale up. Its being 'out of control' was very important.

The international telephone system offers a decent analogy. The reason we can plug in a telephone pretty much anywhere in the world is because industry agreed on certain standard interfaces. The voltages and signals on the wire are almost exactly the same everywhere. And given the right adapter, we can plug in a wide range of devices from different companies that send all sorts of information, from voice to fax to video. The phone system defines what it has to, but then leaves how it is used up to the devices. That's what we needed for computers on the Web.

On 15 December, the day after the first consortium meeting, Netscape released the commercial version of Mozilla, renamed Navigator 1.0. It was compatible with Microsoft's Windows operating system, the X Windows system on Unix, and Macintosh. The browser was significant not so much for its technical features, but for the way in which Mosaic released it. Rather than shrink-wrap and ship it, Netscape released it over the

Internet. And rather than charge for it, it was free. Within several months the majority of people on the Web were using it.

Andreessen was following the model by which all previous Web software had been released, except that this time the software was coming from a commercial company that was supposed to make money. People wondered where the profit was going to come from.

Andreessen and Clark had realised that browsers would rapidly become a commodity. NCSA had licensed the Mosaic code to other startups, and Microsoft was developing its own browser. Netscape couldn't hope to make its living from the browser market. What it could do was get its browser out before the others. If it was rapidly and widely accepted, then the company would have a platform from which to launch other products for which it would charge money. It would also bring millions of people to Netscape's home page – the default first screen when Navigator was opened. There, Netscape could display ads from companies that would pay to reach a large viewership. The site also would instantly notify browsers of Netscape's other services, which the company would charge for. Netscape also would charge companies for a commercial grade of the browser, which was more powerful, and for setting up and supporting a company's Web server.

In taking this position, Netscape was wisely acknowledging that on the Web, it was more profitable to be a service company than a software company. Andreessen and Clark may not have been completely clear on this at the beginning, though, because people who downloaded the browser were told that they could use it free for only three months. After that they were expected to pay, or they would be in violation of the licensing agreement.

I didn't know what reaction Netscape was getting to this. I assumed that some people paid, but many did not, and simply downloaded the next version of the software, which also turned out to be free. Netscape allowed this to happen for fear of losing fans to other browsers, and as time went on its appeal for payment was minimised.

This approach set the tone for the Web companies that would follow: release beta versions for review, which put a nascent software program in the hands of hundreds of professional and amateur users, who would (for free) send suggestions for improvements; give away basic software to get customers on board; distribute the software fast and cheap over the Internet; then try to make money from the millions of visitors through ads or services.

On 16 December 1994, a third day in an incredible week, CERN announced major news. After negotiating for several years, the CERN Council had unanimously approved the construction of the Large Hadron Collider, a new accelerator. It would be the next leap towards investigating the even smaller scales of matter. I would soon learn, however, that to accomplish such a mammoth undertaking CERN would impose stringent budget conditions across the organisation. No programme that wasn't central to high-energy physics could be supported. That meant that CERN, regretfully, could not continue to support Web development, or the consortium.

In a way, it was probably in everybody's best interests for it to opt out. CERN, at its heart, had always concentrated on high-energy physics, and had never developed great experience with industry or a general policy about working with it. But I felt that CERN deserved the credit for letting me develop the Web, and for maintaining such a tremendously creative environment. Continued involvement in the consortium would have cemented its place in the Web's ongoing history. I would rather have seen the organisation get a pat on the back than go quietly into the night. For his part, Robert would remain very involved with the Web community, by continuing to organise the annual WWW Conference series.

CERN's resignation left the consortium without a European base, but the solution was at hand. I had already visited the Institut National de Recherche en Informatique et en Automatique (INRIA), France's National Institute for Research in Computer Science and Control, at its site near Versailles. It had world-recognised expertise in communications: their Grenoble site had developed the hypertext browser/editor spun off as Grif that I had been so enamoured with. Furthermore, I found that Jean-François Abramatic and Gilles Kahn, two INRIA directors, understood perfectly well what I needed. INRIA became cohost of the consortium. Later, in early 1996, we would arrange that Vincent Quint and Irene Vatton, who had continued to develop Grif, would join the consortium staff. They would further develop the software, renamed Amaya, replacing Arena as the consortium's flagship browser/editor.

The whirlwind of events that had taken place in a mere seventy-two hours was exciting yet daunting. The consortium had to get moving with a sense of urgency if it was going to stay ahead of the large forces that were gathering.

I had to wait only two months for confirmation that the Web had become a global juggernaut. In February 1995 the annual meeting of the G7, the world's seven wealthiest nations, was held in Brussels. The world's governments were rapidly becoming aware of the technology's influence, and Michael Dertouzos, LCS's director, was invited to join the US delegation there. As Michael describes in his book *What Will Be*, the keynote speaker was Thabo Mbeki, then deputy president of South Africa. Mbeki delivered a profound speech on how people should seize the new technology to empower themselves; to keep themselves informed about the truth of their own economic, political and cultural circumstances; and to give themselves a voice that all the world could hear. I could not have written a better mission statement for the World Wide Web.

CHAPTER 9

Competition and Consensus

History often takes dramatic turns on events that, at the time, seem ordinary. Microsoft wanted to license Netscape's browser, buy a share of the company and take a seat on Netscape's board. In return, Netscape would be the browser on Microsoft's Windows 95, an entirely new operating system, which would launch Netscape into the huge personal-computer industry. But Jim Clark and Netscape's new CEO, Jim Barksdale, who had been hired to raise money and make deals, were wary. The proposal fell through, and Microsoft redoubled its efforts to offer its own browser.

Other deals, however, did go through, further shaping the competitive landscape. In April, Compaq announced that its new line of personal computers would come with Navigator – the first time a browser would be bundled directly with hardware.

In May, with little fanfare, Sun Microsystems introduced Java, a new programming language. Java was a repackaging of James Gosling's Oak language, originally designed for applications such as phones, toasters and wristwatches. Small application programs written in Java, called *applets*, could be sent directly between computers over the Internet, and run directly inside a Web page on a browser. That was the theory. It met the need for applications in which a hypertext page was not sufficiently interactive, and some programming on the client was necessary. The excitement was that even if computer A and computer B had different operating systems, an applet written on computer A could run on computer B, because the Java language set up a virtual computer on computer B that required only minimal support from computer B's operating system. Many languages, however, had tried to achieve this goal in the past, but the effort of standardising all the facilities they needed was often their demise.

Initially, Java worked. Suddenly, a professional or amateur programmer could create a Java application, post it on a Web site, and people everywhere could download and use it. Java opened up a wide world of potential Web applications that would be simple and inexpensive. Netscape immediately licensed Java, and incorporated it into its next version of Navigator. I was very excited because Java is an object-orientated language, a more powerful programming technique that I had used to write 'World Wide Web' but had abandoned due to lack of standardisation.

In theory, a computer would not need a substantial hard disk and working memory (RAM) to store and run volumes of software for various applications such as word processing, bookkeeping and the like. Instead, a computer with minimum memory and RAM could call up a Web site and download a Java applet for writing documents or keeping books. Personal computers could therefore be made with less hardware and thus at a lower price. Some people even thought this new development could erode the power of the large software companies, like Microsoft, since popular software programs such as word processors could be got in Java rather than from the shrink-wrap market. Java also meant that people with all sorts of different pocket devices, which couldn't support a lot of hardware or software, could communicate and work with each other over the Web from anywhere.

Meanwhile, great anxiety was growing among a group of technology companies that for several years had been leading the way towards the Information Age: the online service providers. CompuServe, Prodigy, America Online and others that offered prepackaged content such as news, an encyclopedia, travel information and e-mail tended to represent the Internet as some 'other' network that was arcane and complex, certainly not worth hassling with. But the Web suddenly made the Internet easy. It also enlightened subscribers to the fact that these online companies were either isolated islands or just a small part of the Internet. To keep their customers, the online service providers grudgingly provided access to the Web, though they still tried to represent it as something that was part of their kingdom. As press coverage of the Web increased, the services became more careful about not misrepresenting the Web to a smarter public. They had to reverse their stance, repositioning themselves as providing organised and safe content, so that people didn't have to venture out alone on to the Web to find what they wanted.

As part of the general upheaval, America Online (AOL) bought Navisoft, the company that had developed the Navipress browser that also worked as an editor. AOL changed the product name to AOLpress. (It is the software that I used to draft early parts of this book.)

At one point, there were even rumours that AOL was trying to start a consortium like W3C, with a similar name. I sent an e-mail to AOL's chief executive, Steve Case, to try to bridge the cultural gap. They gave up on the idea, realising that all the Web companies were already part of W3C, and were far too big a group for them to try to control.

Realising that Netscape had to grow fast if it was going to compete with the big guys like Microsoft, Netscape's chief executive, Jim Barksdale, decided the company should go public, to get a big cash infusion. The initial public offering (IPO) was held on 9 August, only sixteen months after the company was formed. This was extremely early for an IPO, but Wall Street was paying premium prices for high-technology stocks, and Netscape needed ammunition to compete with Windows 95 and the browser that would come with it, which were due out very soon with heavy Microsoft promotion.

The stock was set to open at twenty-eight dollars a share, already a high price, but demand rapidly pushed it to seventy-one dollars. Morgan Stanley, the investment house managing the offering, could not issue shares fast enough. Scores of large institutions wanted large percentages of ownership. They kept buying more until, at the close of trading, 38 million shares were on the market. Netscape, after a single day of trading, was worth $4.4 billion. It was the largest IPO in history, and the company had yet to show a profit.

If the World Wide Web had not yet got the public's full attention, this remarkable story put it on centre stage. It also sent an undeniable message to the commercial world: the Web was big business. The gold rush was on. The flood of cash enabled Netscape to buy small companies that had developed specialised

products for the Web, create joint ventures with larger corporations and broaden its product line to support big contracts from major corporate buyers. By the end of 1996, when it settled into its full business model, Netscape would employ more than two thousand people and report revenues of $346 million. Its inflated stock price would come down to reasonable levels over the coming years, but in one fell swoop the Web had become a major market.

After Netscape's IPO, people began to ask me whether I was upset by the Web 'going commercial'. They still ask today. One part of the question means: 'Are you upset that people have to pay money for certain Web products, or at least for commercial support for them?' Of course I am not. The free-software community was fundamental to the development of the Web, and is a source of great creativity. But it was inevitable and important that if the Web succeeded, there would be a variety of free and commercial software available.

A second meaning to the question related to the fact that for a long time Web pages were posted by individuals and not-for-profit organisations, which pointed to each other with no thought of commercial gain. Academics who had used the Internet from its early stages felt it was an open, free, pure space for their use, and they worried that the bountiful information space they had enjoyed for these righteous uses would now become unavailable, swamped by junk mail and advertising. Certain people felt that commercially motivated material polluted the Web. I had little time for this point of view. The Web was designed as a universal medium. A hypertext link must be able to point to anything. Information that is put up for commercial gain can't be excluded.

People have sometimes asked me whether I am upset that I

have not made a lot of money from the Web. In fact, I made some quite conscious decisions about which way to take my life. These I would not change – though I am making no comment on what I might do in the future. What does distress me, though, is how important a question it seems to be to some. This happens mostly in America, not Europe. What is maddening is the terrible notion that a person's value depends on how important and financially successful they are, and that that is measured in terms of money. That suggests disrespect for the researchers across the globe developing ideas for the next leaps in science and technology. Core in my upbringing was a value system that put monetary gain well in its place, behind things like doing what I really want to do. To use net worth as a criterion by which to judge people is to set our children's sights on cash rather than on things that will actually make them happy.

It can be occasionally frustrating to think about the things my family could have done with a lot of money. But in general I'm fairly happy to let other people be in the Royal Family role (as it were), as long as they don't abuse the power they have as a result. The consortium is the forum where people setting the agenda meet. It's not as if I can just make decisions that change the Web … but I can try to get an entire industry organisation to do it. My priority is to see the Web develop in a way that will hold us in good stead for a long time. If someone tries to monop-olise the Web – by, for example, pushing a proprietary variation of network protocols – they're in for a fight.

Two weeks after Netscape's IPO, Microsoft released Windows 95, and with it Microsoft's browser, Internet Explorer. Bill Gates was turning his back on his earlier strategy of creating a dial-up service, the Microsoft Network, patterned after AOL.

The first version of Internet Explorer had very little functionality. I could tell it was put together in a hurry, but it got Microsoft's toe in the water. In December 1995, Gates made what would later be seen as a famous speech to the press, in which he announced that his company was going to 'embrace and extend' the Internet. To certain people in the computer industry, 'embrace' meant that Microsoft's products would start off being compatible with the rest of Web software, and 'extend' meant that sooner or later, once they had market share, Microsoft's products would add features to make other people's systems seem incompatible. Gates was turning the company around very rapidly and forcefully, to fully exploit the Web. The business community was impressed that Gates was getting into this so personally.

By mid-1996, millions of people were accessing the Web, thousands of companies were serving it, and the press was writing about it constantly. Internet service providers, ISPs, sprouted everywhere, offering Web access for twenty to twenty-five dollars a month. Computer jocks in small towns around the globe started putting up their own homepages, and soon enough offered to do the same for businesses, the local shop, and individuals.

The consortium had positioned itself to help the Web move positively forward. We were holding meetings and issuing briefings packages. But our head of communications, Sally Khudairi, realised we needed more than an efficient Web site to get our message across. She rapidly set up relationships with the press and channels to all those we needed to tell about W3C work. The members suddenly found out all kinds of things about their consortium they never knew, and people who really needed to know about W3C Recommendations but had never heard of us were soon using our name as a household word.

Al Vezza was an effective chair and in essence CEO for the first years; he was succeeded by INRIA's Jean-François Abramatic, whom I had met when I first visited INRIA. Alan Kotok, who was one of the four people from Digital Equipment who had shown up at my office in Geneva, ended up being on the Advisory Committee, and is now on the staff as associate chair. Dale Dougherty, who chanted, 'We can change it' in that Edinburgh bar, would later join the Advisory Board, a small group elected from the full Advisory Committee.

The consortium soon began to develop and in turn codify its process for developing future technology and recommendations. From then on the process would continuously evolve and be refined. Any member could raise the idea of pursuing an issue. Members or staff would draw up a briefing package, which explained why it was important to address a certain matter. It would address what the market conditions were, the technical issues, why the consortium rather than someone else should tackle this, how we could help the situation, what the next step would be – a workshop, a working group, a slew of working groups – and how much it would cost us to pursue.

A briefing package would be distributed to the whole membership. Members would review the package, returning comments as to their support and likely participation. If there was sufficient support and no serious problems, we would most often create a new *activity*. Activities could contain any number of working groups, co-ordination groups, interest groups and staff so as to get the job done in an open, high-quality and efficient way.

In addition to considering the core technical issue, the consortium had to consider the impact on the society being built over the Web, and political questions such as whether governments were likely to do rash things if a technology was not developed correctly. With every new activity, the mix of pressures would be different. The consortium had to be able to respond in a very flexible way to put together a structure and strategy that were appropriate.

Working groups could offer their specifications for wider and wider review by other groups, the membership and the public. The final phase occurred when a solution became a *Proposed Recommendation*, up for formal member review. All the members then would be asked to comment within thirty days. It would either become a W3C Recommendation, be sent back for changes, or be dropped altogether. In theory, the outcome was my decision, based on the feedback (much as the monarch, in theory, rules Britain!), but in fact we would put the member review comments through an internal process of review with the domain and activity leads and working-group chair. In most cases there would be clear consensus from the membership anyway. In a few cases we would go ahead despite objections of a minority, but then only after having delivered a detailed analysis of the opinion overruled. Once a Recommendation was passed, the membership was informed, a press release would go out, and Sally's PR machine would encourage everyone everywhere to adopt it.

One day Dan Connolly arrived very disgruntled at the consortium staff's regular Tuesday meeting at LCS. I had met Dan way back at the hypertext conference in San Antonio where Robert and I had soldered together the modem so we could demonstrate the Web. A red-haired navy-cut Texan, Dan had been very active on the Internet and was an expert in many areas key to Web technology, including hypertext systems and markup languages. He had since joined the W3C staff and was leading our Architecture domain. On this day, he came in saying the consensus process had broken down in a working group, and all hope of meeting the deadlines promised to other groups seemed lost. One company was becoming a big problem, though he couldn't tell for exactly which reasons. The specification wouldn't be able to come out, and the failure would be a blow for the consortium and the Web community.

Dan didn't really want to talk about it, but the rest of the team dragged him back to the subject. This sort of problem was the crux of the job. Technical issues might be more fun, but this was the stuff of building consensus, of making progress in an open community.

Did the problem company really not want to agree? Was there no way to arrive at consensus? Each of us interrogated Dan. We diagrammed what was happening on the whiteboard. The whole staff worked through it with him. By the end of the meeting, Dan and the team had developed a way to bring the spec forward. The companies agreed within two weeks. It was rewarding for me to see that the process worked even in times of controversy, and it meant a great deal to me that the staff could work so well together.

Of course, at times there was tension when people from different companies had different technical views on how to settle a recommendation. It was often difficult to predict which company representative might play the good guy or bad guy. But finding a technically sound, common solution was the job we were about. Indeed, the consortium thrived on the tensions. The competitive struggles for chunks of a lucrative market now provided the financial backdrop for the technological revolution, which itself was the backdrop for a real social revolution. Everyone had a common need to see that the technology evolved.

During 1996, Netscape released Navigator 2.0, which had easy-to-use e-mail and supported Java applications. Bit by bit, the online service providers were giving up and providing gateways to the Web. Bill Gates agreed with AOL's Steve Case to provide AOL with a version of the Explorer browser so that AOL subscribers who accessed the Web through AOL's gateway could browse. An unfortunate outcome of this arrangement, however, was the death of AOLpress, one of the few commercial browsers that provided simple online editing.

The consortium's biggest social test came in response to possible government overreaction to the public's rapidly rising concern about pornography on the Web. John Patrick from IBM was the first W3C member to broach the topic. Sitting to one side of the small room at LCS at that first meeting of twenty-five people, John mentioned that there might be a problem with kids seeing indecent material on the Web. Everyone in the room turned towards him with raised eyebrows: 'John, the Web is open. This is free speech. What do you want us to do, censor it?'

Underlying his concern was the fact that IBM was trying to install computers in classrooms across America, and it was meeting with resistance because parents and teachers were worried about access to inappropriate material. 'Something has to be done,' he maintained, 'or children won't be given access to the Web.'

This was a sobering and new concern for many of us. We decided to return to the topic at a later meeting, but then *Time* magazine published Marty Rimm's article alleging more or less that a large proportion of students spent a large proportion of their time browsing the Web, and a large proportion of what they were viewing was pornography.

Exaggerated though this take on the situation may have been, a group of companies quickly came to the consortium asking to do something now, because they knew Congress had plans to draw up legislation very soon that would be harmful to the Internet. Already, Web sites acceptable to people in Finland were appalling to people in Tennessee, and the idea of Washington trying to decide what was 'indecent' for everyone in the world was indeed sinister.

The consortium companies realised that as an industry they had to demonstrate that they could produce a solution. They had to show that, with simple technology, they could give parents the means to control what their children were seeing, with each parent using their own definition of what material was appropriate, not Washington's. The idea was to create a simple program that could be installed on or in any browser and would let parents block the display of sites that carried a certain rating, like the 'R' or 'X' rating of a movie. However, the program would allow parents to choose from any number of rating schemes that would be devised by different commercial, civic, even governmental groups. A rating service would simply be found at the group's URI.

The consortium would define the languages for writing the ratings and for serving them up on the Web. We called this work the Platform for Internet Content Selection (PICS) and released it to the public in March 1996. Member companies would incorporate the technology into their products.

The legislation everyone was terrified of surfaced as the Communications Decency Act, which rode on the big Telecommunications Act that was certain to be passed. Proposed by both the Democratic and Republican parties, it would regulate content on the Net. We rapidly promoted PICS, and a number of the companies that had members on the PICS working group funded press events. The Communications Decency Act passed, but then civil rights groups challenged it in the courts. Ultimately, it was overthrown as unconstitutional. The existence of PICS was an important factor in helping the courts see that the act was inappropriate, that protection could be provided without regulation and in a manner more in keeping with the Bill of Rights.

Ratings schemes were subsequently devised, and a number of companies incorporated the technology. Other companies that specialised in child-protection software sprang up. But the furore calmed down, people relaxed and industry didn't push PICS technology. Still, PICS had shown that the consortium could work very rapidly, effectively, and in a new arena – the overlapping area of technology, society and politics.

Just after the consortium released PICS, I made the mistake of talking about it to a reporter who found the principle difficult to understand. I thought it was rather simple: W3C develops the protocols, some other party develops the rating schemes, other parties like civic groups would issue ratings, the protocols would be incorporated into commercial products, and parents would choose which rating scheme and levels they would use to block material for each child. Combining this with the conditions on W3C's sample code, the reporter translated it into the statement that W3C was producing a product for safe Web surfing that would be distributed free to all parents, and by the end of the year! The story suggested that W3C would be undermining the market for child-protection software. Although it ran in a small, local paper, that paper belonged to a syndicated news wire, and, unbeknownst to me, the story showed up all over the place, even internationally.

The next afternoon, still unaware of the article, I got a phone call from *Market Wrap*, a fast-paced daily financial programme on CNBC. They asked me if I would answer a few questions for the evening's programme. Acting on the mistaken believe that all publicity is good publicity, I agreed.

I went down to the basement of a local television studio, where I was going to be hooked up so I'd appear to viewers as a guest in a window on the television screen. There I sat, in this grey windowless box of a room, waiting for the slot to come on the air. There was an unmanned camera pointing at me, and a television monitor that showed the programme in progress. My rising unease with the situation suddenly spiked when I heard the anchor break in and say, 'We'll be back in a few minutes with Tim Berners-Lee, and his plans to control the Internet.'

From there it only got worse. When the anchor came back to start the segment with me the monitor went blank. I tried to concentrate on the anchor's voice in my ear and the camera in front of me, with no visual clues as to what was going on.

Suddenly, they cut me in. The anchor's first words were: 'Well, Tim Berners-Lee, so you actually invented the World Wide Web. Tell us, exactly how rich are you?'

Clearly, the fine points of PICS were not what they were after. I was flummoxed. They were annoyed, then eager to hustle me off as the milliseconds fled by. My debut as a talking head was a disaster. Since then, I have not been eager to return to live television. The next day, as the botched news-wire article made ever-wider rounds, there was a large outcry from software companies that we were undercutting their market by (supposedly) releasing competitive products for free. We fought a hard rearguard action to explain how the story was totally wrong. But this was a big headache we didn't need. I had learned how difficult it is to determine what a reporter does and does not understand, and how vital it is to get one's story across in no uncertain terms. I had also learned the fundamental truth about life at W3C: we never would know when it would be a quiet day or when the phone would be ringing off the hook.

More companies from Japan and the Pacific Rim were joining the consortium, enough so that there was a need for an Asian host. Keio University in Japan filled the bill, becoming our third host institution, with Professor Nobuo Saito as associate chair and Tatsuya Hagino as associate director for Japan. Suddenly, finding a good time for global telephone conferences became even more difficult.

The Web industry was growing. The browser companies such as Netscape were broadening into server software, and Web intranets for corporations. Hundreds of large companies, from

Chrysler to Federal Express, were starting Web operations. Conventional groupware products, such as Lotus Notes, which had been taken over by IBM, were reconfigured so they could be accessed with a browser and used to create a Web site.

Through the consortium's work, HTML steadily became more robust. We built on various early work, such as Dave Raggett's handling of tables and figures in his Arena browser, Marc Andreessen's handling of images embedded in the text of Mosaic, and style sheets for different fonts and formatting that Håkon Lie had championed since the early days and taken far beyond the crude form in my original browser on the NeXT, as well as new innovations. By mid-1997 Web sites routinely carried beautiful photographs, animated graphics, tabular information, audio and order forms. Hypertext glued them all together in a multimedia sensation. Though less visible, development of better servers was advancing just as quickly.

By autumn, Microsoft's Internet Explorer had garnered a third of the browser market. But the company turned heads when it began to promote its new operating system, Windows 98, scheduled for release in the spring of 1998. According to Microsoft, this new version would include an upgraded browser, Explorer 4.0. The browser would no longer be a program that came bundled with the system's software, but would be an integrated part of the operating system, one and the same with the program that ran the Windows desktop. This piqued the interest of the US Department of Justice. The DOJ had investigated Microsoft a few years earlier on potential antitrust violations. It had more recently issued a consent decree that forbade tight product integration. Was Explorer 4.0 truly integrated, or just another bundle?

The US Attorney General Janet Reno announced that the

Justice Department would take Microsoft to court, on charges of violating the decree. Investigations, injunctions and hearings would extend the case into 1999.

Whatever the merits of the Department of Justice case, integrating a browser with an operating system was connected with the consistency of user interface for local and remote information. Back at the Boston Web conference in December 1995, I had argued that it was ridiculous for a person to have two separate interfaces, one for local information (the desktop for their own computer) and one for remote information (a browser to reach other computers). Why did we need an entire desktop for our own computer but get only a window through which to view the entire rest of the planet? Why, for that matter, should we have folders on our desktop but not on the Web? The Web was supposed to be the universe of all accessible information, which included, especially, information that happened to be stored locally. I argued that the entire topic of where information was physically stored should be made invisible to the user. This did not, though, have to imply that the operating system and browser should be the same program.

The Justice Department wasn't concerned with the merits of software design. The question it raised was whether or not Microsoft was using its market dominance to destroy competition. By including the browser with Windows 98, it maintained, the company effectively eliminated any reason for anyone to purchase Netscape Navigator.

In January 1998 Netscape made a surprise move reminiscent of the original Internet ethos: rather than just give away the compiled code for its browser, it said it would make all the source code – the original text of the programs as written by the programmers – completely public. This *open source* policy meant that anyone promoting a new technology could create their own version of Navigator for it. It meant that any student doing research or simply a class project could create his or her own versions of specific parts of the browser, and regenerate Navigator with his or her own ideas built in. It meant that anyone who was infuriated by a Navigator bug that Netscape didn't fix could fix it themselves, and send the fix to Netscape if they wanted, for future versions. The open release would allow thousands of people to improve Netscape's products. Microsoft was bigger than Netscape, but Netscape was hoping the Web community was bigger than Microsoft.

The Netscape and Microsoft stories made for dramatic reading, so they were the constant focus of the press. But they were only a small part of the Web story. By its nature, the work at the consortium took a much lower profile, but it stuck to the evolving technology. The Web is built on technical specifications and smooth software co-ordination among computers, and no marketing battle is going to advance either cause.

By the end of 1998 the consortium had produced a dozen Recommendations. W3C's technical strength was broader. There were more than three hundred commercial and academic members worldwide, including hardware and software vendors, telecommunications companies, content providers, corporate users and government and academic entities. Advisory Committee meetings had moved from meeting rooms to a large auditorium, with questions coming from attendees standing at microphones posted in the aisles.

The consortium has learned how to let the outside world put pressure on a member that may not be acting in an open manner. We produce Recommendations – not Standards or regulations – and we have no way to require anybody to abide by them. But journalists can look at a company's statements about openness and compliance, then check its newest product to see if the company is delivering on those promises. Vendors are driven by buyers, and buyers are largely driven by the press, which can lay into anybody it feels is playing a game. The consortium, the press and the user community all work as part of a cycle that helps the public make reasonable judgements about how honest a company is being with them.

One of the major technical advances to come from the consortium is a simpler language to supersede SGML, called XML – the Extensible Markup Language. Like SGML, XML is a base for defining languages like HTML. Dan Connolly, a Web architect from early days, had an understanding of the SGML tradition. Jon Bosak came from a tradition of SGML in ISO committees but saw that the Web needed something cleaner. They formed the nucleus of what had seemed such a remote hope when Dale Dougherty had muttered, 'We can change it,' in that Edinburgh pub.

The XML revolution that followed has been greeted with great enthusiasm, even by the SGML community, since it keeps the principles of SGML in place. When Tim Bray, editor of the XML specification, waved it at the attendees at the WWW6 conference in April 1997, he was greeted with applause – because the spec was thin enough to wave. XML has gone on to become one of the most widely known of W3C's activities, and has spawned books, conferences and a nascent XML software industry.

The consortium has also developed its own set of advanced Web tools, which we use to test proposed technology as it is brought to the group. It tries to use its limited resources to develop at the leading edge where others have not yet ventured. We can't do this all the time, but we have some pretty good minds at work, and good links with all the major companies and universities.

In 1996 we negotiated the right to the Grif code from INRIA and renamed it 'Amaya'. It is designed completely around the idea of interactively editing and browsing hypertext, rather than simply processing raw incoming HTML so it can be displayed on the user's screen. Amaya can display a document, show a map of its structure, allow the viewer to edit it, and save it straight back to the Web server it came from. It is a great tool for developing new features, and for showing how features from various text-editing programs can be combined into one superior browser/editor, which will help people work together. I switched from AOLpress to Amaya.

One Web server we use is Apache. When NCSA were developing Mosaic, they called me at one point and asked if I would mind if they made a server. My policy, of course, was that I wanted as many people as possible writing Web software, so I said, 'Of course, go right ahead.' What they meant, but left unsaid, was that they'd be writing another server that would be competing for 'market share' with the server I had written. But NCSA's subsequent development slowed down, so a bunch of people from all over the Net got together to create 'patches' for NCSA's server, and the result, Apache, became a server in its own right. It was maintained by a distributed group of people on the frontier of Web development, very much in the Internet style.

Apache to this day has a huge number of users, and is a powerful and flexible server system – again, a tremendous testimony to the whole idea of open-source software.

We use Apache as our main server that is accessible to the public. We use our open-source 'Jigsaw' server for collaborative editing of all kinds of documents, from W3C Recommendations to our meeting minutes. Jigsaw is a Java-based server, originally written for the consortium by Anselm Baird-Smith, a slight, enthusiastic French wizard who can write code at lightning speed. Anselm wrote Jigsaw initially as background exercise to help him get used to Java and HTTP. In the two months before he actually joined the consortium staff he had already rewritten it four times. Jigsaw allows members and staff to read and write documents back and forth, and to keep track of all changes behind the scenes. Jigsaw has had great success as a development and test platform among the Java and HTTP cognoscenti, because the server is so flexible.

Written into the consortium's constitution is the stipulation that all the software it produces in support of its work be available to the public. This is a way of promoting recommendations, discussion and experimentation. It allows anyone to join in the testing of new protocols, and allows new companies to rapidly get into the swing of Web software creation. All anyone has to do is go to the consortium's site, www.w3.org, and download these tools for themselves.

The consortium's world does sometimes fill up with politics – industrial and governmental. Companies occasionally make technical statements for commercial reasons. Marketers tamper with the facts and confuse the public as they fence with the others in the field. But underneath, the consortium's members are still pursuing exciting technological advances. Engineers move from company to company, sometimes with projects their employers are abandoning due to lack of understanding, sometimes leaving a trail of claims to their ideas made by each place where they worked. The web of life continues to grow in all this activity. And despite commercial pressures, the technical ideas, the consortium's principles and the social motivations behind them continue to hold centre stage.

CHAPTER 10

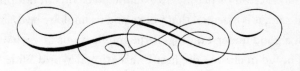

Web of People

The Web is more a social creation than a technical one. I designed it for a social effect – to help people work together – and not as a technical toy. The ultimate goal of the Web is to support and improve our weblike existence in the world. We clump into families, associations and companies. We develop trust across the miles and distrust around the corner. What we believe, endorse, agree with and depend on is representable and, increasingly, represented on the Web. We all have to ensure that the society we build with the Web is of the sort we intend.

When technology evolves quickly, society can find itself left behind, trying to catch up on ethical, legal and social implications. This has certainly been the case for the World Wide Web.

Laws constrain how individuals interact, in the hope of allowing society to function. Protocols define how computers interact. These two tools are different. If we use them correctly, lawyers do not tell computer programmers how to program, and programmers do not tell legislators how to write laws. That is on an easy day. On a difficult day, technology and policy become connected. The Web Consortium tries to define protocols in ways that do not constrain the norms or laws that govern the interaction of people. We define mechanism, not policy. That said, it is essential that policy and technology be designed with a good understanding of the implications of each other. As I noted in closing the first International World Wide Web Conference at CERN in May 1994, technologists cannot simply leave the social and ethical questions to other people, because the technology directly affects these matters.

Since the Web is a work in progress, the consortium seeks to have a dialogue with policy makers and users about what sort of social interactions the Web should enable. Our goal is to assure that the Web accommodates the maximum diversity of public policy choices. In areas like freedom of expression, privacy, child protection, intellectual property and others, governments do have a role. The kinds of tools we make available can help assure that those laws are effective, while also ensuring that individuals retain basic control over their online experience.

Through 1996, most of what happened to the Web was driven by pure excitement. But by 1998, the Web began to be seen as a battleground for big business and big government interests. Religious and parental groups began to call for the blocking of offensive material on the Web, while civil rights groups began to object strongly to these objections. For this reason, among others, many people in business, government, and society at large would like to 'control' the Web in some way.

Unfortunately, these power plays are almost all we hear about in the media: the Justice Department's antitrust case against Microsoft, the merger mania and soaring stock prices of Internet companies, and the so-called battle of the portals – the attempts by mammoth Web sites such as Yahoo!, service providers like

America Online, and content companies like Disney to provide the widest window to the Web's content.

While these manoeuvres certainly affect the business of the Web, in the larger picture they are the background, not the theme. Some companies will rise, some will fall, and new ones might spring from the shadows and surprise them all. Company fortunes and organisational triumphs do not matter to our future as Web users nearly as much as fundamental sociotechnical issues that could make or break the Web. These have to do with information quality, bias, endorsement, privacy and trust – fundamental values in society, much misunderstood on the Web, and alas highly susceptible to exploitation by those who can find a way.

Bias on the Web can be insidious and far-reaching. It can break the independence that exists among our suppliers of hardware, software, opinion and information, corrupting our society. We might be able to hold bias in check if we all could judge the content of Web sites by some objective definitions. But the process of asserting quality is subjective, and is a fundamental right upon which many more things hang. It is asserted using systems of endorsement, such as the PICS protocol the consortium developed to show that government censorship was not necessary. The large number of filtering software tools now available show that government censorship is not even as effective: a nation's laws can restrict content only in that country; filters can block content no matter where it comes from on the Web. Most important, filters block content for users who object to it without removing the material from the Web. It remains available to those who want to see it.

I would like to see similar endorsement techniques used to express other subjective notions such as academic quality.

The essence of working together in a weblike way is that we function in groups – groups of two, twenty and twenty million. We have to learn how to do this on the Web. Key to any group's existence is the integrity of the group itself, which entails privacy and confidentiality. Privacy involves the ability of each person to dictate what can and cannot be done with their own personal information. There is no excuse for privacy policies not to be consensual, because the writing, checking and acceptance of such policies can all be done automatically.

Agreements on privacy are part of the greatest prerequisite for a weblike society: trust. We need to be able to trust the membership of groups, the parties engaging in e-commerce, the establishment of who owns what information, and much more. Nowhere is the difference between the old tree-orientated model of computing and the web model more apparent – and nowhere is society so completely tied to technology – as the online structure that decides who and what we trust. The criteria a person uses to assign trust can range from some belief held by their mother to a statement made by one company about another. Freedom to choose one's own trust criteria is as important a right as any.

A key technology for implementing trust is *public key cryptography* (PKC), a scheme for encoding information so no one else can read it unless he or she has the key to decode it. How we can use it directly affects what we can do socially. With this tool, we can have completely confidential conversations at a distance – vouch for the authenticity of messages, check their integrity and hold their authors accountable. However, it is not available, largely for political reasons explained in the next chapter.

∞

For all its decentralised growth, the Web currently has one centralised Achilles' heel by which it can all be brought down or controlled. When the URI such as http://www.lcs.mit.edu/foo is used to find a web page, the client checks the prefix, and when, as often, it is 'http' it then knows that the www.lcs.mit.edu part is the 'domain name' of a Web server. The domain name system runs on a hierarchical set of computers, which may be consulted to find out the actual Internet address (one of those numbers like 18.23.189.58) to which packets may be sent. At the top of the hierarchy are five computers that store the master list – and an operator error on one of them did once black out the system, causing huge disruption. That technical weakness is itself less of a concern than the social centralisation that parallels it.

Both the domain names and the Internet addresses are given out in a delegated way. To set up the name www.lcs.mit.edu, one registers it with the Lab for Computer Science, which is the owner of the lcs.mit.org domain. LCS got its domain name in turn from MIT, which is the registered owner of mit.edu. MIT got its domain from the owner of edu. Control over the 'top-level' domains such as .com and .edu indirectly gives control over all domain names, and so is something of great power. Who should exercise that power?

During the entire growth of the Internet, the root of an Internet address was administered by a body known as the Internet Assigned Numbers Authority. IANA was set up, was run by and basically *was* the late Jon Postel, an Internet pioneer and guru at the University of Southern California. Jon managed IANA as a public trust, a neutral party. Much of the growth of the Web and Internet depended on his integrity as the ultimate trusted authority who saw to it that the delegation of domain names was fair, impartial, and as unfettered as possible. Because of the sort of person Jon was, it worked. The Web and Internet as a whole owe a lot to Jon, who died in October 1998 at age fifty-five.

Potential problems of unfair control over domain names loomed larger when the US government decided in late 1998 that IANA should be privatised. The potential problem was exacerbated by URI prospectors. The registration of domain names had always been done on a first-come, first-served basis. Increasingly, everyone realised that short, memorable URIs were valuable commodities; the scramble for recognisable domain names, like *candy.com* and *gamble.net*, reached fever pitch. Speculators began to register any name they could think of that might someday be worth more than the one-hundred-dollar registration fee. Domain names like *soap.com* and *sex.com* were snapped up, in hopes of later holding out for a lucrative offer. Select names have since changed hands for large sums of money.

One problem is that the better domain names will wind up with the people or companies that have the most money, crippling fairness and threatening universality. Furthermore, the ability to charge for a domain name, which is a scarce, irreplaceable resource, has been given to a subcontractor, Network Solutions, which not surprisingly made profits but does not have the reputation for accountability, or meeting its obligations. It is essential that domain names be primarily owned by the people as a whole, and that they be governed in a fair and reasonable way by the people, for the people. It is important that we not be blind to the need for governance where centralisation does exist, just because the general rule on the Internet is that decentralisation makes central government unnecessary.

Technically, much of the conflict is due to the mismatch between the domain name structure and the rules of the social mechanism for dealing with ownership of names: the trademark law. Trademark law assigns corporate names and trademarks within the scope of the physical location of businesses and the markets in which they sell. The trademark-law criterion of separation in location and market does not work for domain names, because the Internet crosses all geographic bounds and has no concept of market area, let alone one that matches the existing conventions in trademark law. There can be a Joe & Sons hardware company in Bangor, North Wales, and a Joe & Sons fish restaurant in San Francisco. But there can only be one joeandsons.com.

Whatever solution is found must bridge the gap between law and technology, and the chasm is fairly wide. Suppose a commercial entity is limited to just one domain name. Although under those circumstances it might be hard to manage the persistence of domain names when companies changed hands, companies also might be prevented from snapping up names with every English word related to their area of business. There are some devices in the existing domain name system that can ease the problem. For example, if a widget company in Boston, Massachusetts, can't get the name *widget.com* because it's already taken, it could try the geographically based name *widget.boston.ma.us*.

A neutral, not-for-profit organisation to govern the domain-naming process is currently being put together by the community at large. The original US-centric nature of the domain name service has worried some non-Americans, so any new body will clearly have to be demonstrably international.

There has been a working proposal to create new *top-level*

domains – the *.com* or *.org* or *.net* suffixes on domain names. This would add top-level domains for distinct trades, such as *.plastics*. In this way, *jones.plastics* and *jones.electrical* could be separate entities, easing the crush a little. However, the effect would be a repeat many times over of the ridiculous gold rush that occurred for *.com* names, making it necessary for holders of real trademarks to protect themselves from confusion by registering not just in three domains (*.com*, *.org* and *.net*) but in many more. Unless it was accompanied by a legal system for justifying the ownership of a name on some real grounds, such a scheme would hurt everyone – except those standing on the sidelines ready to make a fast buck by grabbing names they never intend to use.

This is a relatively isolated problem with the Web, and one the W3C has stayed almost completely clear of to date. It does serve as a good illustration of the way a single centralised point of dependence put a wrench in the gears of an otherwise smoothly running decentralised system. It also shows how a technical decision to make a single point of reliance can be exploited politically for power and commercially for profit, breaking the technology's independence from these things, and weakening the Web as a universal space.

Even without a designed-in central point, the Web can be less neutral, and more controlled, than it may seem. The Web's infrastructure can be thought of as composed of four horizontal layers: from bottom to top, they are the transmission medium, the computer hardware, the software and the content. The transmission medium connects the hardware on a person's desk, software runs Web access and Web sites, while the Web itself is only the information content that exists thanks to the other three layers. The independence of these layers is important. From the software engineering point of view, this is the basic principle of modularity. From the point of view of economics, it is the separation of horizontal competitive markets from anticompetitive vertical integration. From the information point of view, think of editorial independence, the neutrality of the medium.

The Microsoft antitrust case was big news in 1999, much of it an argument about the independence in the software layer of an operating system and a browser. In the same year, scarcely a month went by without the announcement of a proposed merger or acquisition between large companies. Two types of deals were taking place, the first between companies that carry data over phone and cable TV lines, the second between content providers. Each of these deals was happening within one of the Web's layers.

I am more concerned about companies trying to take a vertical slice through the layers than creating a monopoly in any one layer. A monopoly is more straightforward: people can see it and feel it, and consumers and regulators can 'just say no'. But vertical integration – for example, between the medium and content – affects the quality of information, and can be more insidious.

Keeping the medium and the content separate is a good rule in most media. When I turn on the television, I don't expect it to deliberately jump to a particular channel, or to give a better picture when I choose a channel that has the 'right' commercials. I expect my television to be an impartial box. I also expect the same neutrality of software. I want a Web browser that will show me any site, not one that keeps trying to get me to go back to its host site. When I ask a search engine to find the information it can on a topic, I don't expect it to return just the sites of companies that happen to advertise with or make payments to the search engine company. If a search engine is not giving me completely neutral results, then I should be told about it with some notice or icon. This is what magazines do when they run an 'article' that has been paid for by an advertiser; it is labelled 'advertising feature', or 'special advertising section', or some such thing. When companies in one layer expand or merge so they can cross layers, the potential for undermining the quality of information in these ways increases greatly.

The trouble begins when a program that an individual depends on for his use of the Web, such as an operating system or browser, displays an array of icons that will automatically connect him to preferred search engines, Web sites, online programs or ISPs. Such arrangements become more troubling if a user gets a single browser/operating system that is written as one integrated software program, and cannot remove such links or negotiate independent arrangements with other providers of similar services that will work with the browser/operating system.

Even the hardware companies are getting into the act. In 1998, Compaq introduced a keyboard with four special keys: hitting the Search key automatically takes the user to the AltaVista search engine. Suddenly, where a person searches the Web depends on where he bought his computer. A user does not know where he stands when he hits a 'Search the Web' or 'Best of the Web' button on a browser or a keyboard. These buttons or keys take the user into a controlled view of the world. Typically they can be set by the user to point to any search engine – but few users change the default.

More insidiously still, it could also be possible for my ISP to give me better connectivity to sites that have paid for it, and

I would have no way of knowing this: I might think that some stores just seemed to have slow servers. It would be great to see some self-regulation or even government regulation in these areas.

The Web's universality leads to a thriving richness and diversity. If a company claims to give access to the world of information, then presents a filtered view, the Web loses its credibility. That is why hardware, software and transmission companies must remain unbiased towards content. I would like to keep the conduit separate from the content. I would like there always to be a choice of the unbiased way, combined carefully with the freedom to make commercial partnerships. And, when other people are making a choice for me, I would like this to be made absolutely clear to me.

Some might argue that bias between the layers is just the free market in action. But if I bought a radio and found that it accessed only certain stations and not others, I'd be upset. I suppose I could have a half dozen radios, one for each set of stations. It makes no more sense to have a half dozen computers or different operating systems or browsers for Web access. This is not just impractical: it fragments the Web, making it cease to be universal. I should be able to buy whichever computer, software and transmission service I want and still have access to the entire content of the Web.

The portals represent the self-reinforcing growth of monopolies, especially those that integrate vertically. In its greater context, the battle of the portals is a battle for brand names on the Web. It is difficult for someone to judge the quality of information, or Web software and services, without extended experience and comparison. As a result, software or transmission companies with existing reputations can capitalise by using their names to attract people to their information services. The extreme would be a company that offered transmission, hardware, software and information, and then tried to brand itself as more or less equivalent to the Web. It would also be a repeat of the dial-up service world of AOL and CompuServe that existed before the Web, on a larger scale. So far, the urge to achieve dominance has driven the quality on the Web upward, but any one company's attainment of it would destroy the Web as we know it.

Happily, the Web is so huge that there's no way any one company can dominate it. All the human effort people and organisations have put in all over the world to create Web sites and home pages is astoundingly large, and most of the effort has to do with what's in the Web, not the software used to browse it. The Web's content, and thus value, will continue despite any one company's actions.

But consider what could happen in a year or two when search engines get smarter. I click the Search button on my keyboard, or tell a search engine, 'I want to buy a pair of shoes.' It supposedly heads out on to the Web to find shoe stores, but in fact brings me only to those shoe stores that have deals with that search engine or hardware company. The same with booksellers. Insurers. News. And so on. My choice of stores and services has thus been limited by the company that sells the computer or runs the search service. It's like having a car with a Go Shopping for Shoes button on the dashboard; when pushed, it will drive only to the shoe store that has a deal with the carmaker. This doesn't help me get the best pair of shoes for the lowest price, it doesn't help the free market, and it doesn't help democracy.

While there are commercial incentives for vertically integrating the layers into one business, legal liability can complicate the picture. In 1998 a Bavarian court convicted Felix Somm, a former head of the German division of CompuServe, of complicity in knowingly spreading pornography via the Internet. The two-year suspended sentence marked the first time in Germany that an online company manager had been held responsible for providing access to content deemed illegal. The material was obtained from computers in other countries, but through CompuServe's gateway to the Internet. When the boundary between the medium and the content is blurred, every ISP or telecommunications company is in danger of being liable for content.

Somm said he had even notified German authorities about the illegal material and aided them in their investigation. CompuServe also provided its subscribers with software they could use to block access to offensive material. Somm may have a chance for acquittal under a new German multimedia law that was passed after he was charged. It says that Internet service providers can be held responsible for illegal material on their servers only if they are aware of it, it is technically feasible to stop it, and they do not take reasonable measures to block access to it – which is what Somm and CompuServe said they did. Somm's defence lawyers argued that no one can be aware of everything on the Internet, and that blocking access to any one bit of it is an exercise in futility.

Since the Web is universal and unbounded, there's all sorts of junk on it. As parents, we have a duty to protect our young children from seeing material that could harm them psychologically. Filtering software can screen information under control of the reader, to spare the reader the grief of having to read what he or she deems junk. People use filters on e-mail to automatically categorise incoming information. An individual clearly has the personal right to filter anything that comes at him, just as he would do with regular mail: some he opens, some he tosses into the bin. Without this right, each day would be chaos. In the future, good browsers will be able to help the user avoid links to Web sites that have attributes he has indicated he doesn't want to have to confront, whether it's the presence of a four-letter word or the fact that the site shows ads.

But when someone imposes involuntary filters on someone else, that is censorship. If a library is supposed to provide a computer that gives citizens access to the Internet, but it prevents access to certain types of material such as pornography, then the library is deciding for the citizenry what they should be able to read. Here the library is installing itself as a central authority that knows better than the reader.

In 1998 patrons of the Loudon County, Virginia, public library filed a suit seeking to remove a filter program installed on Internet computers at six county library branches. They claimed that, while the filter blocked them from accessing pornographic sites, it also blocked them from sites with information on sex education, breast cancer and gay and lesbian rights. The principle here is more interesting than the bickering over details: the suit charged that the library's policy was an unconstitutional form of government censorship.

Just how thorny these qualitative decisions can be was illustrated by a 1998 case described in the *New York Times*: 'The

American Family Association, a conservative Christian group, has been a vocal supporter of filtering products. So it was with some surprise that officials at the group recently discovered that their own Web pages were being grouped with white-supremacist and other "intolerant" sites blocked by a popular filter called Cyber Patrol. Researchers at Cyber Patrol decided the site met the filter's definition of intolerance, which includes discrimination based on sexual orientation.' It seems researchers had found statements on the group's page that spoke out against homosexuality. Cyber Patrol bans up to twelve categories of material it considers inappropriate for the typical twelve-year-old, from gambling to cult sites.

The subjective nature of these decisions is why we set up the PICS system to allow anyone to customise their own objectives without imposing them on others. The key to PICS, and to any attempt to filter, is to give the reader control, and to make different filters available from different groups. With PICS, parents aren't limited to a given label provider, or even a given system of ratings. They have a range of commercially available surveillance programs to choose from – a choice of whom we trust.

The larger point to remember is that laws must be written in relation to actions, not technology. The existing laws that address illegal aspects of information are sufficient. Activities such as fraud and child pornography are illegal offline and online. I don't like the idea of someone else controlling the kinds of information I can access. I do believe, however, that a parent has to protect his or her child on the Internet, just as they would guard where their child goes physically. But the decision as to what information adults can access needs to be up to them.

This principle was at the centre of First Amendment disputes about the constitutionality of Internet censorship laws. When the first effort to censor the Internet was challenged in court, members of the consortium felt it was important that the courts understand how filters could act as an effective alternative to censorship. We provided background information during the deliberations. In 1996 the United States Supreme Court overturned the censorship law, in part because filters enable parents to protect their kids without requiring the government to step in and play nanny. But in 1998 Congress passed another censorship law. It's been challenged again, so that issue is far from settled.

The debate has become more complex, too. Some civil libertarian groups claim that repressive governments could use programs like PICS to squelch political or social communications on the Web that the government doesn't want read. One group, the Global Internet Liberty Campaign (GILC), wrote an open letter to the Web Consortium saying that, to avoid this danger, W3C should not release PICS Rules. PICS Rules is the part of the PICS technology that allows a person or group to store their preferences on a floppy disk, and give them to someone else to use. GILC was worried that the software for doing this could be misused by repressive governments against their own people. GILC also worried, according to Amy Harman of the *New York Times*, that if PICS technology was widely promulgated, Congress could pass a law requiring parents to adopt a particular set of PICS Rules. Since this would constitute government control, GILC said the consortium should not make PICS Rules a standard. We should just bury it.

Here the liberals seem to be wanting to leverage technology in order to constrain government. I find it troubling when

Americans of any party don't trust their political system and try to go around it rather than get it right. The consortium is not going to prevent bad laws by selectively controlling what technology it develops and when to release it. Technologists have to act as responsible members of society, but they also have to cut themselves out of the loop of ruling the world. The consortium deliberately does this. It tries to avoid acting as a central registry, a central profit taker, or a central values setter. It provides technical mechanisms, not social policies. And that's the way it will stay.

The openness of the Web also means there must be a strong concern about business standards. Companies involved in electronic commerce are well aware of this, and some are making attempts to avoid possible governmental imposition of ethical standards by trying to regulate themselves, primarily with endorsements.

The Netcheck Commerce Bureau, for example, is a site where companies can register their commitment to certain standards, and receive a corresponding endorsement. Customers can lodge complaints against such companies with Netcheck. The long-established US Better Business Bureau has a Web site that provides similar tools. Ideally, complaints to these sites will be monitored so that if a company doesn't do right by its customers, it will lose the seal of approval.

Some large companies are taking it upon themselves to establish what is in essence a branding of quality. Since the fundamental issue is determining which site to trust, if someone trusts a large company such as IBM, and IBM brands other companies as ethical, then the person will trust those companies, too. Indeed, IBM has developed what it calls an *e-business mark*, which it bestows on companies it does business with that have shown a commitment to delivering a secure and reliable environment for e-commerce. It's like the Underwriters Laboratory symbol or the Good Housekeeping Seal of Approval.

Unlike regulation, endorsement can be done by anyone, of anything, according to any criteria. This three-way independence makes systems of endorsement very open. An individual can trust a product, or an endorser, or a particular endorsement criterion.

Self-regulation works when there is freedom to set different standards and freedom of consumer choice. However, if 'self-regulation' simply becomes an industry version of government, managed by big business rather than by the electorate, we lose diversity and get a less democratic system.

The e-business mark may be a harbinger of the way many endorsements will go. People in general will not be able to figure out whether they trust a specific online store. So they'll resort to 'trusted' brand names – or endorsements from them.

PICS was the consortium's mechanism to allow endorsements to be coded and checked automatically. It was aimed initially at showing that a Web site meets certain criteria for lack of nudity, violence and such. It hasn't been implemented widely because there is no tremendous economic incentive for people to rate sites. But there may be a huge incentive when it comes to protecting the privacy of personal data someone gives to an online clothing store. The question is whose ratings, or settings, to trust.

As a consumer, I'd like to be made aware of the endorsements that have been given to a site – but without being distracted from the content. Perhaps icons could appear in a window I leave open

while I access a site, or in the border around the page I'm viewing. Endorsements could be made in all fields, not just business.
There could be academic endorsements: when I'm browsing
through research papers on heart disease, an endorsement could
appear that says a given paper has been published in a reputable
journal. Each reader picks the journals he trusts. An individual
would do the same with endorsements from associations in his
profession. And if his medical association, say, happened to
ignore a particular branch of alternative medicine that he believes
in, then he could use an endorsement that is based on a given
journal of alternative medicine. That's the beauty of the Web:
it's a web, not a hierarchy.

Endorsements, as a way of transmitting judgements of quality,
work easily on the Web, because they can be made with hypertext links. However, important though this facility is, it is even
more important to understand that a link does not have to imply
any endorsement. Free speech in hypertext implies the 'right to
link', which is the very basic building unit for the whole Web.

In hypertext, *normal* links are between a hypertext document
and another external document. *Embedded* links are those that
cause something to appear with a document; a picture appears
in a Web page because of an embedded link between the page
and the picture. Normal hypertext links do not imply that the
linked document is part of, endorsed by, or related in ownership
to the first document. This holds unless the language used in
identifying the contents of the linked document carries some
such meaning. If the creator of the first document writes, 'See
Fred's web page [link], which is way cool,' that is clearly some

kind of endorsement. If he writes, 'We go into this in more detail on our *sales brochure* [link],' there is an implication of common authorship. If he writes 'Fred's *message* [link] was written out of malice and is a downright lie,' he is denigrating (possibly libellously) the linked document. Clarifying the relative status of a linked document is often helpful to readers, but the person has to be responsible about what he says, just as he would in any medium.

For embedded links, however, the author of the document has responsibility, even if the contents have been imported from another Web site, and even if the document gives the URI for the embedded text or image so a browser can check the original source. If I write about the growth of the Web and show a graph, the graph is part of my document. It is reasonable to expect me to take responsibility for the image just as for the text. They are logically part of the same document. Advertising embedded in a site is the exception. It would be great if the HTML distinguished links to 'foreign' documents from links to documents with common authorship, and if browsers passed this information on to users in some way.

But beyond this distinction between normal and embedded links, certain misunderstandings still persist. Here are three myths that have crept into the 'common wisdom' about the Web, and my opinion as to the way hypertext protocols should be interpreted.

Myth One: 'A normal link is an incitement to copy the linked document in a way that infringes copyright.' The ability to refer to a document (or a person or anything else) is a fundamental right of free speech. Making the reference with a hypertext link is efficient, but changes nothing else.

Nonetheless, in September 1998, ABC News told the story of a photographer who tried to sue the department store JC Penny, which had a link from its site to the Movie Database Ltd site, which in turn had a link to a Web site run by the Swedish University Network, which was said to have an illegally copied image of the photographer's. Fortunately, the suit was thrown out. A good default rule is that legality online is the same as it is offline. Users, information providers and lawyers need to reach consensus on this. Otherwise, people will be afraid to make links for fear of legal implications. It would soon become impossible to even discuss things.

Myth Two: 'Making a link to an external document makes the first document more valuable, and therefore is something that should be paid for.' It is true that a document is made more valuable by links to other relevant, high-quality documents, but this doesn't mean anything is owed to the people who created those documents. If anything, they should be glad that more people are being referred to them. If someone at a meeting recommends me as a good contact, does that person expect me to pay him for making reference to me? Hardly.

Myth Three: 'Making a link to someone's publicly readable document is an infringement of privacy.' The Web servers can provide ways to give Web site access only to authenticated people. This technology should be used, and Web site hosting services should give publishers control over access. 'Security by obscurity' – choosing a weird URI and not telling people about it – is not conventional, and so a very explicit agreement must be made with anyone who is given the URI. Once something is made public, one cannot complain about its address being passed around.

I do feel it is right to have protection for confidential information that has become public by accident, illegal act, or force of law such as a subpoena. The current assumption that once information has 'accidentally' escaped it is free to be used is unfortunate.

These are my personal feelings about how hypertext should be interpreted, and my intent. I am not an expert on the legalities in each country. However, if the general right to link is not upheld for any reason, then fundamental principles of free speech are at stake, and something had better be changed.

CHAPTER 11

Privacy

When the Web started, one of the things holding it back was often people's unwillingness to be open about their workings – their sources and reasons behind their work. I found this frustrating myself, and would carry the banner for openness of information while I was promoting the Web as one way of fostering this openness. However, I rapidly separated the two, as the Web does not and should not imply that all information must always be shared. To maintain integrity, a group needs a respected border, which in the Web is a border of information flow. Groups need to be able to talk among themselves, and have their own data when necessary.

Perhaps the greatest privacy concern for consumers is that, after they have ordered enough products, companies will have accumulated enough personal information to harm or take advantage of them. With consequences ranging from the threat of junk mail to the denial of health insurance, the problem is serious, and two aspects of the Web make the worry worse. One is that information can be collected much more easily, and the other is that it can be used very easily to tailor what a person experiences.

To see just what can happen to my personal information, I have traced how some online purveyors have used my address. When I provide my address to a Web site, I put a bogus line in it, like an apartment number. Their computer regurgitates it verbatim, so I can tell, when I get junk mail later, who has furnished my address.

There are more threatening scenarios. Burglars could find it very handy to know who has been buying what recently. More likely is the sort of abuse that occurs when a doctor divulges someone's medical condition to the patient's insurance company to justify the claim. Two years later, the insurance company picks the information out of its database when a prospective employer wants to check that person's record. The person doesn't get the job because of a previous medical condition and never even knows what happened.

Software can even track the pattern of clicks a person makes on a Web site. If a user opens an online magazine, the publishers can watch which items he reads, tell which pictures he calls up and in what order, and extract information about him that he would never volunteer on a form. This is known as 'click stream' information. Net Perceptions, started by a former head of Microsoft's programming languages division, is one firm that makes software that companies can use to monitor all sorts of online behaviour, from the amount of time a visitor spends reading about a product to what pages they print on their printer.

If an advertiser runs ads on different sites and finds a person's click stream on a certain selection of the sites, it can build up an accurate profile of sites that person visits. This information can then be sold to direct marketers, or whomever. A famous cartoon drawn early in the Internet's life depicts two dogs sitting at a computer. One explains to the other, 'The great thing about the Internet is no one knows you're a dog.' It has been followed recently by another cartoon in which one dog has clicked to a page with a picture of dog food. Because of this, the server now does know it's a dog. Pretty soon the server also knows it's a dog that prefers a certain brand of dog food, elm trees and Siamese cats.

In the basic Web design, every time someone clicks on a link, their browser goes from server to server afresh, with no reference to any previous transactions. The controversial tool for consumer tracking that changes all that is the *cookie*. A cookie is just a code such as a reference number or account number that the server assigns to the browser so as to recognise it when the same person returns. It is much like getting an account number when opening a bank account. The cookie is automatically stored on the consumer's hard drive, with or without his knowledge, depending on his preferences.

Most transactions between a consumer and a store involve some continuity, and the cookie makes it possible to accumulate things in a shopping trolley, or send items to the same address as last time. Normally, merchants we trade with know what we have bought, and with whom we bank, and where we live, and we trust them. The fact that cookies are often installed on a person's hard drive, and talk back to the server, without any form of permission is also valuable: it's the difference between going into a store and being recognised as creditworthy, and going in and having to fill out identification forms all over again.

However, some commentators see cookies as entirely evil. By default, most browsers accept all cookies automatically, but then again most also offer the user the option of prompting them with an alert notice before the computer accepts a cookie, or of simply refusing it. The problem is not in the cookie itself, over which the user has control. The problem is that there is no knowing what information the server will collect, and how it will use that information. Without that information the user can make choices based only on fear and doubt: not a stable basis for building society on the Web.

A Web site also can change chameleon-like according to who is looking at it, as if it were a brochure being printed for that one person. Imagine an individual visiting the Web page of a political candidate, or a controversial company. With a quick check of that person's record, the politician or company can serve up just the right mix of propaganda that will warm that particular person's heart – and tactfully suppress points he or she might object to. Is this just effective targeted marketing, or deception? It depends on whether we know it is happening.

Europe has tried to solve part of this problem with strict regulation. European companies have to keep secure the information they hold on customers, and are barred from combining databases in ways that are currently quite legal in the United States. Consumers in Europe also have the right to look at and correct databases that contain information about them. In the United States, laws that protect consumers from having their information resold or given away are very weak. The government has hoped that some sort of self-regulation will come into force.

The good news is that the Web can help. I believe that the privacy I require of information I give away is something I ought to have choice about. People should be able to surf the Web anonymously, or as a well-defined entity, and should be able to control the difference between the two. I would like to be able to decide who I will allow to use my personal information and for what.

Currently, a responsible Web site will have a privacy policy one click from the bottom of the home page. One site might sell any information it gets to direct-mail firms or advertisers. Another may record every page a visitor views. Another might not distribute any information under any circumstances. I could read this carefully and decide whether to proceed, but in practice I usually don't have time to read it before rushing in.

The next step is to make it possible for my browser to do this for me – not just to check, but to negotiate for a different privacy policy, one that will be the basis for any subsequent release of information. With privacy software, a Web site provider and browser can do just that.

Consider a company selling clothing over the Internet. It might declare its privacy policy as follows: 'We collect your name, age and gender to customise our catalogue pages for the type of clothing you are likely to be interested in and for our own product development. We do not provide this information to anyone outside our organisation. We also collect your shipping information. We may distribute this information to others.'

For these things to be negotiated automatically, the preferences set by a user and the privacy policy have to be set up in machine-readable form using some common set of categories for different sorts of data and different ways of using it.

The World Wide Web Consortium is creating a technology that will allow automatic negotiation between a user's browser and a store's server, leading to an agreement about privacy. The Platform for Privacy Preferences Project (P3P) will give a computer a way of describing its owner's privacy preferences and demands, and give servers a way of describing their privacy policies, all done so that the machines can understand each other and negotiate any differences without a person at either end getting involved.

I believe that when a site has no privacy policy there ought to be a legally enforced default privacy policy that is very protective of the individual. Perhaps this view shows my European roots. And it may sound counter to my normal minimalist tendencies. But lack of such enforcement allows a company to make whatever use it can of whatever private data it can somehow extract.

In 1998 the Federal Trade Commission did a survey of Web sites and found that very few had a privacy policy, including sites that took information from children. The findings were so dramatic that President Clinton called a two-day Internet privacy meeting in Washington with industry and government officials. The results also prompted the Federal Trade Commission to consider regulating privacy policies.

As is so often the case, the possibility of regulation has prompted industry to make some moves towards self-regulation. In June 1998, Christine Varney, a former FTC commissioner, put together a group of about fifty companies and trade groups called the Online Privacy Alliance. Members included AOL, AT&T, Microsoft, Netscape, the Direct Marketing Association and the US Chamber of Commerce. They said they would clearly reveal what information they collected on all their various Web sites and how it would be used. They also said they would give consumers some choice about how personal data could be used, including the ability to not allow their information to be sold to third parties. The Better Business Bureau Online is also addressing the matter with an endorsement service – a privacy seal it will grant to worthy Web sites. The programme features privacy-standard setting, verification, monitoring and review of complaints.

Some regulators maintain that since there is no mechanism for enforcement, this kind of effort does not go far enough. Tighter control, they say, is needed, especially when it comes to protecting information about children. They maintain that any abuse of information about adults or children should be illegal. But the Online Privacy Alliance is a good start, at least in creating a system of endorsements, which will cause more consumers to gravitate towards sites that comply. This will put pressure on others to do the same. Ideally, such groups will set privacy practices that will be automatically checkable with P3P.

Of course, any privacy negotiation is only as trustworthy as the site's proprietor. However, if a company has, through its Web server, made an undertaking to preserve privacy, and broken that undertaking, then it has acted fraudulently. There are conventional laws to deal with this transgression. Software can't solve this problem. And it should not be up to the consortium or any other technical body to solve it.

Perhaps the most notorious violation of privacy over the Web was the sudden release late in 1998 of details from the US Independent Counsel's report about President Clinton's sexual activities. This information was purposely exposed to millions of people, contrary to many people's concepts of respect for the individual or family. We can use the power of the Web to connect anything and everything to great effect, or to do devastating damage. Episodes like this help us recognise how rapidly the widespread distribution of information could cripple our

society – and each of us personally – if absolutely all information remains public.

No one will take part in the new weblike way of working if they
do not feel certain that private information will stay private. In
a group, they will also remain on the sidelines if they feel that
what they say or write will not remain confidential, or if they
can't be sure of whom they are communicating with.

Public key cryptography (PKC) offers one way to achieve the
four basic aspects of security: authenticity, confidentiality,
integrity of messages and nonrepudiatability. Each person has
a number that everyone knows (the *public key*), and another,
related number that no one else ever has (the *private key*). Devised
more than two decades ago, PKC provides a form of encryption
in which an outgoing message is scrambled according to the
receiver's public key. The scrambled message can then be decoded
only by a receiver who has the unique matching private key to
unlock it. A leading form of public key cryptography is RSA,
named after its developers, Ron Rivest, Adi Shamir, and Leonard
Adleman, all of whom were at MIT's Laboratory for Computer
Science in 1977 when they invented it.

Deducing whether someone or some place is authentic begins
with common sense. If a Web site offers a deal that seems too
good to be true, it probably is. Tougher, however, is figuring out
whether the Web site of a well-known clothing store is indeed
operated by that store. Anyone can make a site that looks like a
clothing store. Crooks could even have an elaborate impostor site
that takes an order, passes it to the real store, sends the store's
communication back, and in the meantime steals the credit-card

number. And unlike a physical facade, the fake store will look and feel indistinguishable from the real one. Currently there is some attempt to make the domain name system more secure, but at the moment authenticity relies mainly on the security from intrusion of the domain servers (which tell the browser where, for example, *www.acme.com* is on the Internet) and the connections between them. Public key authentication would be much better.

Confidentiality consists in knowing that no one else can access the contents of a communication. Once again, criminals or spies can intercept a communication to a clothing store and skim off credit-card numbers being sent electronically, or eavesdrop on supposedly private conversations between people in a group. Encryption technology prevents this by scrambling the messages. Anyone browsing a site whose URI starts with *https:* is using an encryption technology called Secure Socket Layer. Normally, however, cryptography is used only to make sure no one except the server can read the communication – not to verify that the server is really who it says it is.

The integrity of messages involves making sure no one can alter a message on the Internet without being detected, and non-repudiatability means that if I have sent a message, I can't later maintain that I did not. PKC provides technology to assure these, too. If I use the software to add to a message I send (or a Web page I write), a number at the end called a *digital signature* allows the receiver to verify that it was I who sent it and that it has not been tampered with. The consortium has a project for applying digital signatures to documents.

If PKC is so well understood, why are we not using it? One reason is the US government's fear of loss of control. It is easy to use, and virtually impossible to crack – so impossible, in fact, that since its development more than twenty years ago the US government has blocked the export of strong cryptography by classifying it as 'munition'. Some other governments have reacted in similar ways, blocking export, or banning its use, for fear that terrorist groups will be able to communicate without government being able to tap into their conversations.

The counterargument points to George Orwell's vision in his book *1984*, in which the National Security Agency becomes Big Brother, able to monitor a person's every move. It argues that without the basic right of the citizen to discuss what he or she wants, the people are left at the mercy of potential dictatorial tendencies in government.

The balance in governmental power is always a tricky thing. But the debate is almost moot in this case, because encryption technology has been written in many countries of the free world. The US export ban frustrates people who simply want, say, to buy clothes from another country. It infuriates software manufactures who have to make two versions of each product, one with strong PKC and the other with a specifically weakened version for export, and then devise ways of trying to prevent the strong one from crossing borders. It hobbles the Open Source community, in which distribution of the source code (original written form) of programs is a basic tenet. To ridicule the export law, PKC programs have been printed on T-shirts, and in machine-readable fonts in books – which cannot be subject to export controls.

There is another reason why PKC has not been adopted: it can only be used in conjunction with a system for telling your computer which public keys to trust for which sorts of things. This is, of course, a very important but also difficult thing to express. An individual's ability to express trust is essential, because without that trust many uses of the Web, from collaborative work to electronic commerce, will be socially impossible.

Authenticity and confidentiality are not problems new to the Web. They have been solved, in principle, for electronic mail. Pretty Good Privacy (PGP) and Secure MIME are two standards for digitally signing mail (to authenticate the person who sent it) and encrypting it (to stop anyone else from reading it).

PGP is more or less a grassroots system. It is a *web of trust*. An alternative, Public Key Infrastructure (PKI), is basically a treelike way of doing things. In either PGP or PKI, a user's computer associates a key with a person by holding a file called a certificate. It typically carries the person's name, co-ordinates and public key. The certificate itself is digitally signed with another public key of someone else the user trusts. He knows that it is the other person's key because it says so on a certificate that was signed with a key of a different party he trusts. And so on, in a chain.

The social structure assumed by PGP is that chains of trust will be made through anyone – a person's family, friends, college, employer. If an individual was authenticating a message from a colleague, he probably would use a certificate signed by their common employer. That is the path of trust.

The PKI system, planned by industry to enable electronic commerce, assumes that people trust just a few basic 'roots' from which all authority flows. A few certificate authorities delegate the right to issue certificates to their commercial partners. They in turn can delegate the right to issue certificates to other, smaller authorities. There is a tree, and money and authority flow up and down it.

Browsers are now slowly being equipped to work with the Public Key Infrastructure. If I open the browser preferences on my Internet Explorer now, I see that I can chose to accept certificates signed by Microsoft, ATT, GTE, MCI, Keywitness Canada Inc., Thawte and Verisign. In the equivalent list in Netscape, I see ATT, BBN, BelSign, Canada Post, Certisign, GTE, GTIS, IBM, Integrion, Keywitness, MCI Mall, Thawte Uptime and Verisign. All these certificate authorities will vouch for the identity of people and their keys. They generally sell certificates, which expire after a certain number of months. But I don't see a button to set myself up to issue a certificate to a friend or relative whom I also trust. PGP would allow this.

The Web worked only because the ability of anyone to make a link allowed it to represent information and relationships however they existed in real life. The reason cryptography is not in constant use in representing trust on the Web is that there is not, yet, a weblike, decentralised infrastructure.

The PGP system relied on electronic mail, and assumed that everyone held copies of certificates on their hard disks. There were no hypertext links that allowed someone to point to a certificate on the Web. Clearly, it should be much easier to introduce a Web of Trust given the Web.

I mentioned that both PGP and PKI made two assumptions: that we trust a person, and that if we do, we just have to link a person with a key. Many pointless arguments and stalling points have involved exactly what constitutes a person, and how to establish the identity of a person. In fact, in most situations it does not matter who the person 'is' in any unique and fundamental way. An individual is just interested in the role the person plays, which is represented by a public key. All we need to do is find a language for talking about what can be done with different keys, and we will have a technical infrastructure for a Web of Trust. If we play our cards right, the work at the consortium in languages for the Web (which I will describe in chapter 13) will end up producing a Web of Trust. Then the Web and the Web of Trust will be the same: a web of documents, some digitally signed, and linked, and completely decentralised. The consortium will not seek a central or controlling role in the Web of Trust: it will just help the community create a common language for expressing trust.

The Web of Trust is an essential model for how we really work as people. Each of us builds our own web of trust as we mature from infancy. As we decide what we are going to link to, read or buy on the Web, an element of our decision is how much we trust the information we're viewing. Can we trust its publisher's name, privacy practices, political motivations? Sometimes we learn what not to trust the hard way, but more often we inherit trust from someone else – a friend or teacher or family member – or from published recommendations or endorsements by third parties such as our bank or doctor. The result of all this activity creates a web of trust in our slice of society.

Automated systems will arise so negotiations and transactions can be based on our stated criteria for trust. Once we have these tools, we will be able to ask the computer not just for information, but why we should believe it. Imagine an Oh Yeah? button on a browser. There I am, looking at a fantastic deal that can be mine just for the entry of a credit-card number and the click of a button. I press the Oh Yeah? button. My browser challenges the server to provide some credentials. Perhaps this is a list of documents with digitally signed endorsements from, say, the company's bank and supplier, with the keys to verify them. My browser rummages through these with the server, looking to be convinced that the deal is trustworthy. If it's satisfied, good for me, I got a deal. If not, I probably just saved myself some grief.

It would be wrong to assume that the Web of Trust is important primarily for electronic commerce, as if security mattered only where money is concerned. The Web is needed to support all sorts of relationships, on all levels, from the personal, through groups of all sizes, to the global population. When we are working in a group, we share things we would not share outside that group, like half-baked ideas and sensitive information. We do so because we trust the people in the group, and trust that they won't divulge this information to others. To date, it has been difficult to manage such groups on the Web because it is hard to control access to information. The Web of Trust has to evolve before the Web can serve as a true collaborative medium. It has to be there before we can trust automated agents to help us with our work. These developments, which I discuss in the next two chapters, are for me the next most important developments for the Web as a whole.

CHAPTER 12

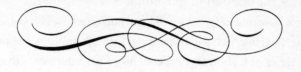

Mind to Mind

I have a dream for the Web ... and it has two parts.

In the first part, the Web becomes a much more powerful means for collaboration between people. I have always imagined the information space as something to which everyone has immediate and intuitive access, and not just to browse, but to create. The initial *WorldWideWeb* program opened with an almost blank page, ready for the jottings of the user. Robert Cailliau and I had a great time with it, not because we were looking at a lot of stuff, but because we were writing and sharing our ideas. Furthermore, the dream of people-to-people communication through shared knowledge must be possible for groups of all sizes, interacting electronically with as much ease as they do now in person.

In the second part of the dream, collaborations extend to computers. Machines become capable of analysing all the data on the Web – the content, links and transactions between people and computers. A 'Semantic Web', which should make this possible, has yet to emerge, but when it does, the day-to-day mechanisms of trade, bureaucracy and our daily lives will be handled by machines talking to machines, leaving humans to provide the inspiration and intuition. The intelligent 'agents' people have touted for ages will finally materialise. This machine-understandable Web will come about through the implementation of a series of technical advances and social agreements that are now beginning (and which I describe in the next chapter).

Once the two-part dream is reached, the Web will be a place where the whim of a human being and the reasoning of a machine coexist in an ideal, powerful mixture.

Realising the dream will require a lot of nitty-gritty work. The Web is far from 'done', It is in only a jumbled state of construction, and no matter how grand the dream, it has to be engineered piece by piece, with many of the pieces far from glamorous.

It is much easier to imagine and understand a more enlightened, powerful Web if we break free of some of the world's current assumptions about how we use computers. When I want to interact with a computer, I have to wait several minutes after turning it on before it is ready to converse. This is absurd. These machines are supposed to be there for us, not the other way around. So let's begin our thinking about a new world by imagining one in which a computer screen is available whenever we want it.

In the same spirit, we should jettison our assumptions about Internet access. Why should we have to wait while a computer connects to the Internet by making a phone call? The Internet isn't designed to be like that. It is made so that, at any time, a little postcardlike packet of a few hundred characters could be dropped into it by one computer, and in a fraction of a second be at its destination on the other side of the world. That is why clicking on an icon can take us very quickly to a Web site. The bother of having to make a phone call wrecks the idea of instant availability.

An essential goal for the telecommunications industry (and regulatory authorities) should be connecting everyone with *permanent* access. The problem till now has not been technology, but rather regulations that control what telephone companies can charge for access, and the lack of agreement about how other companies that might want to provide Internet access can lease the copper wire that goes to every home. With some wiser regulation, in some cases spurred on by competition from cable companies that lay their own cables to people's doors, before too long I should be able to walk up to a screen, see it quickly glow with my home page on it, and follow a link immediately. This simple difference in timing will dramatically change the way we use computers, making the experience more like getting out a pen rather than getting out a lawnmower. Computers will be there when we suddenly have an idea, allowing us to capture it and preventing the world from losing it.

Let's clear our minds about what we will see on these wonderful new computers. Today there is a desktop with various folders and 'applications'. One of these applications is a Web browser. In this scheme, my entire screen is taken up by my local computer, while all the information in the rest of the accessible world is relegated to a small area or icon within it. This is inside out.

The job of computers and networks is to get out of the way, to not be seen. This means that the appearance of the information and the tools one uses to access it should be independent of where the information is stored – the concept of *location independence*. Whether they are hypertext pages or folders, both valid genres of information management, they should look and feel the same wherever they physically happen to be. Filenames should disappear: they should become merely another form of URI. Then people should cease to be aware of URIs, seeing only hypertext links. The technology should be transparent, so we interact with it intuitively.

The next step would be protocol independence. Right now, every time I write something with a computer, I have to choose whether to open the 'electronic mail' application or the 'net news' application or the 'Web editor' application. The mail, news and Web systems use different protocols between computers, and effectively, I am being asked to select which protocol to use. The computer should figure this out by itself.

Location independence and protocol independence would be very simple if all the software on a computer were being re-written from scratch. Unfortunately, it isn't. The required change to the modular design of operating systems and applications would be significant. Indeed, whether or not the terms *operating system* and *application* would survive is not clear. But since software engineers are very inventive, and the stakes – an intuitive interface – are high, I am optimistic.

As we look at the way a person uses the Web, it is simplest to improve the reception of information by adding new forms of graphics and multimedia. It is more difficult to imagine how best to allow a person to interact with the information, to create and modify it. Harder still is imagining how this computer screen can be used to allow one person to interact as one of many people interacting as a group. This is the order in which development has occurred to date, and will occur in the future.

The XML revolution, mentioned in chapter 9, that has taken place over the last few years and is now reaching the mainstream has provided a solid foundation for much of the new design inside and outside the consortium. Even though the computer markup languages for hypertext and graphics are designed for presenting text and images to people, and data languages are designed to be processed by machines, they share a need for a common, structured format. XML is it.

XML is both a boon and a threat to the Web dream. The great thing is that it stems the tide of information loss. It allows anyone to create any kind of tag that can capture the intent of a piece of information. For example, the minutes of a meeting may contain an 'action item'. XML allows the person taking the minutes to make a new document type that includes *<action>* as a new tag. If the minutes are recorded in HTML, this might be lost, because HTML's general set of tags don't include *<action>* and the person taking the minutes can't create one. An XML document is typically richer: the information it contains is more well defined.

This will allow such things as spreadsheets, calendar files, e-mail address books and bank statements that have not used interoperable standard formats to have them developed quickly, dramatically increasing the interoperability in, for example, typical office documents. This is the primary excitement behind the XML revolution: avoiding the information lost when such documents are translated into HTML and thereby lose their ability to be understood as spreadsheets, calendars, bank statements or whatever.

The threat is that when a company introduces a new document type, no one else will understand it. XML makes it easy for everyone to create their own tags or entire markup languages. We might therefore see an end to the idyllic situation that has prevailed thus far on the Web – the predominance of HTML, which has helped all of us share documents easily. Can it be that, a decade into the Web's existence, XML will give us a freedom that forcibly leads us back toward myriad incompatible languages? This is indeed a serious possibility, but one that has been anticipated.

The extensible *X* in *XML* means anyone can invent new tags, but they can't add them to someone else's tags. An XML document can be made of a mixture of tags from more than one *namespace*, but each namespace is identified by a URI. Thus any XML document is completely defined using the Web. This is a huge step forward from the old HTML days in which anyone could make up their own version of what *<table>* meant, for example, with no ambiguity. The XML namespaces change the rules of technology evolution by making every step, whether open or proprietary, well defined.

It is important to remember that XML does not replace HTML. It replaces the underlying SGML on which HTML was built. HTML can now be written as XML. In fact, it is possible to create a valid XML document that will also work with old HTML browsers. (The specification for doing this is XHTML.)

When I proposed the Web in 1989, the driving force I had in mind was communication through shared knowledge, and the driving 'market' for it was collaboration among people at work and at home. By building a hypertext Web, a group of people of whatever size could easily express themselves, quickly acquire and convey knowledge, overcome misunderstandings and reduce duplication of effort. This would give people in a group a new power to build something together.

People would also have a running model of their plans and reasoning. A web of knowledge linked through hypertext would contain a snapshot of their shared understanding. When new people joined a group they would have the legacy of decisions and reasons available for inspection. When people left the group their work would already have been captured and integrated. As an exciting bonus, machine analysis of the web of knowledge could perhaps allow the participants to draw conclusions about management and organisation of their collective activity that they would not otherwise have elucidated.

The intention was that the Web be used as a personal information system, and a group tool on all scales, from the team of two creating a flyer for the local primary school play to the world population deciding on ecological issues.

I also wanted the Web to be used just as much 'internally' as externally. Even though most of the first ten servers, like the one at CERN or SLAC, would be called *intranet* servers today, organisations and families are just beginning to see the power the Web can bring inside their walls. Although it takes a little work to set up the access control for a corporate or family intranet, once that has been done the Web's usefulness is accelerated, because the participants share a level of trust. This encourages more spontaneous and direct communication.

To be able to really work together on the Web, we need much better tools: better formats for presenting information to the user; more intuitive interfaces for editing and changing information; seamless integration of other tools, such as chat rooms, and audio- and videoconferencing, with Web editing. We need the ability to store on one server an annotation about a Web page on another; simple access controls for group membership, and for tracking changes to documents. While some of this work involves leading-edge research, a lot of it consists of trying to adapt existing computer systems to the global hypertext world.

For people to share knowledge, the Web must be a universal space across which all hypertext links can travel. I spend a good deal of my life defending this core property in one way or another.

Universality must exist along several dimensions. To start with, we must be able to interlink any documents – from drafts to highly polished works. Information is often lost within an organisation when a 'final document' of some kind is created at the end of an endeavor. Often, everything from the minutes of meetings to background research vanishes, and the reasoning that brought the group to its endpoint is lost. It might actually still exist on some disk somewhere, but it is effectively useless because the finished document doesn't link to it. What's more, different social and practical systems isolate documents of different levels from each other: we don't insert random notes into finished books, but why not, if they are relevant and insightful? At the consortium today, no one can mention a document in a meeting unless they can give a URI for it. Our policy is 'If it isn't on the Web, it doesn't exist,' and the cry often heard when a new idea is presented is 'Stick it in Team Space!' – a directory for confidentially saving documents not otherwise on the Web. All mail is instantly archived to the Web with a persistent URI. It is already hard to imagine how it could have been any other way. The Web of work and play must be able to intertwine half-baked and fully baked ideas, and Web technology must support this.

Another dimension critical to universality is the ability to link local material to global. When an endeavor is put together that involves groups of different scales – whether a software engineering project such as mine at CERN, or a primary school education project that is part of a town initiative and uses taxpayers' money – information has to come from many levels and has to be cross-linked.

Similarly, universality must exist across the spectrum of cost and intention. People and organisations have different motivations for putting things on the Web: for their own benefit, commercial gain, the good of society or whatever. For an information system to be universal, it can't discriminate between these. The Web must include information that is free, very expensive and every level in between. It must allow all the different interest groups to put together all manner of pricing and licensing and incentive systems … and always, of course, allow the user to 'just say no'.

The reason we need universality on all these levels is that that's how people operate in the real world. If the World Wide Web is to represent and support the web of life, it has to enable us to operate in different ways with different groups of different sizes and scopes at different places every day: our homes, offices, schools, churches, towns, states, countries and cultures. It must also transcend levels, because creative people are always crossing boundaries. That is how we solve problems and innovate.

Information must be able to cross social boundaries, too. Our family life is influenced by work. Our existence in one group affects that in another. Values and actions are fed by all the ideas from these different areas. By connecting across groups, people also provide organisation and consistency to the world. It is unusual for an individual to support environmental policies on a global level but then plan to dump chemicals into the local river.

My original vision for a universal Web was as an armchair aid to help people do things in the web of real life. It would be a mirror, reflecting reports or conversations or art and mapping social interactions. But more and more, the mirror model is wrong, because interaction is taking place primarily on the Web. People are using the Web to build things they have not built or written or drawn or communicated anywhere else. As the Web becomes a primary space for much activity, we have to be careful that it allows for a just and fair society. The Web must allow equal access to those in different economic and political situations; those who have physical or cognitive disabilities; those of different cultures; and those who use different languages with different characters that read in different directions across a page.

The simplest factor controlling the Web as a medium for communication between people is the power of the data formats used to represent hypertext, graphics and other media. Under pressure because of their direct visibility and impact on the user's experience, these have advanced relatively rapidly, because each medium has been essentially independent of the others.

One might have expected that graphics formats would have been standardised long ago, but the Web introduced new stresses that are forcing quite an evolution. Marc Andreessen gave browsers the ability to display graphics right inside a document, instead of relegating them to a separate window. He happened to pick the Graphic Interchange Format (GIF) defined by Compu-Serve. Soon, people also started using the standard JPEG (Joint Photographic Experts Group) format for photographs. These two formats reigned supreme until Unisys announced that it had ended up being the owner of a patent on the compression technology used to make GIF images and that they would be charging licence fees. A small group of enthusiasts proposed an alternative, Portable Network Graphics (PNG), based on an open compression technology, and generally superior to GIF. The consortium members agreed to endorse PNG as a W3C recommendation.

The recent moves to put the Web on everything from televisions to mobile phone screens have made the need for device dependence very clear. This has prompted even newer graphics formats that are more capable of displaying an image on screens of different sizes and technologies. Both JPEG and PNG describe a picture in terms of the square grid of *pixels* that make up a computer screen. The consortium is developing a new format for drawings that will describe them as abstract shapes, leaving the browser free to fill in the pixels in such as way that the image can be shown with optimal clarity on a wristwatch or a drive-in movie screen. The format, called *scalable vector graphics*, is based on XML. It will also dramatically speed up the delivery of documents containing drawings, which will open the door to all sorts of new ways of interacting between a person and a Web site. And because it is in XML, it will be easy for beginners to read and write. We may soon see all kinds of simple animated graphical interfaces.

Virtual Reality Modelling Language (VRML) is another pillar, being created for three-dimensional scenes. I expected 3D to really take off, and still don't quite understand why it hasn't. Sending the details of a 3D scene takes relatively few bytes compared, for example, with video. It does require the user to have a fast computer, to manipulate the scene as the user moves around it. Perhaps the power of the average processor just isn't high enough yet.

Integrating many different text, image, audio and video media into one Web page or show will be greatly helped by the Synchronised Multimedia Integration Language (SMIL; 'smile'). SMIL will make seamless co-ordination simple, even for authors with limited Web design experience. The notorious Clinton tapes, relayed over the Web in windows with mixtures of graphics, text and video, were if nothing else a launch for SMIL. The language can also effectively save bandwidth. Often a TV signal – say, a news broadcast – has a talking head that takes up maybe a quarter of the screen, a still image or map in the background, and perhaps a caption, not to mention football scores scrolling across the bottom of the screen. Transmitting all that as video data takes a lot of bandwidth. SMIL allows the relatively small amount of data about images that are actually moving to be sent as video, and integrated with the still images that are transmitted to the viewer's screen in ways that require much less bandwidth.

Running through all the work on hypertext, graphics and multimedia languages are concerns about access for all, independent of culture, language and disability. The consortium's Web Accessibility Initiative brings together people from industry, disability organisations, government and research labs to devise protocols and software that can make the Web accessible to people with visual, hearing, physical and cognitive or neurological disabilities. The work ranges widely, from review of W3C technologies to ensure that they support accessibility to development of accessibility guidelines for Web sites, browsers and authoring tools, and development of tools to evaluate accessibility. Much of this works only when those building Web sites have taken a little care about how they have done it. The disability and technical communities got together to produce a set of guidelines about the most effective and practical steps to take: recommended reading for webmasters.

The consortium also has an internationalisation activity that checks that new specifications will work in different alphabets, whether they are Eastern or Western, read right to left, left to right or up and down. Conversions can get complicated, but the computer industry is making energetic efforts to extend operating systems to support the display of all kinds of written scripts, including Arabic, Hindi, Korean, Chinese, Japanese, Thai and Hebrew. HTML 4.0 already provides a number of internationalisation features, including the ability to mark text as to which language it is in, and to order text from right to left.

The primary principle behind device independence, and accessibility, is the separation of *form* from *content*. When the significance of a document is stored separately from the way it should be displayed, device independence and accessibility become much easier to maintain. Much of this is achieved with a *style sheet* – a set of instructions on how to present or transform a printed page. Håkon Lie, who worked with me at CERN and later at the consortium, led the development of Cascading Style Sheets (CSS) to make this possible. A new, related language with different capabilities, XSL, is also in the works. There is even an 'aural' style-sheet language, part of CSS2, to explain to a browser how a Web page should sound.

The growing list of graphics formats relate primarily to static displays. But some people feel a Web page isn't sufficiently exciting unless it moves. At a minimum, they want the page to change as a user interacts with it. Pop-up balloons and menus, and forms that fill themselves in, are simple examples we find today on the Web. These work because a small program, or *script*, is loaded with the page. It operates the page like the hand inside a puppet, in response to the user's actions. This has created a crisis in interoperability, however, because the connection between the script and the Web page, the hand and the puppet, is not standard for different kinds of style sheets. To fix this, the consortium is working on a Document Object Model (DOM), a set of standards for that interface. Unfortunately, it is much more difficult to make these animated pages accessible to voice browsers and screen readers. On the positive side, the DOM interface should provide a powerful way for accessibility tools such as document readers to access the document structure within a browser.

The media may portray the Web as a wonderful, interactive place where we have limitless choice because don't have to take what the TV producer has decided we should see next. But my definition of interactive includes not just the ability to choose, but also the ability to create. We ought to be able not only to find any kind of document on the Web, but also to create any kind of document, easily. We should be able not only to follow links, but to create them – between all sorts of media. We should be able not only to interact with other people, but to create with other people. *Intercreativity* is the process of making things or solving problems together. If *interactivity* is not just sitting there passively in front of a display screen, then *intercreativity* is not just sitting there in front of something 'interactive'.

With all this work in the presentation of content, we still have really addressed only the reading of information, not the writing of it. There is little to help the Web be used as a collaborative meeting place. Realising this early on, the consortium held a workshop to find out what was needed. The result was a long shopping list of capabilities, things like strong authentication of group members, good hypertext editors, annotation systems (similar to the little yellow paper sticky notes), and tools for procedures such as online voting and review.

Some of the results have been satisfying. SMIL was one, integrating various media and possibly allowing a real-time collaborative environment, a virtual meeting room, to be constructed. Others are still in the wings. A long-standing goal of mine had been to find an intuitive browser that also, like my *WorldWideWeb*, allows editing. A few such browser/editors had been made, such as AOLpress, but none were currently supported as commercial products. Few items on the wish list for collaborative tools had been achieved. At the consortium we wondered what was wrong. Did people not want these tools? Were developers unable to visualise them? Why had years of preaching and spec writing and encouragement got hardly anywhere?

I became more and more convinced that the only way to find out what was holding back the development of collaborative tools was to try to develop them ourselves. Our policy had always been that we would use whatever commercial tools were available to get our own work done. At a consortium team retreat in Cambridge, I suggested we start trying all the experimental solutions being tinkered with in the community, and even develop them further. Perhaps then we would stumble upon the real problems, showing the way towards solutions.

We concluded that to do this, we needed a nucleus of people who would try various new collaboration technologies, just to see what happened. They would help the entire consortium staff become early adopters of experimental software. This new policy, which we called Live Early Adoption and Demonstration (not coincidentally, LEAD), meant that we entitled ourselves to eat our own dog food, as far as our very limited resources would allow. It meant that we'd be testing new protocols not on their own, but in the context of our actual, daily work. It also meant that, with only a handful of programmers, we would be trying to maintain the reliability of these experimental products at a level high enough to allow us to actually use them!

We are only in the early stages, but we now have an environment in which people who are collaborating with the consortium write and edit hypertext, and save the results back to our server. Amaya, the browser/editor, handles HTML, XML, Cascading Stylesheets, Portable Network Graphics, and a prototype of Scalable Vector Graphics and Math ML. While we have always developed Amaya on the Linux operating system, the Amaya team has adapted it for the Windows NT platform common in business, too. I now road test the latest versions of these tools as soon as I can get them, sending back crash reports on a bad day and occasionally a bottle of champagne on a good one.

We are using our open-source Java-based server, Jigsaw, for

collaborative work. For example, Jigsaw allows direct editing, saves the various edited versions of a document, and keeps track of what has been changed from one version to the next. I can call up a list of all versions, with details about who made which changes when, and revert to an older version if necessary. This provides everyone with a feeling of safety, and they are more inclined to share the editing of a piece of work. Jigsaw and Amaya allow our team space to come alive as our common room, internal library and virtual coffee machine around which staff members who are in France, Massachusetts, Japan or on an aeroplane can gather.

Making collaboration work is a challenge. It is also fun, because it involves the most grassroots and collegial side of the Web community. All Web code, since my first release in 1991, has been open-source software: anyone can scoop up the source code – the lines of programming – and edit and rebuild them, for free. The members of the original www-talk mailing routinely picked up new versions of the original Web code library 'libwww'. This software still exists on the consortium's public server, www.w3.org, maintained for many years by Henrik Nielsen, the cheerful Dane who managed it at CERN and now MIT. Libwww is used as part of Amaya, and the rest of Amaya and Jigsaw are open-source in the same way. There are a lot of people who may not be inclined to join working groups and edit specifications, but are happy to join in making a good bit of software better. Those who are inspired to try Amaya or Jigsaw, want to help improve them, develop a product based on them or pick apart the code and create an altogether better client or server can simply go to the w3.org site and take it from there, whether or not they are members of the consortium.

We create other tools as we need them, and our tool-creation crew is always much in demand. Meeting registration, mailing-list management and control for our Web site are typical examples. We are looking forward to the time when we will use public key cryptography to authenticate collaborators. Every now and again the new systems go down, and we pay the price for being on the bleeding edge by having to wait till they are fixed. But we are gaining more of an understanding of what it will take to achieve the dream of collaboration through shared knowledge.

I expect these tools to develop into a common new genre on the Web. Real life is and must be full of all kinds of social constraint – the very processes from which 'society' arises. Computers help if we use them to create abstract *social machines* on the Web: processes in which the people do the creative work and the machine does the administration. Many social processes can be better run by machine, because the machine is always available, it is free from bias, and no one likes to administer these kinds of systems anyway. Online voting is one example, and it's already beginning to happen: ADP Investor Communications and First Chicago Trust have services that conduct online proxy voting for corporate shareholder meetings, and more than a thousand companies are using them.

People are already experimenting with new social machines for online peer review, while other tools such as chat rooms developed quite independently and before the Web. MUDDs are social tools derived from multiuser games of Dungeons and Dragons where thousands of people take on roles and interact in a global, online fantasy world. By experimenting with these structures we may find a way to organise new social models that not only scale well, but can be combined to form larger structures.

Almost a decade ago now, I asked Ari Luotonen to spend three days writing a discussion tool for the nascent Web. It was to be like a newsgroup, except that it would capture the logic of an argument. I'd always been frustrated that the essential role of a message in an argument was often lost information. When Ari was done, anywhere on the CERN server that we created a subdirectory called Discussion, a new interactive forum would exist. It allowed people to post questions on a given subject, read and respond. A person couldn't just 'reply'. He had to say whether he was agreeing, disagreeing or asking for clarification of a point. The idea was that the state of the discussion would be visible to everyone involved.

I would like any serious issue to be on the Web in hypertext. I would like annotation servers to exist where groups could add links (or sticky yellow things) to documents they want to comment on. Annotation servers are a third-party service allowing a group to share each other's coments on documents anywhere else in the Web. The browser gets the original page and then separately checks annotation servers for comments, which are then superimposed on the page. Imagine having servers for comments in different forums, perhaps family, school and company. Each point and rebuttal is linked, so everyone can see at a glance the direct agreements and contradictions and the supporting evidence for each view, such that anything could be contested by the people involved. If there was some sort of judicial, democratic process for resolving issues, the discussion could be done in a very clear and open fashion, with a computer keeping track of the arguments. Again, the theme is human beings doing the thinking and machines helping it work on a larger scale, but nothing replacing wisdom in the end.

My hope was that the original 'Discussion' idea, and future mechanisms that could evolve from it on the new Web, would move us beyond the historical situation of people hurling mud at each other, of peppering their arguments with personal abuse and vitriol, and replace all that with much more of a reasoned, Socratic debate, in which individual ideas, accusations and pieces of evidence can be questioned or supported.

What Ari and I were trying to do was create a machine that would do the administration for, say, a court, or working group, or parliament. The initial trial was a discussion for the sake of discussion, and it didn't make a big splash. There are now a number of software products for doing some of these things. To actually emulate a courtroom or a democratic voting process, however, the tools need much more development. I long for a move from argument by repetition of sound bites to a hypertext exposition that can be justified and challenged – one that will allow us to look up and compare, side by side, what politicians, or defendants and accusers, actually say, regardless of what is claimed in television commercials and nightly news interviews.

Because of low overhead, social machines will allow us to do things we just couldn't do before. For example, they will allow us to conduct a national plebiscite whose cost would otherwise be prohibitive. This would, of course, like all the benefits of this new technology, be biased towards those with Internet access. This is just an example to show that we can reassess what is possible; I am not advocating a move from representative democracy to direct democracy. We should be careful not to do things just because they are possible.

Perhaps the Web will enable more organic styles of management, in which groups within a company form in a local, rather ad hoc fashion. They could be made self-forming like a newsgroup, but with constraints that ensure that whoever joins is needed for the work of the company and is covered by sufficient budget. Beyond that, the company doesn't have much conventional structure. When someone has a task to perform, they associate with whomever they need to get it done. People make commitments and negotiate them between groups, without having to go to a manager. The whole organic organisation could grow from a seed of a few digitally signed documents on the Web, over the substrate of an electronic constitution that defines how the social machines operate. Provisions for amending the constitution would provide for mutation. A few minimalist rules would ensure fairness.

While there is great excitement because these new social systems are essentially independent of geography, race and religion, they will of course isolate those in developing countries who cannot afford or have no option to access the Internet. At once the great equaliser and the great divider, the Web highlights – as do clean water and health care – the necessity of those better off to care for but not simply control those less advantaged. I do no more than touch on that urgent debate here.

The stage is set for an evolutionary growth of new social engines. The ability to create new forms of social process would be given to the world at large, and development would be rapid, just as the openness of Web technology allowed that to bloom.

My colleagues and I have wondered whether we should seed this process using the consortium itself. We could construct the consortium social machine out of the many machines that make up working groups and staff meetings and so on. We could allow a set of working groups that can be shown to form a tight self-reliant cluster to secede and form a new peer 'clone' consortium. The rules would have to include more than a newsgroup-like vote; budgets and contributions would have to balance, and responsibility would have to be accepted. In theory, we could then generalise this new social form. Then anyone could start a consortium, when the conditions were right, by pushing a few buttons on the Web page of a virtual 'consortium factory'.

Machines and the Web

In communicating between people using the Web, computers and networks have as their job to enable the information space, and otherwise get out of the way. But doesn't it make sense to also bring computers more into the action, to put their analytical power to work making sense of the vast content and human discourse on the Web? In part two of the dream, that is just what they do.

The first step is putting data on the Web in a form that machines can naturally understand, or converting it to that form. This creates what I call a *Semantic Web* – a web of data that can be processed directly or indirectly by machines.

Consider the limited amount of help we have received so far on the Web from machines. Search engines have proven remarkably useful in combing large indexes very rapidly and finding obscure documents. But they have proven remarkably useless, too, in that they have no way to evaluate document quality. They return a lot of junk. The problem is that search engines generally just look at occurrences of words in documents – something that is a hint at but tells very little about what the document really is or says.

A bit more sophisticated are automated brokerage services, which began to emerge in 1998. These are Web sites that try to match buyers and sellers. From the buyer's perspective, such a service can look like a metashop – a store of stores. One metashop to emerge is webmarket.com: give it a book title, and it will search all the online bookstores it knows, check the prices, and present a competitive list. To actually search the bookstores' catalogues, it has to pretend to be a browsing buyer, run their search engines, then extract the resulting data about product, price and delivery. It can then prepare a table comparing each deal.

The trick of getting a computer to extract information from an online catalogue is just that: a trick. It is known as *screen scraping* – trying to salvage something usable from information that is now in a form suitable only for humans. It is tenuous because the catalogue could change format overnight – for example, putting the ISBN number where the price used to be – and the automatic broker would be confused.

As people learn to use the Web, they analyse it in many ways. Ego surfing – looking for occurrences of one's own name – is a simple example. It may seem narcissistic, but it is a reasonable quest, because we have a certain responsibility to figure out where we fit into the world. Online research is a more serious example: one tries to find not only the answer to a question, but also what structures might be out there in the information.

Take a writer who wants to influence decision makers in Pakistan and India who are toying with the possible use of nuclear weapons. He wants to give them a deep awareness of the horrible aftermath of the atomic bombing of Nagasaki. He needs to know the forums in which these people operate, what they read.

He needs sources of information on nuclear weapons. He needs the current connections between the people, forums and information sources. The structures and interrelations are important.

The same sort of Web analysis could uncover new markets. It could help a project team leader evaluate the workings of her team by mapping all the dependencies and relationships among people, meeting minutes, research and other materials involving the group, which together define how the project is going. A CEO would like to be able to analyse his company's entire operation. Imagine receiving a report along the lines of: 'The company looks fine, except for a couple of things. you've got a parts division in Omaha that has exactly the same structure and business patterns as a company in Detroit that just folded: you might want to look at that. There's a product you make that is completely documented but completely unused. And there seem to be a few employees who are doing nothing that contributes to the company at all.'

None of this analysis can be automated today, partly because the form of intelligence that can draw such conclusions is difficult enough to find in people, yet alone in a computer program. But a simpler reason is that very little of the information on the Web is in a form that a machine can understand. The Semantic Web tackles this simpler problem – perhaps in the end as a foundation for tackling the greater problem.

Today, when one person posts a notice on a Web site to sell, say, a yellow car, it is almost impossible for another person to find it. Searching for a 'yellow car for sale in Massachusetts' results in a useless huge list of pages that happen to contain those words, when in fact the page I would want may be about a 'Honda, good runner, any good offer' with a Boston phone number. The search engine doesn't understand the page, because it is written for a human reader with a knowledge of English and a lot of common sense.

This changes when the seller uses a program (or Web site) that allows him to fill out a form about an object for sale. This could result in a Web page, in a machine-readable format, that maintains the significance of the document and its various parts. If all notifications of cars for sale were posted using the same form, then it would be easy for search engines to find, exclusively, yellow cars in Massachusetts. This is the simplest first step towards machine-understandable data.

The next step is a search engine that can apply logic to deduce whether each of the many responses it gets to an initial search is useful. This would allow us to ask general questions of our computerised agents, such as 'Did any baseball teams play yesterday in a place where the temperature was 22°C?' A program – call it a logic engine – would apply mathematical reasoning to each item found. The search engine might find six thousand facts involving baseball teams, and two million data items about temperatures and cities. The logic engine would analyse which bits of data refer to where a baseball team is, ascertain what the temperature was in certain towns, filter both sets of data, strip out all the junk, and respond: 'The Red Sox played in Boston yesterday and the temperature was 22°C. Also, the Sharks played in Tokyo, where it was 22°C.' A simple search would have returned an endless list of possible answers that the human would have to wade through. By adding logic, we get back a correct answer.

While Web pages are not generally written for machines, there is a vast amount of data in them, such as stock quotes and many parts of online catalogues, with well-defined semantics. I take as evidence of the desperate need for the Semantic Web the many recent screen-scraping products, such as those used by the brokers, to retrieve the normal Web pages and extract the original data. What a waste: clearly there is a need to be able to go and publish and read data directly.

Most databases in daily use are *relational databases* – databases with columns of information that relate to each other, such as the temperature, barometric pressure and location entries in a weather database. The relationships between the columns are the *semantics* – the meaning – of the data. These data are ripe for publication as a *semantic* Web page. For this to happen, we need a common language that allows computers to represent and share data, just as HTML allows computers to represent and share hypertext. The consortium is developing such a language, the Resource Description Framework (RDF), which, not surprisingly, is based on XML. In fact it is just XML with some tips about which bits are data and how to find the meaning of the data. RDF can be used in files on and off the Web. It can also be embedded in regular HTML Web pages. The RDF specification is relatively basic, and is already a W3C Recommendation. What we need now is a practical plan for deploying it.

The first form of semantic data on the Web was metadata: information about information. (There happens to be a company called Metadata, but I use the term here as a generic noun, as it has been used for many years.) Metadata consist of a set of properties of a document. By definition, metadata are data, as well as data about data. They describe catalogue information about who wrote Web pages and what they are about;

information about how Web pages fit together and relate to each other as versions, translations and reformattings; and social information such as distribution rights and privacy codes.

Most Web pages themselves carry a few bits of metadata. HTML pages have a hidden space in the document where certain items can be encoded, such as the page's title, its author, what software was used to create it, when it was created and when it was last modified. Often this is also put in human-orientated form, in plain English, at the bottom of a Web page in small type. Legal information, such as the copyright owner and privacy practice of the publisher, might be there, too. Metadata already out there also include catalogue information, such as keywords and classification numbers, and all the things libraries tend to put on library cards. There is endorsement information, such as PICS labels. And there is structural information about which Web pages on a site act as cover page, table of contents and index. There is no end to metadata, and a common RDF language for metadata should make a consistent world out of it.

RDF's introduction has not been straightforward – and there has been a lot of discussion about how and even whether it should be introduced. This is because, like many new languages, it confronts a basic dilemma inherent in the design of any language. HTML is a limiting language: you can use it only to express hypertext documents. Java, by contrast, isn't: you can write a bit of Java to do almost anything. Limiting languages are useful because you can, for example, analyse an HTML page element by element, convert it into other formats, index it and whatever. It is clear what every bit is for. People do all kinds of things with HTML pages that the pages were never originally intended for. A Java applet is different. Because Java is a *complete* programming language, you can use it to do anything, including creating a penguin that does somersaults. However, because Java is so powerful, the only way to figure out what a Java applet will do is to run it and watch. When I designed HTML for the Web, I chose to avoid giving it more power than it absolutely needed – a 'principle of least power', which I have stuck to ever since. I could have used a language like Donald Knuth's 'T_eX', which though it looks like a markup language is in fact a programming language. It would have allowed very fancy typography and all kinds of gimmicks, but there would have been little chance of turning Web pages into anything else. It would allow you to express absolutely anything on the page, but would also have allowed Web pages that could crash, or loop for ever. This is the tension.

There is a fear that one day the big brother of RDF will become a programming language, and library cards will start composing music, and checks will be made payable to a person whose name can be calculated only by using two hundred years of computer time. Looking at my plans for the Semantic Web, computer scientists at MIT and consortium members alike have been known to raise their eyebrows and suggest that we should keep the strength of the total language down. Should we, then, prevent the presence of powerfully descriptive languages on the Web?

The answer is that within many applications on the Web we should, but that in the Web as a whole we should not. Why? Because when you look at the complexity of the world that the Semantic Web must be able to describe, you realise that it must be possible to use any amount of power as needed. A reason for the success of the Web is that hypertext is so flexible a medium that the Web does not constrain the knowledge it tries to represent. The same must be true for the web of meaning. In fact, the web of everything we know and use from day to day is complex: we need the power of a strong language to represent it.

The trick here, though, is to make sure that each limited mechanical part of the Web, each application, is within itself composed of simple parts that will never get too powerful. In many places we need the transparent simplicity of HTML – so each application, like an ATM machine, will work in a well-defined way. The mechanisms for metadata, privacy, payment and so on will all work in a well-defined way. The art of designing applications in the future will be to fit them into the new Web in all its complexity, yet make them individually simple enough to work reliably every time. However, the total Web of all the data from each of the applications of RDF will make a very complex world, in which it will be possible to ask unanswerable questions. That is how the world is. The existence of such questions will not stop the world from turning, or cause weird things to happen to traffic lights. But it will open the door to some very interesting new applications that do roam over the whole intractable, incalculable Web and, while not promising anything, deliver a lot.

To keep a given application simple, RDF documents can be limited so that they take on only certain forms. Every RDF document comes with a pointer at the top to its RDF *schema* – a master list of the data terms used in the document. Anyone can create a new schema document. Two related schema languages are in the works, one for XML and one for RDF. Between them, they will tell any person or program about the elements of a Web page they describe – for example, that a person's name is a string of characters but their age is a number. This provides everything needed to define how databases are represented, and to start making all the existing data available. They also provide the tools for keeping the expressive power of an RDF document limited and its behaviour predictable. It allows us to unleash, bit by bit, the monster of an expressive language as we need it.

As the power is unleashed, computers on the Semantic Web achieve at first the ability to describe, then to infer and then to reason. The schema is a huge step, and one that will enable a vast amount of interoperability and extra functionality. However, it still only categorises data. It says nothing about meaning or understanding.

People 'come to a common understanding' by achieving a sufficiently similar set of consistent associations between words. This enables people to work together. Some understandings that we regard as absolute truths, like the mathematical truth that a straight line is defined by two different points, are simple patterns. Other understandings, such as my understanding of someone's anger at an injustice, are based on complex patterns of associations whose complete anatomy we are not fully aware of.

When people 'understand' something new, it means they can relate it to other things they already understand well enough. Two people from different planets can settle the difference between red and blue by each making a prism, passing light through it, and seeing which colour bends farther. But the difference between love and respect will be hashed out only in interminable discussions. Like words in the dictionary, everything – until we tie things down to the physical world – is defined in terms of other things.

This is also the basis of how computers can 'understand' something. We learn very simple things – such as to associate the word *hot* with a burning feeling – by early 'programming' of our brains. Similarly, we can program a computer to do simple things, like make a bank payment, and then we loosely say it 'understands' an electronic cheque. Alternatively, a computer could complete the process by following links on the Semantic Web that tell it how to convert each term in a document it doesn't understand into a term it does understand. I use the word *semantic* for this sort of machine-processible relative form of 'meaning'. The Semantic Web is the web of connections between different forms of data that allow a machine to do something it wasn't able to do directly.

This may sound boring until it is scaled up to the entirety of the Web. Imagine what computers can understand when there is a vast tangle of interconnected terms and data that can automatically be followed. The power we will have at our fingertips will be awesome. Computers will 'understand' in the sense that they will have achieved a dramatic increase in function by linking very many meanings.

To build understanding, we need to be able to link terms. This will be made possible by *inference languages*, which work one level above the schema languages. Inference languages allow computers to explain to each other that two terms that may seem different are in some way the same – a little like an English-French dictionary. Inference languages will allow computers to convert data from one format to another.

Databases are continually produced by different groups and companies, without knowledge of each other. Rarely does anyone stop the process to try to define globally consistent terms for each of the columns in the database tables. When we can link terms, even many years later, a computer will be able to understand that what one company calls 'mean-diurnal-temperature' is the same as what another company calls 'daily-average-temp'. If HTML and the Web made all the online documents look like one huge book, RDF, schema, and inference languages will make all the data in the world look like one huge database.

When we have the inference layer, finding the yellow car for sale becomes possible even if I ask for a yellow automobile. When trying to fill in a tax form, my RDF-aware computer can follow links out to the government's schema for it, find pointers to the rules and fill in all those lines for me by inference from other data it already knows.

As with the current Web, decentralisation is the underlying design principle that will give the Semantic Web its ability to become more than the sum of its parts.

There have been many projects to store interlinked meanings on a computer. The field has been called *knowledge representation*. These efforts typically use simple logical definitions such as the following: a vehicle is a thing, a car is a vehicle, a wheel is a thing, a car has four wheels – and so on. If enough definitions are entered, a program could answer questions by following the links of the database and, in a mechanical way, pretend to think. The problem is that these systems are designed around a central database, which has room for only one conceptual definition of 'car'. They are not designed to link to other databases.

The Web, in contrast, does not try to define a whole system, just one Web page at any one time. Every page can link to every other. In like fashion, the Semantic Web will allow different sites to have their own definition of 'car'. It can do this because the inference layer will allow machines to link definitions. This allows us to drop the requirement that two people have the same rigid idea of what something 'is'. In this way, the European Commission can draw up what it thinks of as a tax form. The US government can draw up its own tax form. As long as the information is in machine-understandable form, a Semantic Web program can follow semantic links to deduce that line 2 on the European form is like line 3A on the US form, which is like line 1 on the New York State tax form.

Suppose I ask my computer to give me a business card for Piedro from Quadradynamics, but it doesn't have one. It can scan an invoice for his company name, address and phone number, and take his e-mail address from a message, and present all the information needed for a business card. I might be the first to establish that mapping between fields, but now anyone who learns of those links can derive a business card from an e-mailed invoice. If I publish the relationships, the links between fields, as a bit of RDF, then the Semantic Web as a whole knows the equivalence.

Forgive the simplified examples, but I hope the point is clear: concepts become linked together. When, eventually, thousands of forms are linked together through the field for 'family name' or 'last name' or 'surname', then anyone analysing the Web would realise that there is an important common concept here.

The neat thing is that no one has to do that analysis. The concept of 'family name' simply begins to emerge as an important property of a person. Like a child learning an idea from frequent encounters, the Semantic Web 'learns' a concept from frequent contributions from different independent sources. A compelling note is that the Semantic Web does this without relying on English or any natural language for understanding. It won't translate poetry, but it will translate invoices, catalogues and the stuff of commerce, bureaucracy, travel, taxes and so much more.

The reasoning behind this approach, then, is that there is no central repository of information, and no one authority on anything. By linking things together we can go a very long way towards creating common understanding. The Semantic Web will work when terms are generally agreed upon, when they are not, and most often in the real-life fractal mess of terms that have various degrees of acceptance, whether in obscure fields or global cultures.

Making global standards is hard. The larger the number of people who are involved, the worse it is. In actuality, people can work together with only a few global understandings, and many local and regional ones. As with international and federal laws, and the Web, the minimalist design principle applies: try to constrain as little as possible to meet the general goal. International commerce works using global concepts of trading and debt, but it does not require everyone to use the same currency, or to have the same penalties for theft, and so on.

Plenty of groups apart from W3C have found out how hard it is to get global agreement under pressure of local variations.

Libraries use a system called a MARC record, which is a way of transmitting the contents of a library catalogue card. Electronic Data Interchange (EDI) was created a decade ago for conducting commerce electronically, with standard electronic equivalents of things like order forms and invoices. In both cases, there was never complete agreement about all the fields. Some standards were defined, but there were in practice regional or company-wide variations. Normal standards processes leave us with the impossible dilemma of whether we should have just one-to-one agreements, so that a Boeing invoice and an Airbus invoice are well defined but quite different, or whether we should postpone trying to do any electronic commerce until we define what an invoice is globally.

The plan for the Semantic Web is to be able to move smoothly from one situation to another, and to work together with a mixture. XML namespaces will allow documents to work in a mixture of globally standard terms and locally agreed-upon terms. The inference languages will allow computers to translate perhaps not all of a document, but enough of it to be able to act on it. Operating on such 'partial understanding' is fundamental, and we do it all the time in the nonelectronic world. When someone in Uruguay sends an American an invoice, the receiver can't read most of it because it's in Portuguese, but he can figure out that it is an invoice because it has references to a purchase-order number, parts numbers, the amount that has to be paid and whom to pay. That's enough to decide that this is something he should pay, and to enable him to pay it. The two entities are operating with overlapping vocabularies. The invoice is consistent with those drafted in Uruguay, and US invoices are consistent as well, and there is enough commonality between them to allow the

transaction to be conducted. This happens with no central authority that mandates how an invoice must be formulated.

As long as documents are created within the same logical
framework, such as RDF, partial understanding will be possible. This is how computers will work across boundaries, without
people having to meet to agree on every specific term globally.

There will still be an incentive for standards to evolve, although
they will be able to evolve steadily rather than by a series of battles. Once an industry association, say, sets a standard for
metadata for invoices, business cards, purchase orders, shipping
labels and a handful of other e-commerce forms, then suddenly
millions of people and companies with all sorts of computers,
software and networks could conduct business electronically.
Who will decide what the standard fields for an invoice should
be? Not the Web Consortium. They might arise in different ways,
through ad hoc groups or individual companies or people. All
the Web Consortium needs to do is set up the basic protocols
that allow the inference rules to be defined, and each specialised
slice of life will establish the common agreements needed to
make it work for them.

Perhaps the most important contribution of the Semantic
Web will be in providing a basis for the general Web's future evolution. The consortium's two original goals were to help the Web
maintain interoperability and to help it maintain 'evolvability.'
We knew what we needed for interoperability. *Evolvability* was
just a buzzword. But if the consortium can now create an environment in which standardisation processes become a property
of how the Web and society work together, then we will have
created something that not only is magic, but is capable of
becoming ever more magical.

The Web has to be able to change slowly, one step at a time, without being stopped and redesigned from the ground up. This is true not only for the Web, but for Web applications – the concepts, machines and social systems that are built on top of it. For, even as the Web may change, the appliances using it will change much more. Applications on the Web aren't suddenly created. They evolve from the smallest idea and grow stronger or more complex.

To make this buzzword concrete, just take that all too frequent frustration that arises when a version-4 word processor comes across a version-5 document and can't read it. The program typically throws up its hands in horror at such an encounter with the future. It stops, because it figures (quite reasonably) that it cannot possibly understand a version-5 language, which had not been invented when the program was written. However, with the inference languages, a version-5 document will be 'self-describing'. It will be provide a URI for the version-5 schema. The version-4 program can find the schema and, linked to it, rules for converting a version-5 document back into a version-4 document where possible. The only requirement is that the version-4 software needs to have been written so that it can understand the language in which the rules are written. That RDF inference language, then, has to be a standard.

When we unleash the power of RDF so that it allows us to express inference rules, we can still constrain it so that it is not such an expressive language that it will frighten people. The inference rules won't have to be a full programming language. They will be analysable and separable, and should not present a threat. However, for automating some real-life tasks, the language will have to become more powerful.

Taking the tax form again, imagine that the instructions for filling out your tax return are written in a computer language. The instructions are full of *if*s and *but*s. They include arithmetic, and alternatives. A machine, to be able follow these instructions, will need a fairly general ability to reason. It will have to figure out what to put on each line by following links to find relationships between data such as electronic bank statements, pay slips, and expense receipts.

What is the advantage of this approach over, say, a tax-preparation program, or just giving in and writing a Java program to do it? The advantage of putting the rules in RDF is that in doing so, all the reasoning is exposed, whereas a program is a black box: you don't see what happens inside it. When I used a tax program to figure out my 1997 taxes, it got the outcome wrong. I think it got confused between estimated tax paid *in* 1997 and that paid *for* 1997, but I'll never know for sure. It read all my information and filled in the form incorrectly. I overrode the result, but I couldn't fix the program because I couldn't see any of its workings. The only way I could have checked the program would have been to do the job completely myself by hand. If a reasoning engine had pulled in all the data and figured the taxes, I could have asked it why it did what it did, and corrected the source of the problem.

Being able to ask 'Why?' is important. It allows the user to trace back to the assumptions that were made, and the rules and data used. Reasoning engines will allow us to manipulate, figure, find and prove logical and numeric things over a wide-open field of applications. They will allow us to handle data that do not fall into clean categories such as 'financial', 'travel planning', and 'calendar'. And they are essential to our trusting online results, because they will give us the power to know how the results were derived.

The disadvantage of using reasoning engines is that, because they can combine data from all over the Web in their search for an answer, it can be too easy to ask an open question that will result in an endless quest. Even though we have well-defined rules as to who can access the consortium's members-only Web site, one can't just walk up to it and ask for admittance. This would ask the Web server to start an open-ended search for some good reason. We can't allow our Web server to waste time doing that; a user has to come equipped with some proof. Currently, users are asked under what rule or through which member they have right of access. A human being checks the logic. We'd like to do it automatically. In these cases we need a special form of RDF in which the explanation can be conveyed – if you like, a statement with all the whys answered. While finding good argument for why someone should have access may involve large searches, or inside knowledge, or complex reasoning, once that argument has been found, checking it is a mechanical matter we could leave to a simple tool. Hence the need for a language for carrying a proof across the Internet. A proof is just a list of sources for information, with pointers to the inference rules that were used to get from one step to the next.

In the complexity of the real world, life can proceed even when questions exist that reasoning engines can't answer. We just don't make essential parts of our daily business depend on answering them. We can support collaboration with a technical infrastructure that can respect society's needs in all their complexity.

Of course, our belief in each document will be based in the future on public key cryptography digital signatures. A 'trust engine' will be a reasoning engine with a bolted-on signature checker giving it an inherent ability to validate a signature. The trust engine is the most powerful sort of agent on the Semantic Web. There have been projects in which a trust engine used a less powerful language, but I honestly think that, looking at the reality of life, we will need a very expressive language to express real trust, and trust engines capable of understanding such a language. The trick that will make the system work in practice will be to send explanations around in most cases, instead of expecting the receiver to figure out why it should believe something.

Creating the actual digital signature on a document is the simpler part of the trust technology. It can be done regardless of the language used to create the document. It gives the ability to sign a document, or part of a document, with a key, and to verify that a document has been signed with a key. The plan is for a standard way to sign any XML document. The consortium in 1999 initiated this activity, combining earlier experience signing PICS labels with new ideas from the banking industry.

The other part of trust, which actually weaves the Web of Trust, is the mesh of statements about who will trust statements of what form when they are signed with what keys. This is where the meat is, the real mirroring of society in technology. Getting this right will enable everything from collaborating couples to commerce between corporations, and allow us actually to trust machines to work on our behalf. As the Web is used to represent more and more of what goes on in life, establishing trust gets more complicated. Right now, the real-life situation is too complicated for our online tools.

In most of our daily lives, then, even in a complex world, each step should be straightforward. We won't have to unleash the full power of RDF to get our job done. There is no need to fear that using RDF will involve computers in guesswork.

However, now that we are considering the most complex of cases, we must not ignore those in which computers try to give reasonably good answers to open questions. The techniques they use are *heuristics* – ways of making decisions when all the alternatives can't be explored. When a person uses a search engine, and casts her eye over the first page of returns for a promising lead, she is using a heuristic. Maybe she looks at the titles, or the first few lines quoted, or the URIs themselves; in any case, using heuristics is an acquired art. Heuristic programs at a bank are the ones that sound a warning when a person's credit-card spending pattern seems to differ from the usual.

The interplay between heuristic and strictly logical systems will be interesting. Heuristics will make guesses, and logic will check them. Robots will scan the Web and build indexes of certain forms of data, and those indexes will become not definitive, but so good that they can be used as definitive for many purposes. Heuristics may become so good that they seem perfect. The Semantic Web is being carefully designed so that it does not have to answer open questions. That is why it will work and grow. But in the end it will also provide a foundation for those programs that can use heuristics to tackle the previously untacklable.

From here on it gets difficult to predict what will happen on the Semantic Web. Because we will be able to define trust boundaries, we will be inclined, within those boundaries, to give tools more power. Techniques like viruses and chain letters, which we now think of as destructive, will become ways of getting a job done. We will use heuristics and ask open questions only when we have made a solid foundation of predictable ways of answering straightforward questions. We will be sorcerers in our new world when we have learned to control our creations.

Even if the blueprint of technologies to achieve the new Web is not crystal clear, the macroscopic view I've presented should at least convey that a lot of work has to be done. Some of it is far along. Some of it is still a gleam in the eye.

As work progresses, we will see more precisely how the pieces fit together. Right now the final architecture is hypothetical; I'm saying it *could* fit together, it *should* fit together. When I try to explain the architecture now, I get the same distant look in people's eyes as I did in 1989, when I tried to explain how global hypertext would work. But I've found a few individuals who share the vision; I can see it from the way they gesticulate and talk rapidly. In these rare cases I also have that same gut feeling as I did a decade ago: they'll work for whomever they have to work for, do whatever it takes, to help make the dream come true. Once again, it's going to be a grassroots thing.

The blueprint for the new Web is also much like my 1989 proposal for the original Web. It has a social base, a technological plan, and some basic philosophy. A few people get it; most don't. In the very beginning I wrote the World Wide Web code, then went out into the world to promote the vision, made the technology freely available so people could start working on their little piece of it, and encouraged them.

Today the consortium might write some of the code, or at least co-ordinate the writing of the code. Perhaps the computer community will share the vision and complete the pieces according to a business model that spans a number of years. Or perhaps someone watching from the sidelines will suddenly realise: 'I know how I can do this. I don't know how to figure out a business model for it, but I think I can write the code in two weeks.'

Work on the first Web by people in various places progressed in a fairly co-ordinated way because I had written the early code, which gave other people something to write to. Now we have two tools we didn't have then. One is the consortium – a place where people can come together as well as a source of advanced software platforms like Jigsaw and Apache that people can use to try out their new ideas. The second tool is the Web itself. Spreading the word will be so much easier. I can publish this plan to the world even when it's only half finished. The normal academic way Robert Cailliau and I could spread the original proposal was to get it into the hypertext conference proceedings – and it was rejected. This blueprint is not conference ready either, and I'm not inclined to make it so. We'll just get the information out there so people can point to it and discuss it. Once a seed is sown it will contain pointers back to where it came from, so ideas will spread much more rapidly.

Cynics have already said to me, 'You really think this time around people are going to pick up on the architecture, and spend hours and hours on it as Pei Wei and all the others did?' Yes. Because that's just what the cynics said in 1989. They said, 'Oh, well, this is just too much to take on.' But remember, it takes only a half-dozen good people in the right places. Back then, finding that half dozen took a long time. Today, the world can come to the consortium, plug in their ideas, and have them disseminated.

Indeed, the danger this time is that we get six hundred people creating reasoning engines in their garages across the land. But if they try to patent what they're doing, each one of them thinking they've found the grand solution first, or if they build palisades of proprietary formats and use peculiar, undocumented ways of doing things, they will just get in the way. If, through the consortium, they come openly to the table for discussion, this could all work out remarkably soon.

I mention patents in passing, but in fact they are a great stumbling block for Web development. Developers are stalling their efforts in a given direction when they hear rumours that some company may have a patent that may involve the technology. Currently, in the United States (unlike in many countries), it is possible to patent part of the way a program does something. This is a little like patenting a business procedure: it is difficult to define when something really is 'novel'. Certainly among some patents I have looked at I have found it difficult to find anything that gives me that 'ah-ha' feeling of a new idea. Some just take a well-known process (like interlibrary loan or betting on a race) and do it in software. Others combine well-known techniques in apparently arbitrary ways to no added effect – like patenting going shopping in a striped automobile on a Thursday. They pass the test of apparent novelty because there is no existing document describing exactly such a process. In 1980, a device for delivering a book electronically, or a device for online gambling, might have seemed novel, but now these things are just obvious Web versions of well-known things. The US Patent and Trademark Office, ill-equipped to search for 'prior art' (earlier occurrence of the same idea) in this new field, seems to have allowed through patents by default.

It is often difficult to know what a patent is about at all because it is written obscurely using language quite different from that which a normal programmer would use. There is a reason for this: the weapon is fear of a patent suit, rather than the patent itself. Companies cross-license patents to each other without ever settling in court what those patents actually mean. Fear is increased by uncertainty and doubt, and so there is an incentive for obscurity. Only the courts can determine what a patent means, and the legal effort and time involved dwarfs the engineering effort.

This atmosphere is new. Software patents are new. The Internet ethos in the seventies and eighties was one of sharing for the common good, and it would have been unthinkable for a player to ask fees just for implementing a standard protocol such as HTTP. Now things are changing. Large companies stockpile patents as a threat of retaliation against suits from their peers. Small companies may be terrified to enter the business.

The lure of getting a cut of some fundamental part of the new infrastructure is strong. Some companies (or even individuals) make a living only by making up patents and suing larger companies, making themselves immune to retaliation by not actually making or selling any products at all. The original aim of patents – to promote the publication and deployment of ideas and to protect the incentive for research – is noble, but abuse is now a very serious problem.

The ethos now seems to be that patents are a matter of whatever you can get away with. Engineers, asked by company lawyers to provide patentable ideas every few months, resignedly hand over 'ideas' that make the engineers themselves cringe.

It is time for a change, to an ethos in which companies use patents to defend their own valid products, rather than serendipitously suing based on claims even they themselves would have thought applied. The threshold of 'innovation' is too low. Corporate lawyers are locked into a habit of arguing whatever advantage they can, and probably only determined corporate leadership can set the industry back on a sane track. The consortium members have, at the time of writing, been delivering on what to do, but it is not clear what the result will be.

The Semantic Web, like the Web already, will make many things previously impossible just obvious. As I write about the new technology, I do wonder whether it will be a technical dream or a legal nightmare.

CHAPTER 14

Weaving the Web

Can the future Web change the way people work together and advance knowledge in a small company, a large organisation, a country? If it works for a small group and can scale up, can it be used to change the world? We know the Web lets us do things more quickly, but can it make a phase change in society, a move to a new way of working – and will that be for better or for worse?

In a company with six employees, everybody can sit around a table, share their visions of where they're going and reach a common understanding of all the terms they're using. In a large company, somebody defines the common terms and behaviour that make the company work as an entity. Those who have been through the transition know it only to well: it typically kills diversity. It's too rigid a structure. And it doesn't scale, because as the company gets bigger, the bureaucratic boundaries cut off more and more of its internal communications, its lifeblood. At the other extreme is the utopian commune with no structure, which doesn't work either because nobody actually takes out the rubbish.

Whether a group can advance comes down to creating the

right connectivity between people – in a family, a company, a country or the world. We've been trying to figure out how to create this for years. In many ways, we haven't had to decide, as geography has decided for us. Companies, and nations, have always been defined by a physical grouping of people. The military stability of a nation was based on troop placements and marching distances. The diversity of culture we've had also has stemmed from two-dimensional space. The only reason the people in a little village in Switzerland would arise speaking a unique dialect was that they were surrounded by mountains. Geography gave the world its military stability and cultural boxes. People didn't have to decide how large their groups would be or where to draw the boundaries. Now that the metric is not physical distance, not even time zones, but clicks, we do have to make these decisions. The Internet and the Web have pulled us out of two-dimensional space. They've also moved us away from the idea that we won't be interrupted by anybody who's more than a day's march away.

At first, this violation of our long-held rules can be unsettling, destroying a geographical sense of identity. The Web breaks the boundaries we have relied on to define us and protect us, but it can build new ones, too.

The thing that does not scale when a company grows is intuition – the ability to solve problems without using a well-defined logical method. A person, or a small group brainstorming out loud, ruminates about problems until possible solutions emerge. Answers arrive not necessarily from following a logical path, but rather by seeing where connections may lead. A larger company fails to be intuitive when the person with the answer isn't talking with the person who has the question.

It's important that the Web help people be intuitive as well as analytical, because our society needs both functions. Human beings have a natural balance in using the creative and analytical parts of their brains. We will solve large analytical problems by turning computer power loose on the hard data of the Semantic Web.

Scaling intuition is difficult because our minds hold thousands of ephemeral tentative associations at the same time. To allow group intuition, the Web would have to capture these threads – half-thoughts that arise, without evident rational thought or inference, as we work. It would have to present them to another reader as a natural complement to a half-formed idea. The intuitive step occurs when someone following links by a number of independent people notices a relevant relationship, and creates a shortcut link to record it.

This all works only if each person makes links as he or she browses, so writing, link creation and browsing must be totally integrated. If someone discovers a relationship but doesn't make the link, he or she is wiser but the group is not.

To make such a shortcut, one person has to have two pieces of inference in his or her head at the same time. The new Web will make it much more likely that somebody somewhere is browsing one source that has half of the key idea, and happens to have just recently browsed the other. For this to be likely, the Web must be well connected – have few 'degrees of separation'. This is the sort of thing researchers are always trying to do – get as much in their heads as possible, then go to sleep and hope to wake up in the middle of the night with a brilliant idea and rush to write it down. But as the problems get bigger, we want to be able to work this brainstorming approach on a much larger scale.

We have to be sure to design the Web to allow feedback from the people who've made new intuitive links.

If we succeed, creativity will arise across larger and more diverse groups. These high-level activities, which have occurred just within one human's brain, will occur among ever-larger, more interconnected groups of people acting as if they shared a larger intuitive brain. It is an intriguing analogy. Perhaps that late-night surfing is not such a waste of time after all: it is just the Web dreaming.

Atoms each have a *valence* – an ability to connect with just so many other atoms. As an individual, each of us picks a few channels to be involved in, and we can cope with only so much. The advantage of getting things done faster on the Web is an advantage only to the extent that we can accept the information faster, and there are definite limits. By just pushing the amount we have to read and write, the number of e-mails we have to cope with, the number of Web sites we have to surf, we may scrape together a few more bytes of knowledge, but exhaust ourselves in the process and miss the point.

As a group works together, the members begin to reach common understandings that involve new concepts, which only they share. Sometimes these concepts can become so strong that the group finds it has to battle the rest of the world to explain its decisions. At this point, the members may realise for the first time that they have started using words in special ways. They may not realise how they have formed a little subculture until they begin explaining their decisions to colleagues outside the group. They have built a new understanding, and at the same time built a barrier around themselves. Boundaries of understanding have been broken, but new ones have formed around those who share the new concept.

A choice has been made, and there is a gain and a loss in terms of shared understanding.

What should guide us when we make these choices? What kind of a structure are we aiming for, and what principles will help us achieve it? The Web as a medium is so flexible that it leaves the choice to us. As well as the choice of links we make individually, we have a choice in the social machines we create, the variously shaped parts in our construction game. We know that we want a well-connected structure for group intuition to work. We know it should be decentralised, to be resilient and fair.

The human brain outperforms computers by its incredible level of parallel processing. Society, similarly, solves its problems in parallel. For the society to work efficiently on the Web, massive parallelism is required. Everybody must be able to publish, and to control who has access to their published work. There should not be a structure (like a highway system or mandatory Dewey decimal system) or limitation that precludes any kind of idea or solution purely because the Web won't allow it to be explained.

The Internet before the Web thrived on a decentralised technical architecture and a decentralised social architecture. These were incrementally created by the design of technical and social machinery. The community had just enough rules of behaviour to function using the simple social machines it invented. Starting from a flat world in which every computer had just one Internet address and everyone was considered equal, over time the sea of chattering people imposed some order on itself. Newsgroups gave structure to information and people. The Web started with a similar lack of preset structure, but soon all sorts of lists of 'best' sites created a competition-based structure even before advertising was introduced. While the Internet itself seemed to represent a flight from hierarchy, without hierarchy there were too many degrees of separation to prevent things from being reinvented. There seemed to be a quest for something that was not a tree, but not a flat space, either.

We certainly need a structure that will avoid those two catastrophes: the global uniform McDonald's monoculture, and the isolated Heaven's Gate cults that understand only themselves. By each of us spreading our attention evenly between groups of different size, from personal to global, we help avoid these extremes. Link by link we build paths of understanding across the web of humanity. We are the threads holding the world together. As we do this, we naturally end up with a few Web sites in very high demand, and a continuum down to the huge number of Web sites with only rare visitors. In other words, appealing though equality between peers seems, such a structure by its uniformity is not optimal. It does not pay sufficient attention to global co-ordination, and it can require too many clicks to get from problem to solution.

If instead everyone divides their time more or less evenly between the top ten Web sites, the rest of the top one hundred, the rest of the top one thousand and so on, the load on various servers would have a distribution of sizes characteristic of 'fractal' patterns so common in nature (from coastlines to ferns) and of the famous 'Mandelbrot set' mathematical patterns. It turns out that some measurements of all the Web traffic by Digital

Equipment employees on the West Coast revealed very closely this $1/n$ law: the Web exhibits fractal properties even though we can't individually see the patterns, and even though there is no hierarchical system to enforce such a distribution.

This doesn't answer the question, but it is intriguing because it suggests that there are large-scale dynamics operating to produce such results. A fascinating result was found by Jon Kleinberg, a computer scientist at Cornell University who discovered that, when the matrix of the Web is analysed like a quantum mechanical system, stable energy states correspond to concepts under discussion. The Web is starting to develop large-scale structure in its own way. Maybe we will be able to produce new metrics for checking the progress of society towards what we consider acceptable.

The analogy of a global brain is tempting, because Web and brain both involve huge numbers of elements – neurons and Web pages – and a mixture of structure and apparent randomness. However, a brain has an intelligence that emerges on quite a different level from anything that a neuron could be aware of. From Arthur C. Clarke to Douglas Hofstader, writers have contemplated an 'emergent property' arising from the mass of humanity and computers. But remember that such a phenomenon would have its own agenda. We would not as individuals be aware of it, let alone control it, any more than the neuron controls the brain.

I expect that there will be emergent properties with the Semantic Web, but at a lesser level than emergent intelligence. There could be spontaneous order or instability: society could crash, much as the stock market crashed in October 1987 because of automatic trading by computer. The agenda of trading – to make money on each trade – didn't change, but the dynamics did; so many huge blocks of shares were traded so fast that the whole system became unstable.

To ensure stability, any complex electronic system needs a damping mechanism to introduce delay, to prevent it from oscillating too wildly. Damping mechanisms have since been built into the stock-trading system. We may be able to build them into the Semantic Web of co-operating computers – but will we be able to build them into the web of co-operating people? Already the attention of people, the following of links, and the flow of money are interlaced inextricably.

I do not, therefore, pin my hopes on an overpowering order emerging spontaneously from the chaos. I feel that to deliberately build a society, incrementally, using the best ideas we have, is our duty and will also be the most fun. We are slowly learning the value of decentralised, diverse systems, and of mutual respect and tolerance. Whether you put it down to evolution or your favourite spirit, the neat thing is that we seem as humans to be tuned so that we do in the end get the most fun out of doing the 'right' thing.

My hope and faith that we are headed somewhere stem in part from the repeatedly proven observation that people seem to be naturally built to interact with others as part of a greater system. A person who's completely turned inward, who spends all his or her time alone, is someone who has trouble making balanced decisions and is very unhappy. Someone who is completely turned outward, who's worried about the environment and international diplomacy and spends no time sitting at home or in his local community, also has trouble making balanced decisions and is also very unhappy. It seems a person's happiness depends on having a balance of connections at different levels. We seem to have built into us what it takes in a person to be part of a fractal society.

If we end up producing a structure in hyperspace that allows us to work together harmoniously, that would be a metamorphosis. Though it would, I hope, happen incrementally, it would result in a huge restructuring of society. A society that could advance with intercreativity and group intuition rather than conflict as the basic mechanism would be a major change.

If we lay the groundwork right and try novel ways of interacting on the new Web, we may find a whole new set of financial, ethical, cultural and governing structures to which we can choose to belong, rather than having to pick the ones we happen to physically live in. Bit by bit those structures that work best would become more important in the world, and democratic systems might take on different shapes.

Working together is the business of finding shared understandings but being careful not to label them as absolute. They may be shared, but often arbitrary in the larger picture.

We spend a lot of time trying to tie down meanings and fighting to have our own framework adopted by others. It is, after all, a lifelong process to set ourselves up with connections to all the concepts we use. Having to work with someone else's definitions is difficult. An awe-inspiring talent of my physics tutor, Professor John Moffat, was that when I brought him a problem I had worked out incorrectly, using a strange technique and symbols different from the well-established ones, he not only would follow my weird reasoning to find out where it went wrong, but would then use my own strange notation to explain the right answer. This great feat involved looking at the world using my definitions, comparing them with his, and translating his knowledge and experience into my language. It was a mathematical version of the art of listening. This sort of effort is needed whenever groups meet. It is also the hard work of the consortium's working groups. Though it often seems to be no fun, it is the thing that deserves the glory.

We have to be prepared to find that the 'absolute' truth we had been so comfortable with within one group is suddenly challenged when we meet another. Human communication scales up only if we can be tolerant of the differences while we work with partial understanding.

The new Web must allow me to learn by crossing boundaries. It has to help me reorganise the links in my own brain so I can understand those in another person's. It has to enable me to keep the frameworks I already have, and relate them to new ones. Meanwhile, we as people will have to get used to viewing as communication rather than argument the discussions and challenges that are a necessary part of this process. When we fail, we will have to figure out whether one framework or another is broken, or whether we just aren't smart enough yet to relate them.

The parallels between technical design and social principles have recurred throughout the Web's history. About a year after I arrived to start the consortium, my wife and I came across Unitarian Universalism. Walking into a Unitarian Universalist church more or less by chance felt like a breath of fresh air. Some of the association's basic philosophies very much match what I had been brought up to believe, and the objective I had in creating the Web. People now sometimes even ask whether I designed the Web based on these principles. Clearly, Unitarian Universalism had no influence on the Web. But I can see how it could have, because I did indeed design the Web around universalist (with a lowercase *u*) principles.

One of the things I like about Unitarianism is its lack of religious trappings, miracles and pomp and circumstance. It is minimalist, in a way. Unitarians accepted the useful parts of philosophy from all religions, including Christianity and Judaism, but also Hinduism, Buddhism and any other good philosophies, and wrapped them not into one consistent religion, but into an environment in which people think and discuss, argue and always try to be accepting of differences of opinion and ideas.

I suppose many people would not classify 'U-Uism' as a religion at all, in that it doesn't have the dogma, and is very tolerant of different forms of belief. It passes the Test of Independent Invention that I apply to technical designs: if someone else had invented the same thing independently, the two systems should work together without anyone having to decide which one was 'central'. For me, who enjoyed the acceptance and the diverse community of the Internet, the Unitarian church was a great fit. Peer-to-peer relationships are encouraged wherever they are appropriate, very much as the World Wide Web encourages a hypertext link to be made wherever it is appropriate. Both are philosophies that allow decentralised systems to develop, whether they are systems of computers, knowledge or people. The people who built the Internet and Web have a real appreciation of the value of individuals and the value of systems in which individuals play their role, with both a firm sense of their own identity and a firm sense of some common good.

There's a freedom about the Internet: as long as we accept the rules of sending packets around, we can send packets containing anything to anywhere. In Unitarian Universalism, if one accepts the basic tenet of mutual respect in working together towards some greater vision, then one finds a huge freedom in choosing one's own words that capture that vision, one's own rituals to help focus the mind, one's own metaphors for faith and hope.

I was very lucky, in working at CERN, to be in an environment that Unitarian Universalists and physicists would equally appreciate: one of mutual respect, and of building something very great through collective effort that was well beyond the means of any one person – without a huge bureaucratic regime. The environment was complex and rich; any two people could get together and exchange views, and even end up working together somehow. This system produced a weird and wonderful machine, which needed care to maintain, but could take advantage of the ingenuity, inspiration and intuition of individuals in a special way. That, from the start, has been my goal for the World Wide Web.

Hope in life comes from the interconnections among all the people in the world. We believe that if we all work for what we think individually is good, then we as a whole will achieve more power, more understanding, more harmony as we continue the journey. We don't find the individual being subjugated by the whole. We don't find the needs of the whole being subjugated by the increasing power of an individual. But we might see more understanding in the struggles between these extremes. We don't expect the system to eventually become perfect. But we feel better and better about it. We find the journey more and more exciting, but we don't expect it to end.

Should we then feel that we are getting smarter and smarter, more and more in control of nature, as we evolve? Not really. Just better connected – connected into a better shape. The experience of seeing the Web take off by the grassroots effort of thousands gives me tremendous hope that if we have the individual will, we can collectively make of our world what we want.

Information Management: A Proposal

Tim Berners-Lee, CERN

March 1989, May 1990

This proposal concerns the management of general information about accelerators and experiments at CERN. It discusses the problems of loss of information about complex evolving systems and derives a solution based on a distributed hypertext system.

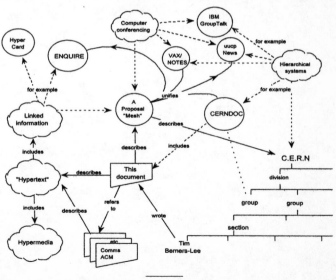

Overview

Many of the discussions of the future at CERN and the LHC era end with the question – "Yes, but how will we ever keep track of such a large project?" This proposal provides an answer to such questions. Firstly, it discusses the problem of information access at CERN. Then, it introduces the idea of linked information systems, and compares them with less flexible ways of finding information.

It then summarises my short experience with non-linear text systems known as "hypertext", describes what CERN needs from such a system, and what industry may provide. Finally, it suggests steps we should take to involve ourselves with hypertext now, so that individually and collectively we may understand what we are creating.

Losing Information at CERN

CERN is a wonderful organisation. It involves several thousand people, many of them very creative, all working toward common goals. Although they are nominally organised into a hierarchical management structure, this does not constrain the way people will communicate, and share information, equipment and software across groups.

The actual observed working structure of the organisation is a multiply connected "web" whose interconnections evolve with time. In this environment, a new person arriving, or someone taking on a new task, is normally given a few hints as to who would be useful people to talk to. Information about what facilities exist and how to find out about them travels in the corridor gossip and occasional newsletters, and the details about what is required to be done spread in a similar way. All things considered, the result is remarkably successful, despite occasional misunderstandings and duplicated effort.

A problem, however, is the high turnover of people. When two years is a typical length of stay, information is constantly being lost. The introduction of the new people demands a fair amount of their time and that of others before they have any idea of what goes on. The technical details of past projects are sometimes lost forever, or only recovered after a detective investigation in an emergency. Often, the information has been recorded, it just cannot be found.

If a CERN experiment were a static once-only development, all the information could be written in a big book. As it is, CERN is constantly changing as new ideas are produced, as new technology becomes available, and in order to get around unforeseen technical problems. When a change is necessary, it normally affects only a small part of the organisation. A local reason arises for changing a part of the experiment or detector. At this point, one has to dig around to find out what other parts and people will be affected. Keeping a book up to date becomes impractical, and the structure of the book needs to be constantly revised.

The sort of information we are discussing answers, for example, questions like:

- Where is this module used?
- Who wrote this code? Where does he work?
- What documents exist about that concept?
- Which laboratories are included in that project?
- Which systems depend on this device?
- What documents refer to this one?

The problems of information loss may be particularly acute at CERN, but in this case (as in certain others), CERN is a model in miniature of the rest of the world in a few years time. CERN meets now some problems which the rest of the world will have to face soon. In 10 years, there may be many commercial solutions to the problems above, while today we need something to allow us to continue.[1]

---

[1] The same has been true, for example, of electronic mail gateways, document preparation, and heterogeneous distributed programming systems.

Linked information systems

In providing a system for manipulating this sort of information, the hope would be to allow a pool of information to develop which could grow and evolve with the organisation and the projects it describes. For this to be possible, **the method of storage must not place its own restraints on the information.**

This is why a "web" of notes with links (like references) between them is far more useful than a fixed hierarchical system. When describing a complex system, many people resort to diagrams with circles and arrows. Circles and arrows leave one free to describe the interrelationships between things in a way that tables, for example, do not. The system we need is like a diagram of circles and arrows, where circles and arrows can stand for anything.

We can call the circles nodes, and the arrows links. Suppose each node is like a small note, summary article, or comment. I'm not over concerned here with whether it has text or graphics or both. Ideally, it represents or describes one particular person or object. Examples of nodes can be:

- People
- Software modules
- Groups of people
- Projects
- Concepts
- Documents
- Types of hardware
- Specific hardware objects

The arrows which link circle A to circle B can mean, for example, that A ...

- depends on B
- is part of B
- made B
- refers to B
- uses B
- is an example of B

These circles and arrows, nodes and links,[2] have different significance in various sorts of conventional diagrams:

Diagram	Nodes are	Arrows mean
Family tree	People	"Is parent of"
Dataflow diagram	Software modules	"Passes data to"
Dependency	Module	"Depends on"
PERT chart	Tasks	"Must be done before"
Organisational chart	People	"Reports to"

The system must allow any sort of information to be entered. Another person must be able to find the information, sometimes without knowing what he is looking for.

In practice, it is useful for the system to be aware of the generic types of the links between items (dependences, for example), and the types of nodes (people, things, documents ...) without imposing any limitations.

---

[2] Linked information systems have entities and relationships. There are, however, many differences between such a system and an "Entity Relationship" database system. For one thing, the information stored in a linked system is largely comment for human readers. For another, nodes do not have strict types which define exactly what relationships they may have. Nodes of similar type do not all have to be stored in the same place.

The problem with trees

Many systems are organised hierarchically. The CERNDOC documentation system is an example, as is the Unix file system, and the VMS/HELP system. A tree has the practical advantage of giving every node a unique name. However, it does not allow the system to model the real world. For example, in a hierarchical HELP system such as VMS/HELP, one often gets to a leaf on a tree such as:

```
HELP COMPILER SOURCE_FORMAT PRAGMAS DEFAULTS
```

only to find a reference to another leaf: "Please see

```
HELP COMPILER COMMAND OPTIONS DEFAULTS PRAGMAS"
```

and it is necessary to leave the system and re-enter it. What was needed was a link from one node to another, because in this case *the information was not naturally organised into a tree*.

Another example of a tree-structured system is the uucp News system (try 'rn' under Unix). This is a hierarchical system of discussions ("newsgroups") each containing articles contributed by many people. It is a very useful method of pooling expertise, but suffers from the inflexibility of a tree. Typically, a discussion under one newsgroup will develop into a different topic, at which point it ought to be in a different part of the tree. (See Fig 1.)

```
From mcvax!uunet!pyrdc!pyrnj!rutgers!bellcore!geppetto!duncan Thu Mar ...
Article 93 of alt.hypertext:
Path: cernvax!mcvax!uunet!pyrdc!pyrnj!rutgers!bellcore!geppetto!duncan
>From: duncan@geppetto.ctt.bellcore.com (Scott Duncan)
Newsgroups: alt.hypertext
Subject: Re: Threat to free information networks
Message-ID: <14646@bellcore.bellcore.com>
Date: 10 Mar 89 21:00:44 GMT
References: <1784.2416BB47@sishq.FIDONET.ORG> <3437@uhccux.uhcc ...
Sender: news@bellcore.bellcore.com
Reply-To: duncan@ctt.bellcore.com (Scott Duncan)
Organization: Computer Technology Transfer, Bellcore
Lines: 18

Doug Thompson has written what I felt was a thoughtful article on
censorship -- my acceptance or rejection of its points is not
particularly germane to this posting, however.

In reply Greg Lee has somewhat tersely objected.

My question (and reason for this posting) is to ask where we might
logically take this subject for more discussion. Somehow alt.hypertext
does not seem to be the proper place.

Would people feel it appropriate to move to alt.individualism or even
one of the soc groups. I am not so much concerned with the specific
issue of censorship of rec.humor.funny, but the views presented in
Greg's article.

Speaking only for myself, of course, I am ...
Scott P. Duncan (duncan@ctt.bellcore.com OR ... !bellcore!ctt!duncan)
                (Bellcore, 444 Hoes Lane RRC 1H-210, Piscataway, NJ ...)
                (201-699-3910 (w)   201-463-3683 (h))
```

Fig 1. An article in the UUCP News scheme.

The subject field allows notes on the same topic to be linked together within a "newsgroup". The name of the newsgroup (all.hypertext) is a hierarchical name. This particular note expresses a problem with the strict tree structure of the scheme: this discussion is related to several areas. Note that the "References", "From" and "Subject" fields can all be used to generate links.

The problem with keywords

Keywords are a common method of accessing data for which one does not have the exact coordinates. The usual problem with keywords, however, is that two people never chose the same keywords. The keywords then become useful only to people who already know the application well.

Practical keyword systems (such as that of VAX/NOTES for example) require keywords to be registered. This is already a step in the right direction.

A linked system takes this to the next logical step. Keywords can be nodes which stand for a concept. A keyword node is then no different from any other node. One can link documents, etc., to keywords. One can then find keywords by finding any node to which they are related. In this way, documents on similar topics are indirectly linked, through their key concepts.

A keyword search then becomes a search starting from a small number of named nodes, and finding nodes which are close to all of them.

It was for these reasons that I first made a small linked information system, not realising that a term had already been coined for the idea: "hypertext".

A solution:
Hypertext

Personal Experience with Hypertext

In 1980, I wrote a program for keeping track of software with which I was involved in the PS control system. Called *Enquire*, it allowed one to store snippets of information, and to link related pieces together in any way. To find information, one progressed via the links from one sheet to another, rather like in the old computer game "adventure". I used this for my personal record of people and modules. It was similar to the application *Hypercard* produced more recently by Apple for the Macintosh. A difference was that *Enquire*, although lacking the fancy graphics, ran on a multiuser system, and allowed many people to access the same data.

```
Documentation of the RPC project                    (concept)

Most of the documentation is available on VMS, with the two
principal manuals being stored in the CERNDOC system.

 1) includes: The VAX/NOTES conference VXCERN::RPC
 2) includes: Test and Example suite
 3) includes: RPC BUG LISTS
 4) includes: RPC System: Implementation Guide
    Information for maintenance, porting, etc.
 5) includes: Suggested Development Strategy for RPC Applications
 6) includes: "Notes on RPC", Draft 1, 20 Feb 86
 7) includes: "Notes on Proposed RPC Development" 18 Feb 86
 8) includes: RPC User Manual
    How to build and run a distributed system
 9) includes: Draft Specifications and Implementation Notes
10) includes: The RPC HELP facility
11) describes: THE REMOTE PROCEDURE CALL PROJECT in DD/OC

Help Display Select Back Quit Mark Goto_mark Link Add Edit
```

Fig 2. A screen in an Enquire scheme.

This example is basically a list, so the list of links is more important than the text on the node itself. Note that each link has a type ("includes" for example) and may also have comment associated with it. (The bottom line is a menu bar.)

Soon after my re-arrival at CERN in the DD division. I found that the environment was similar to that in PS, and I missed *Enquire*. I therefore produced a version for the VMS, and have used it to keep track of projects, people, groups, experiments, software modules and hardware devices with which I have worked. I have found it personally very useful. I have made no effort to make it suitable for general consumption, but have found that a few people have successfully used it to browse through the projects and find out all sorts of things of their own accord.

Hot spots

Meanwhile, several programs have been made exploring these ideas, both commercially and academically. Most of them use "hot spots" in documents, like icons, or highlighted phrases, as sensitive areas. Touching a hot spot with a mouse brings up the relevant information, or expands the text on the screen to include it. Imagine, then, the references in this document, all being associated with the network address of the thing to which they referred, so that while reading this document you could skip to them with a click of the mouse.

"Hypertext" is a term coined in the 1950s by Ted Nelson [...], which has become popular for these systems, although it is used to embrace two different ideas. One idea (which is relevant to this problem) is the concept:

"Hypertext": Human-readable information linked together in an unconstrained way.

The other idea, which is independent and largely a question of technology and time, is of multimedia documents which include graphics, speech and video. I will not discuss this latter aspect further here, although I will use the word "Hypermedia" to indicate that one is not bound to text.

It has been difficult to assess the effect of a large hypermedia system on an organisation, often because these systems never had seriously large-scale use. For this reason, we require large amounts of existing information that should be accessible using any new information management system.

CERN Requirements

To be a practical system in the CERN environment, there are a number of clear practical requirements.

Remote access across networks

CERN is distributed, and access from remote machines is essential.

Heterogeneity

Access is required to the same data from different types of system (VM/CMS, Macintosh, VAX/VMS, Unix).

Non-Centralisation

Information systems start small and grow. They also start isolated and then merge. A new system must allow existing systems to be linked together without requiring any central control or coordination.

Access to existing data

If we provide access to existing databases as though they were in hypertext form, the system will get off the ground quicker. This is discussed further below.

Private links

One must be able to add one's own private links to and from public information. One must also be able to annotate links, as well as nodes, privately.

Bells and Whistles

Storage of ASCII text, and display on 24x80 screens, is in the short term sufficient, and essential. Addition of graphics would be an optional extra with very much less penetration for the moment.

Data analysis

An intriguing possibility, given a large hypertext database with typed links, is that it allows some degree of automatic analysis. It is possible to search, for example, for anomalies such as undocumented software or divisions which contain no people. It is possible to generate lists of people or devices for other purposes, such as mailing lists of people to be informed of changes.

It is also possible to look at the topology of an organisation or a project, and draw conclusions about how it should be managed, and how it could evolve. This is particularly useful when the database becomes very large, and groups of projects, for example, become so interwoven as to make it difficult to see the wood from the trees.

In a complex place like CERN, it's not always obvious how to divide people into groups. Imagine making a large three-dimensional model, with people represented by little spheres, and strings between people who have something in common at work.

Now imagine picking up the structure and shaking it, until you make some sense of the tangle: perhaps, you see tightly knit groups in some places, and in some places weak areas of communication spanned by only a few people. Perhaps a linked information system will allow us to see the real structure of the organisation in which we work.

Live links

The data to which a link (or a hot spot) refers may be very static, or it may be temporary. In many cases at CERN, information about the state of systems is changing all the time. Hypertext allows documents to be linked into "live" data so that every time the link is followed, the information is retrieved. If one sacrifices portability, it is possible to make following a link fire up a special application, so that diagnostic programs, for example, could be linked directly into the maintenance guide.

Non requirements

Discussions on Hypertext have sometimes tackled the problem of copyright enforcement and data security. These are of secondary importance at CERN, where information exchange is still more important than secrecy. Authorisation and accounting systems for hypertext could conceivably be designed which are very sophisticated, but they are not proposed here.

In cases where reference must be made to data which is in fact protected, existing file protection systems should be sufficient.

Specific Applications

The following are three examples of specific places in which the proposed system would be immediately useful. There are many others.

Development Project Documentation

The Remote procedure Call project has a skeleton description using *Enquire*. Although limited, it is very useful for recording who did what, where they are, what documents exist, etc. Also, one can keep track of users, and can easily append any extra little bits of information which come to hand and have nowhere else to be put. Cross-links to other projects, and to databases which contain information on people and documents would be very useful, and save duplication of information.

Document retrieval

The CERNDOC system provides the mechanics of storing and printing documents. A linked system would allow one to browse through concepts, documents, systems and authors, also allowing references between documents to be stored. (Once a document had been found, the existing machinery could be invoked to print it or display it.)

The "Personal Skills Inventory"

Personal skills and experience are just the sort of thing which need hypertext flexibility. People can be linked to projects they have worked on, which in turn can be linked to particular machines, programming languages, etc.

The State of the Art in Hypermedia

An increasing amount of work is being done into hypermedia research at universities and commercial research labs, and some commercial systems have resulted. There have been two conferences, Hypertext '87 and '88, and in Washington DC, the National Institute of Standards and Technology (NST) hosted a workshop on standardisation in hypertext, a follow-up of which will occur during 1990.

The *Communications of the ACM* special issue on Hypertext contains many references to hypertext papers. A bibliography on hypertext is given in [NIST90], and a uucp newsgroup alt.hypertext exists. I do not, therefore, give a list here.

Browsing techniques

Much of the academic research is into the human interface side of browsing through a complex information space. Problems addressed are those of making navigation easy, and avoiding a feeling of being "lost in hyperspace". Whilst the results of the research are interesting, many users at CERN will be accessing the system using primitive terminals, and so advanced window styles are not so important for us now.

Interconnection or publication?

Most systems available today use a single database. This is accessed by many users by using a distributed file system. There are few products which take Ted Nelson's idea of a wide "docuverse" literally by allowing links between nodes in different databases. In order to do this, some standardisation would be necessary. However, at the standardisation workshop, the emphasis was on standardisation of the format for exchangeable media, not for networking. This is prompted by the strong push toward publishing of hypermedia information, for example on optical disk. There seems to be a general consensus about the abstract data model which a hypertext system should use.

Many systems have been put together with little or no regard for portability, unfortunately. Some others, although published, are proprietary software which is not for external release. However, there are several interesting projects and more are appearing all the time. Digital's "Compound Document Architecture" (CDA), for example, is a data model which may be extendable into a hypermedia model, and there are rumours that this is a way Digital would like to go.

Incentives and CALS

The US Department of Defence has given a big incentive to hypermedia research by, in effect, specifying hypermedia documentation for future procurement. This means that all manuals for parts for defence equipment must be provided in hypermedia form. The acronym CALS stands for "Computer-aided Acquisition and Logistic Support).

There is also much support from the publishing industry, and from librarians whose job it is to organise information.

What will the system look like?

Let us see what components a hypertext system at CERN must have.

The only way in which sufficient flexibility can be incorporated is to separate the information storage software from the information display software, with a well defined interface between them. Given the requirement for network access, it is natural to let this clean interface coincide with the physical division between the user and the remote database machine.[3]

This division also is important in order to allow the heterogeneity which is required at CERN (and would be a boon for the world in general).

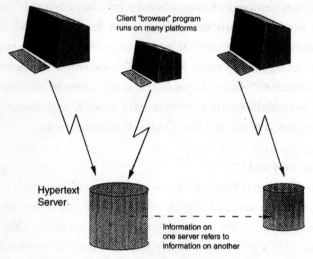

Client "browser" program
runs on many platforms

Hypertext
Server

Information on
one server refers to
information on another

Fig 3. A client/server model for a distributed hypertext system.

Therefore, **an important phase in the design of the system is to define this interface.** After that, the development of various forms of display program and of database server can proceed in parallel. This will have been done well if many different information sources, past, present and future, can be mapped onto the definition, and if many different human interface programs can be written over the years to take advantage of new technology and standards.

[3] A client/server split at this level also makes multi-access more easy, in that a single server process can service many clients, avoiding the problems of simultaneous access to one database by many different users.

Accessing Existing Data

The system must achieve a critical usefulness early on. Existing hypertext systems have had to justify themselves solely on new data. If, however, there was an existing base of data of personnel, for example, to which new data could be linked, the value of each new piece of data would be greater.

What is required is a gateway program which will map an existing structure onto the hypertext model, and allow limited (perhaps read-only) access to it. This takes the form of a hypertext server written to provide existing information in a form matching the standard interface. One would not imagine the server actually generating a hypertext database from an existing one: rather, it would generate a hypertext view of an existing database.

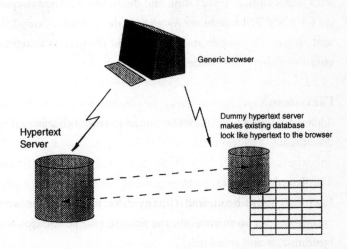

Generic browser

Dummy hypertext server makes existing database look like hypertext to the browser

Hypertext Server

Fig 4. A hypertext gateway allows existing data to be seen in hypertext form by a hypertext browser.

Some examples of systems which could be connected in this way are:

uucp News
This is a Unix electronic conferencing system. A server for uucp news could make links between notes on the same subject, as well as showing the structure of the conferences.

VAX/Notes
This is Digital's electronic conferencing system. It has a fairly wide following in FermiLab, but much less in CERN. The topology of a conference is quite restricting.

CERNDOC
This is a document registration and distribution system running on CERN's VM machine. As well as documents, categories and projects, keywords and authors lend themselves to represention as hypertext nodes.

File systems
This would allow any file to be linked to from other hypertext documents.

The Telephone Book
Even this could be viewed as hypertext, with links between people and sections, sections and groups, people and floors of buildings, etc.

The unix manual
This is a large body of computer-readable text, currently

organised in a flat way, but which also contains link information in a standard format ("See also..").

Databases

A generic tool could perhaps be made to allow any database which uses a commercial DBMS to be displayed as a hypertext view.

In some cases, writing these servers would mean unscrambling or obtaining details of the existing protocols and/or file formats. It may not be practical to provide the full functionality of the original system through hypertext. In general, it will be more important to allow read access to the general public: it may be that there is a limited number of people who are providing the information, and that they are content to use the existing facilities.

It is sometimes possible to enhance an existing storage system by coding hypertext information in, if one knows that a server will be generating a hypertext representation. In 'news' articles, for example, one could use (in the text) a standard format for a reference to another article. This would be picked out by the hypertext gateway and used to generate a link to that note. This sort of enhancement will allow greater integration between old and new systems.

There will always be a large number of information management systems – we get a lot of added usefulness from being able to cross-link them. However, we will lose out if we try to constrain them, as we will exclude systems and hamper the evolution of hypertext in general.

Conclusion

We should work toward a universal linked information system, in which generality and portability are more important than fancy graphics techniques and complex extra facilities.

The aim would be to allow a place to be found for any information or reference which one felt was important, and a way of finding it afterwards. The result should be sufficiently attractive to use that if the information contained would grow past a critical threshold, the usefulness of the scheme would in turn encourage its increased use.

The passing of this threshold accelerated, by allowing large existing databases to be linked together with new ones.

A Practical Project

Here I suggest the practical steps to go to, in order to find a real solution at CERN. After a preliminary discussion of the requirements listed above, a survey of what is available from industry is obviously required. At this stage, we will be looking for systems which are futureproof:

- portable, or supported on many platforms
- extendable to new data formats

We may find that with a little adaptation, parts of the system we need can be combined from various sources; for example, a browser from one source with a database from another.

I imagine that two people for 6 to 12 months would be sufficient for this phase of the project.

A second phase would almost certainly involve some programming in order to set up a real system at CERN on many machines. An important part of this, discussed below, is the integration of a hypertext system with existing data, so as to provide a universal system, and to achieve critical usefulness at an early stage.

(...and yes, this would provide an excellent project with which to try our new object oriented programming techniques!)

References

[NEL67]   Nelson, T. H. "Getting it out of our system" in *Information Retrieval: A Critical Review*, G. Schechter, ed. Thomson Books, Washington D.C., 1967, 191-210.

[SMISH88]   Smish, J.B and Weiss, S. F, "An Overview of Hypertext", in *Communications of the ACM*, July 1988 Vol 31, No. 7, and other articles in the same special "Hypertext" issue.

[CAMP88]   Campbell, B and Goodman, J, "HAM: a general purpose Hypertext Abstract Machine", in *Communications of the ACM*, July 1988 Vol 31, No. 7.

[ASKCYN88]   Akscyn, R. M, McCracken, D and Yoder, E. A, "KMS: A distributed hypermedia system for managing knowledge in orig- inations," in *Communications of the ACM*, July 1988 Vol 31, No. 7.

[HYP88]   *Hypertext on Hypertext*, a hypertext version of the special Comms of the ACM edition, is available from the ACM for the Macintosh or PC.

[RN]   Under unix, type man rn to find out about the rn command which is used for reading uucp news.

[NOTES]   Under VMS, type HELP NOTES to find out about the VAX/NOTES system.

[CERNDOC]   On CERNVM, type FIND DOCFIND for information about how to access the CERNDOC programs.

[NIST90]   J. Moline et. al. (ed.) *Proceedings of the Hypertext Standard- isation Workshop January 16-18, 1990*, National Institute of Standards and Technology, pub. U.S. Dept. of Commerce.

Glossary

For background information and references for this book, please see http://www.w3.org/People/Berners-Lee/Weaving.

access control The ability to selectively control who can get at or manipulate information in, for example, a Web server.

accessibility The art of ensuring that, to as large an extent as possible, facilities (such as, for example, Web access) are available to people whether or not they have impairments of one sort or another.

ACSS (Audio Cascading Style Sheets) A language for telling a computer how to read a Web page aloud. This is now part of CSS2.

Amaya An open source Web browser editor from W3C and friends, used to push leading-edge ideas in Web client design.

Apache An open-source Web server originally formed by taking all the 'patches' (fixes) to the NCSA Web server and making a new server out of it.

browser A Web client that allows a human to read information on the Web.

CERN The European Particle Physics Laboratory, located on the French–Swiss border near Geneva, Switzerland.

Click-stream Information collected about where a Web user has been on the Web.

client Any program that uses the service of another program. On the Web, a Web client is a program, such as a browser, editor or search robot, that reads or writes information on the Web.

CSS (Cascading Style Sheets) A W3C recommendation: a language for writing style sheets. *See also* style sheet.

Cyc A knowledge-representation project in which a tree of definitions attempts to express real-world facts in a machine-readable fashion. (Now a trademark of Cycorp Inc.)

digital signature A very large number created in such a way that it can be shown to have been done only by somebody in possession of a secret key and only by processing a document with a particular content. It can be used for the same purposes as a person's handwritten signature on a physical document. Something you can do with public key cryptography. W3C work addresses the digital signature of XML documents.

DOM (Document Object Model) Within a computer, information is often organised as a set of 'objects'. When transmitted, it is sent as a 'document'. The DOM is a W3C specification that gives a common way for programs to access a document as a set of objects.

domain name A name (such as 'w3.org') of a service, Web site or computer, and so on in a hierarchical system of delegated authority – the Domain Name System.

DTD In the SGML world, a DTD is a metadocument containing information about how a given set of SGML tags can be used. In the XML world this role will be taken over by a schema. Sometimes, but arguably, 'document type definition'. *See also* schema.

Dublin Core A set of basic metadata properties (such as title, etc.) for classifying Web resources.

EBT (Electronic Book Technology) A company started by Andries Van Dam and others to develop hypertext systems.

EDI (Electronic Data Interchange) A pre-Web standard for the electronic exchange of commercial documents.

Enquire A 1980 program, named after the Victorian book *Enquire Within upon Everything*.

filtering The setting up of criteria to select a subset of data from a broad stream of it. Filtering information is essential for everyone in daily life. Filtering by parents of small children may be wise. Filtering by others – ISPs or governments – is bad, and is called censorship.

GIF (Graphics Interchange Format) A format for pictures transmitted pixel by pixel over the Net. Created by CompuServe, the GIF specification was put into the public domain, but Unisys found that it had a patent on the compression technology used. This stimulated the development of PNG.

GILC (Global Internet Liberty Campaign) A group that has been laudably vocal in support of individual rights on the Net (though occasionally tending to throw out the baby with the bathwater).

graphics Two- or three-dimensional images, typically drawings or photographs. *See also* GIF, PNG, SVG and VRML.

HTML (Hypertext Markup Language) A computer language for representing the contents of a page of hypertext; the language that most Web pages are currently written in.

HTTP (Hypertext Transfer Protocol) A computer protocol for transferring information across the Net in such a way as to meet the demands of a global hypertext system. Part of the original design of the Web, continued in a W3C activity, and now a HTTP 1.1 IETF draft standard.

hypertext Nonsequential writing; Ted Nelson's term for a medium that includes links. Nowadays it includes other media apart from text and is sometimes called hypermedia.

information space The abstract concept of everything accessible using networks: the Web.

INRIA (Institut National de Recherche en Infomatique et Automatique) The French national research laboratory for computer science and control. Cohost of W3C and developers of Amaya.

Internet A global network of networks through which computers communicate by sending information in packets. Each network consists of computers connected by cables or wireless links.

Intranet A part of the Internet or part of the Web used internally within a company or organisation.

IP (Internet Protocol) The protocol that governs how computers send packets across the Internet. Designed by Vint Cerf and Bob Khan. (IP may also stand for *intellectual property*; *see* IPR.)

IPR (Intellectual Property Rights) The conditions under which the information created by one party may be appreciated by another party.

ISO (International Standards Organisation) An international group of national standards bodies.

ISP (Internet service provider) The party providing one with connectivity to the Internet. Some users have a cable or some sort of wireless link to their ISP. For others, their computer may dial an ISP by phone and send and receive Internet packets over the phone line; the ISP then forwards the packets over the Internet.

Java A programming language developed (originally as 'Oak') by James Gosling of Sun Microsystems. Designed for portability and usability embedded in small devices, Java took off as a language for small applications ('applets') that ran within a Web browser.

Jigsaw Open-source Web server of great modularity, written in Java. From W3C and friends.

JPEG (Joint Photographic Experts Group) This group defined a format for encoding photographs that uses fewer bytes than the pixel-by-pixel approaches of GIF and PNG, without too much visible degradation in quality. The format (JFIF) is casually referred to as JPEG.

Keio University Near Tokyo, Japan. Cohost of W3C.

LCS (Laboratory for Computer Science) A laboratory at the Massachusetts Institute of Technology. Cohost of W3C.

LEAD (Live Early Adoption and Demonstration) A W3C policy to eat our own cooking to find out how it can be better.

libwww The library (collection) of WWW-related program modules available for free use by anyone since the start of the Web.

line-mode In high and far-off times, people did not see computer programs through windows. They typed commands on a terminal, and the computer replied with text, which was displayed on the screen (or printed on a roll of paper) interleaved with the commands, much as though the person were in a chat session with the computer program. If you have seen a 'DOS window', then you have some idea of how people did their communicating with computers in those days, before they learned how to drag and drop. Line-mode is still a very respectable way to communicate with a computer.

line-mode browser A Web client that communicated with the user in line-mode and could run all kinds of computers that did not have windows or mice.

link A reference from one document to another (external link), or from one location in the same document to another (internal link), that can be followed efficiently using a computer. The unit of connection in hypertext.

MARC record A standard for machine-readable library catalogue cards.

meta- A prefix to indicate something applied to itself; for example, a metameeting is a meeting about meetings.

metadata Data about data on the Web, including but not limited to authorship, classification, endorsement, policy, distribution terms, IPR and so on. A significant use for the Semantic Web.

micropayments Technology allowing one to pay for Web site access in very small amounts as one browses.

minimal constraint, principle of The idea that engineering or other designs should define only what they have to, leaving other aspects of the system and other systems as unconstrained as possible.

MIT (Massachusetts Institute of Technology) *See* LCS. Cohost of W3C.

mobile devices Pagers, phones, handheld computers and so on. All are potentially mobile Internet devices and Web clients.

Mosaic A Web browser developed by Marc Andreessen, Eric Bina and their colleagues at NCSA.

NCSA (National Center for Supercomputing Applications) A centre at the University of Illinois at Urbana-Champaign whose software development group created Mosaic.

Nelson, Ted Coiner of the word *hypertext*; guru and visionary.

Net Short for *Internet*.

NeXT Name of the company started by Steve Jobs, and of the computer it manufactured, that integrated many novelties such as the Mach kernel, Unix, NeXTStep, Objective-C, drag-and-drop application builders, optical disks and digital signal processors. The development platform I used for the first Web client.

NNTP (Network News Transfer Protocol) A protocol that defines how news articles are passed around between computers. Each computer passes an article to any of its neighbours that have not yet got it.

node Thing joined by links. In the Web, a node is a Web page, any resource with a URI.

open source Software whose source code is freely distributed and modifiable by anyone. W3C sample code is open-source software. A trademark of opensource.org.

packet A unit into which information is divided for transmission across the Internet.

partial understanding The ability to understand part of the import of a document that uses multiple vocabularies, some but not all of which are understood.

PGP (Pretty Good Privacy) An e-mail security system that uses public key cryptography and has the philosophy that individuals can choose whom they trust for what purpose – the 'web of trust'.

PICS (Platform for Internet Content Selection) W3C's technology that allows parents to select content for their children on the basis of an open set of criteria, as opposed to government censorship. See filtering.

PKC (public key cryptography) A very neat bit of mathematics on which is based a security system in which there is no need to exchange secret keys; instead, people have one 'private' key that only they know and one 'public' key that everyone knows.

PKI (Public Key Infrastructure) A hierarchy of 'certification authorities' to allow individuals and organisations to identify each other for the purpose (principally) of doing business electronically.

PNG (Portable Network Graphics) A format for encoding a picture pixel by pixel and sending it over the Net. A recommendation of the W3C, replacing GIF.

protocol A language and a set of rules that allow computers to interact in a well-defined way. Examples are FTP, HTTP and NNTP.

RDF (Resource Description Framework) A framework for constructing logical languages that can work together in the Semantic Web. A way of using XML for data rather than just documents.

RPC (remote procedure call) When one part of a program calls on another part to do some work, the action is called a procedure call. RPC is a set of tools that allow you to write a program whose different parts are on different computers, without having to worry about how the communication happens. A generic technique, not a specific product.

RSA A public key encryption system invented by Ron Rivest, Adi Shamir and Leonard Adleman. RSA algorithms have been patented, and so its inventors have licensed its deployment.

schema (pl., schemata) A document that describes an XML or RDF vocabulary.

Semantic Web The Web of data with meaning in the sense that a computer program can learn enough about what the data means to process it.

separation of form from content The principle that one should represent separately the essence of a document and the style with which it is presented. An element in my decision to use

SGML and an important element in the drive for accessibility on the Web.

server A program that provides a service (typically information) to another program, called the client. A Web server holds Web pages and allows client programs to read and write them.

SGML (Standard Generalised Markup Language) An international standard in markup languages, a basis for HTML and a precursor to XML.

SMIL (Synchronised Multimedia Integration Language) A language for creating a multimedia presentation by specifying the spatial and temporal relationships between its components. A W3C recommendation.

style sheet A document that describes to a computer program (such as a browser) how to translate the document markup into a particular presentation (fonts, colours, spacing etc.) on the screen or in print. *See also* CSS, XSL, separation of form from content.

SVG (Scalable Vector Graphics) A language for describing drawings in terms of the shapes that compose them, so that these can be rendered as well as possible.

Tangle A program I wrote for playing with the concept of information as consisting only of the connections.

TCP (Transmission Control Protocol) A computer protocol that allows one computer to send the other a continuous stream of information by breaking it into packets and reassembling it at the other end, resending any packets that get lost in the Internet. TCP uses IP to send the packets, and the two together are referred to as TCP/IP.

URI (Universal Resource Identifier) The string (often starting with *http:*) that is used to identify anything on the Web.

URL (Uniform Resource Locator) A term used sometimes for certain URIs to indicate that they might change.

Viola An interpreted computer language (like Java) developed by Pei Wei at the University of Berkeley. Also, a Web browser built using Viola.

virtual hypertext Hypertext that is generated from its URI by a program, rather than by recourse to a stored file.

VRML (Virtual Reality Modelling Language) An idea for 3D compositional graphics on the Web, proposed by Dave Raggett as 'Virtual Reality Markup Language', and implemented by Mark Pesce as a variant of Silicon Graphics' 'Inventor' format; later managed by the VRML consortium, now 'Web 3D' consortium.

W3C (World Wide Web Consortium) A neutral meeting of those to whom the Web is important, with the mission of leading the Web to its full potential.

WAI (Web Accessibility Initiative) A domain of W3C that attempts to ensure the use of the Web by anyone regardless of disability.

WAIS (Wide Area Information Servers) A distributed information system designed by Brewster Kahle while at Thinking Machines. WAIS was like a Web of search engines, but without hypertext.

Web Short for *World Wide Web*.

World Wide Web (three words; also known as WWW) The set of all information accessible using computers and networking, each unit of information identified by a URI.

WorldWideWeb (one word; no spaces) The name of the first Web client, a browser/editor that ran on a NeXT machine.

X The X Window system, invented by Bob Scheifler; a standard

interface between a program and a screen that was ubiquitous on Unix systems. Unlike Microsoft's Windows, from the
beginning X allowed programs running on one machine to
display on another, across the Internet. Scheifler ran the X
Consortium from MIT/LCS for many years, then spun it off,
and eventually closed it.

Xanadu Ted Nelson's planned global hypertext project.

XML (Extensible Markup Language) A simplified successor to
SGML. W3C's generic language for creating new markup languages. Markup languages (such as HTML) are used to
represent documents with a nested, treelike structure. XML
is a product of W3C and a trademark of MIT.

XSL (Extensible Style Sheet Language) A style sheet language,
like CSS, but also allowing document transformation.

Index

MUDDs, 186
National Center for Supercomputing
    Applications (NCSA), University
    of Illinois, 74, 75, 76–7, 78, 81, 82,
    83, 84, 86, 89, 99, 107
Navisoft Inc., 87, 113
Navipress, 87, 113
Nelson, Ted, 5, 6, 22, 70–2
Net Perceptions, 156
Netcheck Commerce Bureau, 149
Netscape, 89–90, 99, 100
    free release of, 89–90
    IPO and stock, 114–15
    Microsoft and, 99, 111
    Mozilla (Navigator 1.0), 103, 104,
        106, 107
    Navigator 2.0, 121
    open source policy, 128
    security issues and Secure Sockets
        Layer (SSL), 104, 163
Network Solutions, 138
Newcastle University, 78
Newman, Clifford, 44
NeXT Inc., 25–6 computer,
    WorldWideWeb code written on,
    25–6, 30, 33, 49, 51, 53, 60, 62
failure of despite product, 30
Nielsen, Henrik Frystyk, 63, 103, 185
NLS (on line System), 6
NNTP, 42, 43

Online Privacy Alliance, 161
Online research, 192–3
Online voting, 186
Open source software, 185
    community, 164
Operating systems, 21
    communication between different,
        19, 21
O'Reilly Associates 69, 82, 83, 87, 102
Owl Ltd, 28, 29, 102

Patents, 213–15
Patrick, John, 121
PCs (IBM and clones), 49, 83

Pellow, Nicola, 32, 47, 53, 63
Pesce, Mark, 94
PGP (Pretty Good Privacy), 165–6
PICS (Platform for Internet Content
    Selection), 123, 125, 135, 147, 148,
    150, 196, 209
PKC (public key cryptography), 136,
    162, 163–4
    government fear of loss of control
        and, 163–4
    RSA, 162
PKI (Public Key Infrastructure), 165
Plessey Telecommunications, 4
PNG (Portable Network Graphics),
    179
Pollerman, Bernd, 35
Poole, John, 12–13
Pordes, Ruth, 76
Pornography on the Web, 121–3, 146
    liability, 145
Portals, 134, 143
Postel, Jon, 137
Privacy issues, 135–6, 155–68
    click stream information, 156
    confidentiality, 163
    cookies, 157
    European regulations, 158
    hypertext protocols and, 152
    P3P (Platform for Privacy
        Preferences Project), 152
    PKC (public key cryptography), 136,
        162, 163–6
    software for, 159
    Web site privacy policy, 159
Prodigy, 98, 113
Prospero, 44
Protocols, 20, 21, 38, 133–4
    Document Object Model (DOM),
        182
    elements for the Web, list, 39
    global systems, 38
    graphics formats, 178–9, 180
    independence, 172, 181
    Internet, 39, 44
    standardization of WWW's, 57–8,

Foreword

Ross-shire Writers, a dynamic group of local writers, present here their third collection of short stories and poetry.

"Ross-shire Reflections" follows the highly successful "Along the Lines" (2007) and "Further Along the Lines" (2009).

Over the last three years new members have joined the group and it is exciting to see their writing alongside that of contributors who have appeared in the previous publications.

We hope you enjoy the stories and poems that follow, selected from a wide range of work reflecting the diverse talents and interests of the group.

Preface
Chris Powici

Writing is unique among the arts. The saxophone virtuoso is unlikely to need their instrument outside of the concert hall; the portrait artist won't need any brushes and paints on a shopping trip. But all of us need words to get by. Just about any conversation will involve telling a story of some kind, and this is as true for the teenager at the bus stop as it is for the Nobel prize-winner. We are, by nature, story-making animals. Indeed I rather think that Ernest Hemingway, Gabriel Garcia Marquez, Seamus Heaney, Toni Morrison have all, at some point, been teenagers at bus stops talking about their lives.

Ross-shire Reflections is a fine demonstration that, at heart, we show off our human-ness by telling stories and making poems. But there is more to this collection than bus stop chatter! All the writers have brought craft and art to bear upon the urge to describe the world – in its 'real' and in its 'fictional' guises. The raw, funny, terrible, poignant stuff of life is amply represented in these pages, from junior football heroics to the sombre dignity of herons, from witch-burnings to the human racket in the Quiet Coach of a train.

If there is a theme that bubbles under the surface of all of these writings it is the pleasure, and sometimes the pain, of memory. Memory, imagination and story are oxygen for the soul, and Ross-shire Writers are to be congratulated for producing a book that can help you to breathe!

The Memory Hollow
Janet Macdonald

When we spend time with people we love,
their parting leaves a hollow.
Its shape,
the space they filled in our lives.
Its contents,
the things they did or said,
the way that they spoke.
It holds joy, laughter, loss,
or a general disquiet.
A place to visit,
remembering, enjoying, grieving.
The hollow may heal in weeks,
or maybe in hours.
Tears can fill it,
help to heal it,
embedding memory,
becoming a part of us.

The Ticket Tout

Louise James

"You did get good seats for tomorrow night's performance of La Bohème didn't you darling?" Grant poured himself a whisky and sighed, not noticing Elspeth's flinch. "I've booked the pre-theatre meal at The Roasted Chestnut for six-fifteen. Finlay and Barbara are coming here for drinks just after five and the cab will be here for back of six. God! I hope the evening goes well. I'll be surprised if my promotion doesn't hinge on this."

"But why should it affect your job, my love?" Elspeth managed not to croak her response.

"Finlay has a very low opinion of culture in the Highlands and I need to convince him we're right up there with his Edinburgh set. He's done some blasted management course and has this theory about building teams of – what did he call it - 'diverse but complementary players, each bringing their own perspectives to the table'. He has me down as an action man: 'completer-finisher' in the jargon! Bloody hell, can you believe it?" Grant sighed and downed his rather large whisky in two swift gulps.

Elspeth composed herself, and managed a smile, while her mind whirled. She knew there was something else she was supposed to be doing when she was in town last week having a rather long lunch with Annette. Never mind – she continued her silent internal monologue – they never sell out of anything highbrow at the Oriole Centre. It's just the stand-up comics and the so-called mediums that pack the house. Don't panic, girl, for goodness sake.

"All in hand, darling, all in hand," she replied breezily. Then, with practised deception, she glanced at her watch and exclaimed:

"Oh goodness, I promised Nicola I'd pop this book over to her. I'll leave you in peace to watch the rugby or whatever. Won't be long!"

Elspeth grabbed her handbag and hurried out the door before Grant could pursue the matter further. Buckling herself in quickly she was soon gunning it down the eastern distributer road, airily dismissing the 40mph speed limit as ridiculous. Parking was an unexpected problem in the vicinity of the theatre. Tonight was the first of two performances and it did look rather busy. Perhaps she had underestimated local demand, but there was still someone at the box office so that was a good sign. She joined the short queue, standing behind an elderly chap, impatiently waiting her turn. Intermission was over and the theatre-goers had returned to their seats. The only other person loitering in the foyer was a watchful chap in his late twenties, eyeing the queue, which by this time had dwindled down to Elspeth and the posh older gentleman in his tweed jacket. Elspeth studied the opera flyer while waiting, reading with alarm that the soprano playing Mimi was originally from the Highlands and these rare performances had been arranged as a tribute to her local roots. That would account for the demand, she realised with a sinking feeling in the pit of her stomach.

The man in front finished his transaction and beamed at her as he pocketed his tickets. "Last four!" he exclaimed. "There's a huge waiting list and I was first on it – just got a call an hour ago and picked up these cancellations. Good luck, but looks a bit hopeless I'm afraid." He patted his pocket again and made for the door.

Elspeth felt ill. "But please," she begged the box office attendant who had begun closing down her computer.

"Sorry Madam, it's been so popular, we sold out ten days ago. That chap just got lucky, a party of four cancelled. It won't happen again, I doubt very much." She smiled her professional wish-I-could-be-more-helpful look and exited into the back office.

Elspeth staggered outside, gasping for breath. However flippant she had been to Grant, she knew that this promotion was crucial to his career, not to mention their financial well-being. Paying for the extensive renovations to their large villa had cost a fortune and she'd already made further inroads into their savings than she had admitted to, so confident was she that the new job was in the bag. She really must stop these liquid lunches, they were addling her memory.

The concourse outside the main entrance was almost deserted. She watched the elderly gentleman move into the shadowy system of paths leading to the car park when suddenly he staggered, and with a moan, crumpled to a motionless heap. Two thoughts entered Elspeth's head almost simultaneously. She rushed to his side, shouting loudly to anyone who might be within hearing distance:

"I'm a first-aider! Someone call an ambulance!" She could see one or two people out of the corner of her eye as she rolled the poor man into the recovery position, whilst very smoothly extracting the envelope with the tickets from his pocket and transferring it rapidly to hers.

The young man seen earlier in the foyer was on the scene very quickly too. He rapidly dialled 999 and summoned an ambulance, then, rolling the ill man onto his back, he began cardiac resuscitation. Elspeth reddened as he threw her a knowing look. What had he seen? Hopefully just her out-of-date first aid skills.

She wondered if she could slip away quietly, but the ambulance was arriving and a crowd had gathered. Clearly the man was in a bad way – the paramedics got to work but it looked hopeless. One or two people commended her on her quick action but she graciously acknowledged the skilful young man and backed away towards her car. Her heart was pounding and she rested her head on her arms for a moment to calm herself down.

"Well done you!" came a soft voice at her elbow.

"Oh! It was...I mean… no, you must take all the credit. I am clearly out of date with my first aid skills. But please excuse me, it's all been rather upsetting and I…" her voice strangled in her throat. "Take your hand off me, or I'll scream!"

"Oh, I wouldn't if I were you madam. I really wouldn't. Let's see now, four seats at £40.00 each. I could turn those for at least twice that for tomorrow's little gig. Regular little earner, opera is, best tout of the year. I was just counting myself unlucky till our mutual friend had the misfortune to keel over and you spotted the same golden opportunity as I did. Don't even think of lying to me, it takes one to know one and I have to say I was very impressed. Your left jacket pocket, I believe?"

Elspeth was on the point of denying everything but something told her that would be to no avail. "I refuse to incriminate myself, I have done nothing wrong. But as you are threatening me, I am prepared to pay you –what did you say – double. I'll give you £350 if you'll just go away." With shaking hands she pulled out her purse.

"Double is my minimum, darlin', absolute minimum. Tell you what I'll do, now that I see you are a woman of principle, let's make it an even five hundred, no questions asked. That way we are both happy. There's a cash point just over the road – I don't think you have quite enough on you, am I right?"

The next evening, relaxed and confident, Grant escorted his beautiful wife and elegant friends from the taxi to the front entrance. Elspeth had been in a strange mood all day, rather bordering on the hysterical, he thought, but he was glad to see she was only slightly tipsy and had calmed herself down before Finlay and Barbara arrived. As they swept up the path, Grant commented, rather loudly, on the presence of the usual touters flogging tickets to waiting opera lovers who had not the foresight to purchase their tickets in time. A jaunty young chap, just completing a transaction, actually had the nerve to wink at his wife.

Moving On
Sandra Bain

Sarah eased herself on to the sofa. It felt good to put her feet up and relax. She was almost finished with the packing, black bin bags having swallowed up much of the accumulation of thirty years.

"It shouldn't take long to do this place," she thought. She was glad she had left the conservatory to the last. It was pleasant to rest here between stints of emptying drawers and cupboards.

The most difficult part had been deciding what to keep and what could be disposed of. Each bundle of papers resurrected memories. The linen, the china and the ornaments all told a story, and it was small consolation that charity shops were going to benefit.

The furniture was easier. Large pieces had to go. She looked round the conservatory. She didn't want any of these chairs or coffee tables. Of the plants on the shelves and sills, she knew exactly which ones she would take. The others were going to the Ladies' Group coffee morning in two weeks' time.

But there were the shells. Their future would be more difficult. In a blue bowl were those she had picked up as a small child on the very beach which lay just beyond her garden. A little girl wearing brown sandals and a pretty cotton dress, she must have been seven or was it eight? They had been staying at the Marine Hotel. The sun had shone every day – or so it seemed – and she and her brother had spent hours building sand castles and looking for attractive shells. She remembered the tears when several of her treasures disappeared before the holiday ended. No one knew anything about them. She now examined those which had survived all those years.

She was older when they went to the west coast of Scotland for a summer holiday. The pink and mauve sea urchin was a souvenir of that time. She blew off the layer of dust. Yes, this past week had been a busy one with no time for dusting. As she put the shell to one side she noticed the shimmering "mother-of-pearl". What romance was associated with that little shell! She was sixteen again, sitting on the rocks watching the surging tide, waiting for Ralph, the boy she had met in the ice-cream shop two days before. He came running along the water's edge, splashing on to her rock. They remained there for a while. Then as they walked back along the beach she found the shell. It was unusual and she put it in the pocket of her shorts. By the time they reached the path up to her hotel the sun was down. In the half light he kissed her – her first kiss. In her room she could still feel the glow. The delicate shell shone in the lamplight and it became a symbol of the light in her life – Ralph. Three days later he went home and despite promises to keep in touch she heard nothing and was heartbroken. Until the following summer...

She must keep the sand dollar, found on a beach in Florida, fifteen years ago. She and Ralph were celebrating their fortieth anniversary. Dear Ralph. It was their last anniversary together. His heart attack, eight months later, took him without warning. How she missed him. The sand dollar was special.

Sarah looked at the images on the shell, remembering the legend. The five holes on one side were said to represent four nail holes and the hole of a Roman spear – the wounds of Christ during His Crucifixion. She could see the Easter Lily and, at its centre, a star representing the Star of Bethlehem. The Poinsettia and bell on the other side were a reminder of

Christmas and she knew if she broke open the shell she would release five little white doves of peace. It had all meant so much to Ralph.

What did the future hold for her now? Ralph believed in a life after death. At times like this she wished she shared his faith. But best not become introspective.

Picking up a little shell turtle she thought of her son. Was Hector, the uncaring businessman, the same person as their little boy who had excitedly collected shells and made little ornaments by gluing them together? She would like to have given them to his children but she seldom saw them. All their holidays were spent in exotic places – never at Grandma's. Her thoughts focussed on his last visit, three months ago.

"Mother, there are wonderful places where you would be well looked after..."

"A home! You think I should go into a home? You think I'm senile."

She had seen he was exasperated. He had stood up and paced the lounge.

"Of course I don't, but I'm worried about you here on your own."

"I can manage perfectly well on my own...and I can't afford one of those homes."

"Have you thought of selling the house? You could use the money to pay...."

"Sell the house? What makes you think I would sell the house?" He had shrugged his shoulders.

"It was just an idea. You would be free of the responsibility."

"What responsibility is there in the house? Mrs Dillon comes in and she sees to anything that needs doing."

"Oh yes. Mrs Dillon." Hector had smirked as he ran his finger over the layer of dust. "But you've just had a fall. What if you had broken a leg and were lying on the floor for hours..."

"Oh, what if...what if... Nothing's going to happen here that couldn't happen in one of those ghastly places."

"Winter's coming on – there's the worry of burst pipes."

"The central heating is good – don't you worry about the pipes."

"Maybe he's right," Sarah had told Mrs Dillon later. "But I know he's so tied up in his work he doesn't want the responsibility of his mother. And he'd rather play golf all weekend than drive over to see me. When was he here last? And as for that wife of his…"

"Did you know there's vacancies in the sheltered homes at the other end of town?" Mrs Dillon always seemed to know all that was going on. "That might suit you. I can make enquiries if you like."

Sarah felt sad, as the time had come to leave this house which she and Ralph had snapped up when it came on the market all those years ago. It was a great holiday home but two years after buying it Ralph found work in the town, and they moved here permanently. The shell collection came with them. Perhaps the time had come to return the shells to the beach. There were enough treasures packed for the little place she was going to.

Just then a squally shower hit the window. Should she wait until the rain went over? No. She might change her mind. She carefully placed all the shells in a plastic bag.

In the dust on the empty shelf she could see where the larger shells had been sitting. She could put each one back in its original spot if she wished. She fetched a duster and swept it over the shelf – no trace now of the shells. Only the empty blue bowl remained.

She put on her waterproof coat and a head scarf, locked the door and then checked it. The rain was heavy and as she left the shelter of the house a gust of wind tugged at her scarf. It wasn't a day to be out. But she couldn't go back now.

The sea was rough, and on the open beach the wind was strong in her face. At one point she feared she was going to be blown down. She struggled along the sand until she was past the houses on the sea front, not wanting anyone to wonder what she was doing. Then she dropped a few shells here and there.

She studied the sand dollar and smiled as she thought of someone puzzling over how it came to be there. She thought of Ralph and put the shell into her pocket.

Walking into the wind was becoming more of an effort. She could hear the waves pounding on the rocks which were just ahead. The sound drew her towards them and as she approached she could feel the spray. There was something exhilarating about it. The dark waters were swirling and surging. She and Ralph used to come here on a stormy afternoon to watch the waves. She stepped on to the lower rocks and gazed at the scene. As far back as she could remember, the sea had fascinated her. A few flickers of sunshine broke the blackness before her. She was being drawn forward towards the water. A little nearer and then a little more. She could be with Ralph. No one would ever know what happened. Then she felt the sand dollar in her pocket.

No, she wasn't ready, yet.

Intrusion
Terry Williams

They're drilling a hole in the street
outside this room
where grandfather is dying.

The noise invades our whispers,
pushes between us
and grandfather's last moments.

Murmur of summers spent
in careless glee
of grandfather's lively company.

Scent of bright geraniums
filling the porch
with grandfather's pride and joy.

Brambling down the garden,
purple tongues
and grandfather's basket filling slow.

Sand between our toes,
wooden spades
digging grandfather into the beach.

They're drilling a grave outside this place.
Can't they wait
until grandfather is ready to leave?

Wandering Joan
Catriona Tawse

The fox was at the hens last night, I heard them gok-gawking. What could I have done about it, a man well past his three score years and ten? By the time I had swung the old legs out of the bed and found my slippers and the gun, the rascal would have been over the rigs and beyond. I will ask Jimmy later to look where it might be getting in.

The Lord has blessed me in so many ways. I have a good roof over my head and a pension of money that sees to my needs. And lucky too that a son and a daughter still live here with me though others have put distance between us in the need to find work. It has brought me much happiness that just this week Wilma, my youngest, is here from south of the border. Her husband has been sent to Dubai to "fulfil a contract". Amn't I good with these fine words, they'll be putting me on television next. Anyway, Wilma is here with the children for two weeks, after that they are going ski-ing I think, to some foreign place with a name I find hard to recall.

The boy Christopher is quiet and steady like his uncle Jimmy was in his young day. I would like to see him get out and about a bit more, but he sits most of the time in the house with some noisy contraption that he works with great concentration and watches things jumping about on a little glass screen. Imogen, his sister, is quite the opposite, a tomboy we might have called her even with that fancy name. She wants to be off on Sadie's old bike or hiking up the hill or splashing about in the sea. We were all round the table after supper when she told us she was going to the caves next day, she'd take the big torch and spend time exploring.

"You must be very careful there," I said to her. "Have we told you what happened to Wandering Joan?"

"Who? Never heard of her," Imogen said quite cheekily, but I could see she was curious. And Christopher switched off the sound of gunfire and turned to look my way. I took the cup of tea from Sadie's hand and rested my feet in their socks on that fat leather cushion thing - I can never remember the name they have for it.

She was a girl from this village, a few years older than you are now. Because she had one leg that was shorter than the other the children laughed at her with the big black boot. Her parents tried to keep her close to home as much as they could in case she would come to harm. But Joan was not happy with these restrictions and she'd be off and away as soon as nobody was looking, even when darkness was coming down, and you'd be surprised how fast she could shift herself for someone so lame. More than once they had people out looking for her and she would be in awful trouble when they got her home but that never stopped her, even when she was no longer a child. It seemed as though she was always searching for something beyond what she had.

Early one May morning, the story goes, she set off for the shore, just like you are planning for tomorrow. It was in the Brown Seals' Cave, farther than she had ever gone before, that she found the circle of white stones, and knowing the power they possessed, she stepped inside and shut fast her eyes for a wish. At once her feet were sucked down into the sand and the creeping dark of the cave closed in around her. From somewhere within she could hear a mewling cry as if a kitten was calling and being soft-hearted she wanted to go and look for it. But try as she might her feet remained stuck fast. She became aware that the pillar of rock in front of her was not rock at all but a young man straight and tall like the mast of a boat, his eyes as dark as midnight pools. His strong hands lifted her without effort.

'You are here now and the time of waiting is over,' he said. 'It is right that we will be together.'

He led her up a flight of stony steps and into the open air where the sun beamed down from a wide clear sky. To Joan's great joy the ugly boot had vanished, just as she had wished, and her feet trod lightly.

'This is Daonnan, the land of Always', he said proudly. 'You will be safe here with me, Strong Niall of the Well. Here you will hear no voices raised in anger, no illness will bring you down, no child will cry in the night, no sudden squalls of wet will sweep over from the hills. Youth and beauty will ever be yours in this place but you must not at any time seek the Steps of Return.'

Countless weeks and months and years went by. Their family numbered five, their crops flourished, their cows bore healthy calves every spring. Joan had never known such happiness, and memories of an earlier life did not come to trouble her contentment. Then came the day when she heard a kitten wailing again. It sounded in such desperate plight, so out of the usual for this perfect place. Without a second thought Joan put down her basket of mushrooms and set off to follow the pitiful sound. On and on she walked, all else forgotten, not noticing that the path grew narrow and the sky darkened overhead. She found herself at the top of the steps. The crying of the animal came clearly from somewhere down below. Forgetting the warning that she must never seek the Steps of Return Joan let her feet carry her further away from Daonnan, sure in the knowledge that she would find her way back.

But this was not to be. She felt the smell of the sea and plunged forward through the mouth of the cave where her wondrous journey had begun. To her utmost dismay, the hand she raised to smooth back her tangled hair was old and wrinkled. Her tongue could feel the gaps in her mouth where not long before had been sound, strong teeth. And worst of all, her foot was once again dragged down by the clumsy black boot. She hobbled on and on, finally reaching the place which she recognised as home. At the front door she paused, anxious of the scolding she would surely receive. Her mother, bent and haggard, came at her knocking but showed no sign of recognition, even as Joan ventured to explain all that had befallen her. It was a year and a day since their daughter went missing, she was told. They still prayed each waking hour for her safe return.

'But because you are old and surely have come far we will offer you a bite of food and a resting place till the new day,' the mother went on.

And so it happened. Joan passed the night asleep in the room of her childhood while her parents tip-toed through the house, fearful of what it all meant.

In the morning the mother tapped lightly on the bedroom door and opened it quietly to rouse their ancient guest. She looked all around but could see nothing save for a strange grey cat curled up peacefully upon the quilt. Wandering Joan was never seen again.

The silence lasted only moments before Imogen spoke.

"Thanks Grandfather, that was a great story but you know, I don't believe a word of it and it certainly won't put me off exploring the cave tomorrow. I will watch out for the white stones!"

She picked up an apple from the bowl on the dresser and nodded to her brother to follow her through to the room. They would sit there in front of the television and happily accept for real, events every bit as unlikely as what had just been told to them.

"Well I remember you telling us all that stuff when we were children," Sadie said. "I don't think the young folk today are so likely to take it to heart."

"It's not that," I told her. "It isn't so long till we'll be coming into a new century with its changing ways and modern ideas and it would be a pity if the story-telling tradition was to die away. So much would be lost."

They said how definitely they agreed with me and how they remembered this tale and the other, 'Black Duncan from Skye' had been a big favourite.

"That one can keep for another day."

I left them to their washing up and went off out to see if Jimmy had the hens' place secured. If he hadn't, by Jove he would hear all about it from me.

Ugandan Gin
Reg Holder

The plane landed heavily, slewing across the runway into the driving rain. Angus Taylor stared through the oval windows looking at the runway lights flashing through the rotation of the propellers. Already he was regretting leaving the country. It had been a quick decision and apart from his initial actions, not much planning had gone into it or any thought given as to what the consequences could be. Jack, he knew, would be a problem, and probably by now asking questions as to her whereabouts. However, it was too late to change anything and he would have to lie low for a while. His first move, he had decided, would be to get to Euston station and catch the train to his parents in the North of Scotland and hope the situation would somehow resolve itself.

Late that afternoon the train began its journey from Edinburgh into the Highlands. By now it was snowing in ever increasing intensity, soft flakes blown past by the rush of the train but unnoticed by the other occupants in the compartment. They either slept or remained head down, reading, oblivious to the outside world.

Back in Uganda there would be no question of them remaining in such silence and though he had no wish to involve himself in any deep discussion with his fellow passengers, he felt a sudden need to have some sort of communication with others. He had tried a tentative smile to the girl opposite but she had looked away and buried her head in a magazine. The man in the corner dressed in tweeds ignored his attempt to strike up a conversation and the old lady, two seats down near the window, was snoring gently. He felt very afraid and alone. His frequent trips outside to the corridor to sip from his flask did little to bolster his courage and only served to heighten his sense of foreboding.

The snow turned into a full blizzard; smoke from the engine mixed up in the flakes. He hoped that the driver and his mate were protected and able to keep the engine going. He knew that snow on the long climb into the Highlands could cause problems and they would be in trouble if anything happened.

His thoughts turned back to Uganda and the well cushioned life that he had led there. There was many a happy hour spent below the dam where the Nile came out of Lake Victoria and began its long journey to the Mediterranean. There he would fish for barbel and Nile perch at weekends, though camping was not an option because of the hippos and he would often stay over in the Jinja club for the weekend. There were few worries for him at that time and along with many of his colleagues, he led a carefree existence. Sport was a major part of their lives and after work they usually managed a game of tennis and then drinks in the club before going on to dinner or a party.

'His job!' he mused . 'Yes that was the start of the problem.'

His interview in the Glasgow offices of the trading company had gone well and when the Managing Director had asked to see him after lunch he knew that he would be offered the job. Starting as 'Manager in Charge' of the drinks division meant that he had to travel over the whole country visiting company outlets and ensuring replenishments arrived in timely fashion. He usually stayed over in the town's club and in the evening would join the colonial officials for sundowners and often would be invited out to dinner as well. Back home it was all too easy to keep the house full of booze and in time this was to become his downfall.

His next mistake was to get married on his first leave. He had met Angela in one of the big dancehalls in Sauchiehall Street. Soon he was caught up in the sheer exhilaration of a whirlwind courtship and with little prospect of meeting someone back in Africa, asked her to marry him. Taking her north to meet his parents had been a disaster. He was the product of a conventional Highland family and she was obviously from a different background. Despite all their entreaties, he wouldn't be talked out of it, and they refused to attend the wedding, hastily arranged in Glasgow. He and Angela travelled back together as man and wife, hardly knowing each other and with little idea of how she would adapt to colonial life.

Angela embraced her new life with enthusiasm and in no time was the centre of the many activities that the capital offered. She was popular and in great demand. Too many invitations and constant partying soon took its toll, leaving him in the shadows and unable to keep up with her. Increasingly he resorted to the gin bottle, though visiting his outlets upcountry gave some relief. The long hours driving across indifferent roads in the bush meant that he had to concentrate and drinking was not so much of an issue. However at home he began to have trouble getting to work, especially after the weekend, and often the staff had to endure his bad temper and irrational behaviour.

It all came to a head one night when he arrived home to find that Angela was out. This was not the first time and her behaviour was now becoming intolerable. Coming up the steps to the bungalow he called to the houseboy:

"George, George wapi memsahib?"
"Hapana jua Bwana."

"I don't know," was the reply, but Angus knew there was more to the denial than he was letting on and he was beginning to suspect that there was something going on.

Taking a drink out to the veranda, he sat waiting morosely in one of the cane chairs staring out into the African night. The endless cacophony of cicadas cutting the air mocked him with their message. He reflected bitterly that he had made a major blunder in bringing her back. His parents had been right, and far from enhancing his status in the close-knit colonial community Angela's behaviour had made him the object of scorn and derision.

Eventually he saw the headlights of a car winding up the hill, pulling into the drive at the bottom of the garden. He heard the tinkling of laughter and the sharp intake of breath.

"Stop it Jack, not here you naughty boy, you'll get me into trouble. Ooh, that was nice, but not now. I have to go in."

The car door slammed and she came tripping onto the veranda.

"Angus there you are, sorry I'm late, thought you would be there to pick me up. Had to get Jack to drive me home!"

Her words were slurred and stumbling through into the lounge she fell on the sofa. Angus followed, shouting and full of anger.

"What the hell do you think you are doing?" he shouted "Behaving like a whore that's it, I've finished with you; tomorrow pack your bags and leave."

Barely able to control himself, he picked her up, dragged her through to the bedroom, and threw her across the bed. Her head caught the corner of the steel bedstead and she slumped to the floor, inert and lifeless with a thin trickle of blood running from the corner of her mouth.

My God, what had he done? He dropped down beside her, cradling her head in his lap. "Angela, Angela, wake up, wake up, for God's sake wake up!" he sobbed.

His head cleared and it became obvious that she was dead. He realised that this was not the time to panic and that his life could depend on what he did next. The house boy's quarters were in darkness and he was able to put her body in the boot of his car unseen, as far as he could tell. After a long and difficult night, he called the houseboy and told him that the Memsahib had not come home and that he would leave on his next safari for a few days, adding that on his return he would be going home to Scotland with her.

He drove down the Jinja road, conscious of her in the boot; his every nerve at was at screaming pitch but at the same time he remained strangely calm and focused. Soon he was at the turn off to the dam. He drove down to his favourite fishing spot which he knew was well sheltered and was thankful that there was no traffic as he made his way there. Arriving at the river's edge he lifted her body out and threw it into the water, the current taking her swiftly downstream. He knew the crocodiles would take care of her and there would be little chance of her being found.

From there he drove back to his office and spent the day as normally as possible, telling his staff that he had received word that his father was seriously ill and he needed to leave on the plane that night.

The train ground to a halt, jolting him awake and interrupting his thoughts. Huge snow drifts had built up on the track. The wind shrieked in a howling crescendo, the blizzard piling more snow alongside the train. There was no hope of reaching Inverness that night. Stumbling out to the corridor with flask in hand and a need to relieve himself, Angus opened the outside door of the train. In an instant the wind pulled him out and immediately buried him in the drifting snow.

It was the next day before the storm abated and the track cleared to allow the train to move again. His fellow passengers, more interested in keeping themselves warm and getting through the night, had not taken any interest in his absence and no one thought to report that he had not returned to his seat. They knew he had been drinking and assumed that he had moved to another compartment.

The heavy police presence as the train drew into the platform at Inverness caused some surprise but they would not be able to offer any explanation as to the disappearance of their fellow passenger.

Bun Fight that KO'd Morale
Christina Macdonald

Mrs Euphemia Grubb placed the last of the breakfast dishes in the dish-drainer and turned to pick up a new tea-towel. Glancing up at her kitchen calendar, she gave a sigh of pleasure. It was Easter week, and Tuesday 2nd April was marked in red pencil, her date for making the scones and dainties for the Church Coffee Morning, along with Mrs Mavis Dupe.

The first words of information gave her satisfaction; the rest pained her and to tell the truth, strained her Christian feelings of sisterly love. She and Mavis did not "get on". There was no so-called chemistry between them and in general they avoided each other on social occasions, but unfortunately Euphemia's bosom buddy Daisy had chosen that week to go on a coach holiday to the Cotswolds and the minister's wife had altered the baking rota without prior consultation.

Even if there had been a general discussion about it, Euphemia would have found it difficult to arrange another partner to join in her culinary efforts. All the established church ladies knew her strict standards of excellence and none of the others felt able to produce baking that compared with hers. Euphemia was famed for her feathery scones, her airy meringues and her fruity fly-cemeteries. Mavis was a newcomer to the area and to the group, and had been drawn into the situation through innocence and ignorance. She had not as yet had to prove her baking skills.

The main purpose of tomorrow's event was to provide an Easter treat for a group of old folk who rarely got out and about, but who were transported once a month by minibus to various venues to socialise with others who lived alone.

Euphemia, after a second cup of coffee, opened her cupboards and proceeded to select the ingredients required for her treats. Mavis, on the other side of town in the less fashionable area among the terraced houses of Laburnum Avenue, was looking at her calendar with apprehension. Mavis had always been a church-goer and had soon found her niche among the ladies in St Stephen's where her pleasant modest behaviour was well received. She would definitely not be a challenge to the status quo.

She opened the drawer of the old pine dresser where she kept her well-thumbed recipe books, sat down at the kitchen table and leafed through them. She already knew what Euphemia was making - she had announced her plans on the way out of church on the previous Sunday. "Steer clear of the scones, pastries and meringues" had been the message given and received clearly. What should she make? Her pancakes were always enjoyed. She would make some Hot Cross buns and a big Easter Cake, cover it with yellow icing and decorate it with mini chocolate eggs and fluffy chicks. That would cheer the old folk up.

On Tuesday morning at ten o'clock, Mavis arrived in the old Fiesta with her baking, and carried it carefully into the church kitchen. Some of the other ladies were already in the hall, putting up tables and chairs and setting out teacloths and cups.

Ten minutes later a large silver Honda slid into place in front of the hall door. Euphemia extricated herself elegantly from the passenger seat, while husband Roger, laden with boxes of baking, stumbled up the path. Mavis had started to set out her pancakes and Hot-Cross buns on small plates while her

Easter Cake sat magnificently under its plastic dome, safe from meddling hands. Euphemia eyed it closely, recognising the skill it represented and mentally vowing she would have to keep a close eye on that Mavis Dupe from now on – a potential rival for her catering crown.

Euphemia unveiled her scones from the cocoon of a pristine white tea-towel, her luscious fly-cemeteries and then her "pièce de resistance" – or rather non-resistance she hoped – her slightly brown crisp meringues, mouth-watering even to look at. From a cool-bag she produced a pot of double cream with which to cement the meringues together. Just before coffee was served she'd pop through to the kitchen and make them up.

Everything was now laid out for the coffee morning. The two ladies and their helpers retired to the hall to hear the minister's wife's welcoming speech to the Minibus Group. Some minutes later, the sound of the tea-urn bubbling away in the kitchen cheered up the pensioners. They usually pitched into the goodies right away on a visit. Their modest breakfasts of tea and toast had already lost their impact, and their stomachs were rumbling.

Just as the minister's wife was delivering her last sentence, Euphemia slipped gracefully into the kitchen. The sounds of a loud scream followed by a string of choice words resounded from the hatch.

"You dirty B****R, get out! GET OUT OF HERE!"

A clattering sound followed. There was an ominous crash and an ear-piercing wail. Mavis and the other helpers rushed through to find a scene of devastation. Euphemia was sliding down to the floor in a puddle of cream dripping from the worktop. A mangy black cat shot out of the window, just avoiding Euphemia's high-heeled shoe. The opportunist thief had trodden all over her meringues with his muddy paws, chewed the lid off and managed to demolish most of the tub of cream! The whole sorry episode was described later by Mavis to her amused husband as Operation Catastrophe. Roger was summoned to take his hysterical wife home.

But, as the saying goes, "the show must go on" and so the rest of the delicacies, saved from the marauder's jaws, were duly served up to the Old Brigade.

The trail of events had brightened up the normal monotony of their day and Mavis's Easter Cake, in all its glory as the centrepiece on the table, seemed to swell with justifiable pride. For this day at least, Mavis was the undisputed Culinary Queen.

Out of the Blue

Christine Rolffe-Budd

The branches of the tree stirred gently in the wind, scratching at my window. Daylight sneaked though a chink in the curtains, penetrating the dusty corners of my room. It was time to get up.

The others were already seated for breakfast when I joined them. I felt them all watching as I sat beside my grandmother. Her wrinkled face smiled as she remarked once more that I was the image of her son, who had drowned a decade ago. She patted my hand, her long thin fingers heavily adorned with gold rings inlaid with precious stones. I could feel everyone holding their breath as she took off one of her rings and placed it on my finger – a large blue sapphire in a circle of diamonds.

"Your father gave it to me my dear, and now I'm passing it on to you. The sapphire was the same colour as his eyes – your eyes."

I squeezed her cold hands and thanked her, looking challengingly at the family. I caught their disapproval, but they bowed their heads and continued with their breakfast.

Later that day I sat with my grandmother, admiring the sapphire that sparkled in the light of the fire. This was only the beginning, I thought. I was aware of her leafing through the family album, lingering over the photos of her dead son.

"You're so like him, why did you take so long to find me?"

"I'm sorry. But I'm here now, and I won't leave you." I kissed her on the cheek, remembering my mother's parting words:

"The truth is neither here or there, it's the likeness that matters."

Living in Paradise

June Munro

Mildred is on automatic pilot. The trigger is the unspoken thought - 'It's time to go to the Mini-Market'- and before she knows what is happening she puts on her sandals, fastens the fleece that Susan sent her for Christmas and checks her purse for change. She walks over to the balcony and looks out. It is sunny as usual, 'but you never know until you get out whether there is a bite in the breeze,' she says to herself. Checking that the windows are locked she crosses the room to the door. Drawing back the top and bottom bolts, undoing the two tenant locks and moving the angle bar over, she releases the chain and a couple of turns of the Chubb lock opens the door.

The corridor is dark, but the light switch is by the door and pressing it she slips out and reverses the key in the lock twice. It feels firm, but you have to be sure. The light is timed to stay on until she gets into the lift and if the lift is slow coming sometimes she can press the switch by the left entrance and light comes flooding into the corridor again. If the lift is out of order, walking down the four flights of stairs isn't too bad, but coming up is getting a bit too much these days.

Once in the street she turns left and walks the few hundred yards to Paco's. Metres still confuse her, but she has mastered kilos and grams after a bit of a struggle.

"Hola Doña Mildred, como estas?"

"Muy bueno," Mildred replies, feeling proud of her attempts at the language but pleased that she won't have to try to say much else. Paco speaks excellent English but this little greeting is part of their ritual and helps her feel noticed. Once the season begins in earnest Paco will have a stream of temporary assistants to help and Mildred will pass in and out unnoticed unless Paco himself happens to be around when the usual exchanges will take place. She selects a packet of Horniman's Tea, a jar of jam and a small Bimbo loaf, completing her purchases with a copy of The Daily Mail. She only buys it twice a week, it is so expensive and after all it is printed in Spain so the cost annoys her. She sometimes picks up copies of *The Sur* in English, but it doesn't have much interest for her and some of the advertisements shock her at times - 'Lovely young woman, twenty-five years old, very experienced in all techniques, will visit you in your own home.'

'What sorts of people place those notices and who rings the numbers in the advert?' she asks herself for the umpteenth time.

"How is your daughter, Doña Mildred? Is she coming to see you soon?" asks Paco gently.

"I hope so," she answers, wondering to herself when Susan would be able to fit in a visit. Her daughter isn't married, but has a demanding career and an expensive lifestyle to maintain, and she has hinted that the Costa del Sol is a bit downmarket for her.

"Adios Paco," she smiles.

"Hasta luego," he replies as she steps into the street.

'I'll try a different place for coffee,' Mildred says to herself and walks along the Esplanade. Passing Ye Olde English Tea Shoppe and Molly Malone's, she settles on Stella's, an unpretentious but tidy looking establishment opposite the gardens. Waiting for the coffee to arrive she finds herself thinking how it had all begun. She and Arthur had spent holidays here every year since Susan left home and when Arthur had retired and they had been able to have longer holidays. It had seemed such a natural progression to move out permanently to the sun. They had been told that there would never be any more building around the new development they moved into - what a tale! Within a couple of years their sea view had disappeared and the blocks of apartments that were built had dwarfed the six storeys of their own building. Bars and cafes had sprung up, shops selling beach goods, postcards and hats were all around them and in high season the discos were open all night. The little streets were packed with the young and middle aged of half of Europe all 'having a good time' as they claimed if anyone dared to ask them to make less noise.

She and Arthur had coped, but it was not the paradise they thought that they had bought into. It had been bearable of course when they were together, but her eyes filled with tears as she remembered how Arthur had suddenly collapsed and died, leaving her alone and so lonely.

They had prided themselves on not being 'joiners' and keeping themselves to themselves, but now it had rebounded on her. She looks around the cafe hoping to make eye contact with someone, anyone, but knows she is suffering from elderly blight - she is invisible to the younger folks around her.

"La cuenta, por favor," she mutters searching in her bag for her purse. The young fellow, face immobile, says 'Okay, Grandma' and she recognises the slightly contemptuous familiarity for what it is.

'Ah well, back to the grind' she says under her breath. Smiling to herself she remembers how envious her old neighbours had been when she and Arthur had left for their life in the sun.

If only they knew.

Midwinterings
Terry Williams

springborn home and everlasting flame
summerful milk and fish and children's laughter
autumnsleek cattle and corngold fields
wintersnow
        whisper
             eviction

roof thatch red roaring
hearth ash grey fading
wind

    sibilant

    sweeping

    scouring

scattering broken hearts.

moonraking

        bare fields

frostbiting

        tumbled walls

windsweeping

        empty hearth

stir ember

        fan flame

fill absence

        with net and pail and stack and creel

fill silence

        with laughter and song

greet the awakening land.

Twenty-One Eleven
Reg Holder

By the time the family arrive at the New Life Cryogenic Centre, my body will have been prepared: filled with nitrogen, frozen down and in its casket to wait my reawakening. When I told them of my planned cryogenic future, my family did not believe in the process and had tried to dissuade me from signing up. One hundred and fifty thousand dollars was a huge sum to wager on something that was, in their view, very unlikely to happen. However I had left them well cared for and none of them need ever want for anything. I also opened a trust fund designed to take care of expenses when the time came to re-awaken me. There were risks of course. My family could lose interest and stop monitoring the project and I could be forgotten. More importantly, if the company didn't keep the project going, a lot of us in the centre would be very disappointed. Not that we would know anything about it – only time would tell.

That was a long time ago, one hundred years to be precise, and according to my instructions, it is time for me to return to life. By now the technology should be in place to fulfil the dreams of those who believed that science would solve the mystery of eternal life.The tubes are warming up, a faint swishing signals the arrival of the flushing liquid, coursing through my body. Soon blood will take its place, and the next stage of my life will begin. There is no way of knowing what awaits. My instructions stipulate that as soon as I am recovered (for that's how I look at it) money from the trust will be there to cover the costs. Of course any remaining family will stand to gain as well, but they will have to look after me in exchange. In due course, there will be millions to be made from the media and scientific institutes interested in the process of my revival.

Now I can hear voices. "They" have kept their side of the bargain after all. My heart has been kick-started and feeling is gradually returning to all my extremities. My nose itches intolerably but there is nothing I can do about it. My eyes open and I look out on the operating room. Figures in green gowns bend over me, rubbing my legs, moving my arms and massaging my head. Slowly they bring me to a sitting position. A machine is pumping my blood through my body. It will be a while before my heart can take over, but life is slowly coming back and I must be patient.

The technician completes his work, strips off his gloves, and indicates that I can be wheeled out to the recovery room. He leaves. The nurse leans over and says everything will be alright. Once I am settled they will explain everything. I nod my head. I have no speech, but surely that will come.

I am taken to a room, where I have no idea of time passing. Every so often doctors and scientists look over me, prodding and poking my body. The machine is still connected. I can see and hear but still cannot speak.

Later, the Head of the Centre appears and says they have carried out the resuscitation according to my instructions. He tells me I am the first to undergo the procedure, and explains that they are not far enough advanced yet to take it any further. However, my body is valuable to them and they need to gain as much knowledge as possible so those who follow me may benefit. When they can do nothing more, the machine will be switched off.

This time I will die. I can do nothing but wait.

Mothers and Sons

June Munro

We hug, we kiss
We meet as equals
In an unequal pairing.

One love has come through pain
Time and wonder.
One from security
Acceptance and certainty.

Experiences have sometimes
Been different, difficult,
But never divisive.

Our roles have changed slowly,
Delicate balance of carer
And cared-for.
The face the world sees.

I see within the man
The boy, touching his mother's arm,
And holding her heart forever.

Traplines

Louise James

Clarissa pressed her fingers into the small of her back and tried to stretch away the dull ache that had become her constant companion. She fed more logs into the woodstove and checked her bread; it was the final batch of sourdough and she carefully stored the starter dough for her next baking day. On the range a pot of stew was simmering. It was the last of the caribou and she prayed that Malcolm would be bringing another beast when he arrived, this afternoon, or tomorrow at the latest. It took him four weeks to work his trap line. They timed his absences by the moon and it was full last night. Every so often she looked out the small window, pulling aside the red and white gingham curtains she had brought with her when she came out from the Old Country seven years ago. A mail order bride, organised by the Hudson's Bay Company–their way of populating the back country with Home Settlers and keeping the trappers sober and happy. She'd signed up willingly enough; a future of domestic drudgery and spinsterhood lay before her if she didn't seize this chance and her restless nature made the decision easier. For the most part she was happy with her choice although it had proved to be a life of great challenge, harsh and difficult, and often lonely. A baby had been born every year; four survived. Although Malcolm seemed to truly love her, his life as a trapper suited him, and after a week cooped up in the small cabin with four children, he was itching to get away on the line again.

It was almost dark when she heard the dogs barking and Fraser, the oldest, shouted the arrival of his father. How good it was to hold him close again, and to feel the burden of loneliness and responsibility slip from her shoulders for a week at least.

They ate together as family for the first time in a month: the children noisy, hungry, already knowing that father had brought food to last and anyway spring was on its way. There would be more trips to the trading post for supplies, and they would help their mother plant the Indian corn and root vegetables, trying out new seeds exchanged with neighbours. Wild berries grew in profusion and their hands and faces would be blue with huckleberry juice.

Malcolm played with them for an hour, and then the four of them were piled together like puppies in their closet bed. When the noise of the little ones had died down, Clarissa and Malcolm sat in silence by the fire. Malcolm warmed his hands, as if by habit. The cabin was cosy but he was used to his life in the wilds where keeping the cold at bay was a constant necessity.

"Did you miss me?" This was his preamble to his claim on her for his marital rights. "I missed you so bad it hurts, Clarissa."

She smiled, looking into the fire. She wasn't being coy, but she needed to collect herself, knowing as she did, his secret. He had no clue that she had found out about Nakota, his country wife. Clarissa had been shocked to learn of her existence before travelling north to meet her future husband. All the men, she'd been told, had country wives, Sioux women. She suspected but did not know for certain, that he had children with Nakota, offspring who were growing up in a native community somewhere up along the trap line. Of course the men who worked for the Company were supposed to give up their country wives when they married for good, but many did not. How could they abandon a woman who had been their long term companion during the coldest and loneliest winters of their lives? Clarissa sighed inwardly. It had bothered her for a long time. She had begun to believe, during the first years of their marriage, that he had given the other woman up, but it was when Jock McKinley passed through two years ago and let slip, that her suspicions were confirmed.

Jock worked one of the parallel lines and would generally call in when Malcolm was at home. But from time to time he visited when Malcolm was not there, sometimes just days after he had headed back out. Jock was easy company. He was a reader and something of a poet and he would lend Clarissa books that had been sent out from the Old Country. Starved of mental stimulation, she devoured the books, and read what she could to the older children. Somehow she never told Malcolm about all the extra visits that Jock took to paying. It was wilderness hospitality never to turn a man away from your door. You could die in the backwoods in a few hours. There was a code of chivalry that led men like Malcolm to trust other trappers who would call in, have a meal, warm up by the fire and maybe sleep in the loft for a night or two.

Clarissa turned her thoughts back to her husband, newly back from the lines. Tired, happy, and ready for bed. He was a good man, but he had no conversation. They lay down together, pulling the rough blankets over them and Clarissa gave in willingly to his urgent embraces. She was glad he was never very good at counting. Maybe tomorrow, or perhaps on his next visit home, she'd tell him the news about the baby.

Musical Trees

Janet Macdonald

Welcome to the land of trees!

Clutching rock and crevice,
they fringe the hills with delicate traces.
Ancient trunks, encrusted boughs,
embraced by mist,
generous hosts to lesser plants.

Younger trees, exuberant ferns,
their roots in tangled strings,
surround rocks and other trees,
impatient to reach the ground;
draw moisture,
grow giant leaves,
feed uninvited guests.

Fastidious guests
bore a single hole, then
seek other leafy flavours.

Gentler visitors linger,
lovingly create leaf lacework.

Ruthless jaws gorge greedily,
leave tasteless leaf gristle.

As light fades,
their meal finished,
the guests tune up.
A chorus of semitones
rattle tiny maracas,
shriek or creak,
scrape and whistle.
Discordant drones
insistent, strident,
fade and resume.

You thought trees were silent?

I Don't Do Lunch
Christina Macdonald

"I don't do lunch normally," said the Reverend Cuthbert Prudhomme, eagerly eyeing the side-table on whose crisp white cloth lay an array of delicious cold meats and salads. Inwardly he was recalling that he usually had to settle for Mrs Bluit's watery cock-a-leekie soup and cheese and biscuits at mid-day.

"However, on this occasion I think I could be persuaded to partake."

Rev Prudhomme was settled in one of Mrs Nagberry's green velvet-covered armchairs close to a glowing coal fire. He had been ensconced there for the past half hour, sipping a dainty glass of sherry and as time wore on, his cheeks had turned from the colour of Pink Lady apples to the hue of scarlet cherries. His short legs, dangling from the chair revealed a fleshy gap between his trousers and a pair of bright red socks.

Seated primly on the opposite side of the fire, his hostess took in the view. Quite unbecoming for a vicar, Mrs Nagberry thought. Red indeed! How frivolous for a man of the cloth to be sporting such attachments to his person, though she did approve of the sober black suit and dog-collar.

"I'm very pleased to hear it," she found herself replying "but first there's the matter of the Church Flowers and the Fabric Fund which the Vestry will be discussing at the next meeting."

The Rev.Prudhomme nodded in agreement, trying not to reveal that his thoughts had already turned with longing to the prospect of the meal ahead. Agnes Nagberry continued:

"The ladies are in agreement that they require some money to pay for the floral decorations in the church each Sunday. I am fully aware that Mrs Ponsonby and Lady Gardenia have large gardens from which they can procure flowers and greenery at any time of year, but as Mrs Lumpit says, she doesn't have a garden worth looking at, seeing as she lives in an upper flat in Cardigan Street. She has to buy her flowers, when it is her turn, from Easy-Save and that costs her £6 a bunch at least, that is if there's a cheap offer on. She doesn't have much to spare from her pension these days."

Rev. Prudhomme nodded placidly as this waterfall of words swept over him. He brushed the crumbs of shortbread from his ample stomach; the heat from the fire now threatened to overcome him. By this stage he was almost on the point of agreeing to any proposal if it hastened his access to lunch.

But Mrs Nagberry, in full flow, continued:

"And as for the hall seats, they're a disgrace! We've had them since I was a girl and they are so uncomfortable if you have to sit on them for any length of time – especially at Vestry meetings that seem to go on forever! They are all right no doubt for Mrs Plumtree, whose generous rear is well upholstered but the rest of us, less well endowed, have resorted to bringing our own cushions out of sheer frustration. Surely there must be some money for these worthy causes?"

Rev Prudhomme by now almost totally acquiescent and still intermittently eyeing the enticing spread, as if willing it not to disappear, rose unsteadily to his feet and made his way over to the buffet table.

"I shall do my best to persuade the Vestry to release some money for these worthy causes, Mrs Nagberry, and in the meantime I shall be delighted to partake of this splendid lunch! Bless these mercies for our use and may we be truly thankful. Amen!"

The Last Witch
Christine Rolffe-Budd

It was a cold June day and I was frightened, very frightened, not for myself but for my mother, for I had been pardoned. I stood in the shadow of the Tolbooth, watching the jeering mob, their faces distorted with rage. They had been gathering outside since early morning. Many of them were our neighbours, whose malicious gossip had us arrested, charged with witchcraft.

It was early spring when I accompanied my mother to Dornoch. The air was crisp, like the patches of snow that still clung to the distant hills. A yellow sun dusted the slate sea with silver. I had never seen my mother so happy as she hurried along the shore road, eager to be returning home. She had imagined that there would be a warm welcome from her old neighbours, but she was sadly mistaken. They didn't recognise the old grey-haired woman calling herself Janet Horne, who spoke halting Gaelic in a strange accent. They only remembered a young woman who had left to work as a lady's maid in Italy.

Under the suspicious eyes of the townspeople, we moved into the old family cottage which had been empty since the death of my grandfather. My mother kept mostly indoors, as the cold weather was not to her liking, and as she dozed in her chair by the fireside, it fell to me to do the daily chores.

I never knew my father, for he had left us when I was a baby. Although I often broached the subject, my mother would never speak of him. I only knew that she had met and married him when she had returned from Italy, after her mistress had died. We lived near Helmsdale for most of my childhood, until one fine day my mother took it into her head to return to Dornoch. At first I found my new home quite agreeable. I liked the freedom of wandering across the broad sands, collecting driftwood for our fire and feeling the wind ruffling my hair. I enjoyed the solitude, away from prying eyes, forgetting that I had been born with crooked feet and hands with webbed fingers. It was only when I had to go into town that my appearance bothered me. I became aware of huddles of people whispering as they stared in my direction.

My disabilities, and my mother's reclusiveness, only added to our isolation with our neighbours. Gossip began to spread, and soon whispers of witchcraft were on everyone's lips. It was widely rumoured that my mother turned me into a pony each night so that she could ride me out to do the Devil's work. They believed that my hands and feet looked like ponies' hooves as a result of my mother's failing to return them back to form. It was even speculated that the Devil himself had shod me.

Fearing that we were a threat to their Christian society, the townsfolk, led by the Reverend Robert Robertson, who wholly believed the malicious gossip - had us arrested.

We were thrown into the Tolbooth, a grim stone building in the town square, close to Dornoch Cathedral. Our cell, although warm, was small and cramped, for the building also housed the Court and the Council House. We sat clinging to each other for solace, our feet shackled to an iron bar set in the wall of the cell. Our only comfort was the dirty straw strewn thinly on the floor, but it reeked so strongly of urine that I began to feel sick.

Convinced that we might be hiding charms and implements that could be used for casting spells, the guards took us separately to be searched and examined. I shook with fear when it was my turn. Panic welled up inside and I fought like a wild cat, kicking and screaming. Two guards held me fast, whilst another roughly shaved my head. I cried at the sight of my fair hair falling at my feet. As I struggled I felt the pain of the razor cutting my scalp and the blood running down my face. Not content with my head, they roughly pulled off my clothes and proceeded to shave off all my bodily hair - even my private areas were not spared the razor.

Weak and exhausted, I felt that I could no longer fight them. I stared up at the screen of cobwebs that covered the ceiling above my head. I became numb and detached, imagining myself as a spider looking down, watching the guards as they examined my naked body. With dirty, calloused fingers they pinched and prodded suspicious-looking moles and blemishes which could be perceived as the devil's mark. But their scrupulous search went unrewarded and clutching my torn clothes, I was dragged back to my cell.

In the days that followed, and sometimes during the night, my mother and I were continually harassed to sign confessions of witchcraft. Although starved and deprived of sleep, I stubbornly refused, pleading our innocence. As for my mother, she so was confused that she didn't really understand what was being asked of her. Eventually, anxious to extract an early confession, it was decreed by the Minister and the Council that we should be tortured by pricking.

My mother was chosen first because of her frailty, and they knew that under torture a confession could be easily extracted. At the Council's expense, skilled prickers were hired. I could hear her screams from the room above our cell, begging them to stop as they inserted the long needles. They stabbed them right up to the hilt into her arms, legs, buttocks and breasts, pricking her inch by inch, meticulously looking for an area that was numb, free of pain and bloodless when pierced. An area where they believed Satan himself had touched her – the Devil's mark – if found, would have proved her guilt beyond doubt. But they were unsuccessful, for my feeble mother could not withstand the excruciating pain that was inflicted upon her, and in her confused state she freely signed the documents, confessing everything. Thankfully, I was spared this torture as my mother's full admission was enough to convict us both.

Our trial was a hurried affair and by rights should never have taken place. I later discovered that Captain David Ross, Depute Sheriff of Sutherland, had failed to inform the King's Advocate of the allegations made against us. But despite this oversight, the Minister had strongly persuaded him that we should be brought to trial immediately.

The court was packed, mainly by townsfolk, all shouting and cursing us. During the proceedings, my mother was asked by Captain Ross to recite the Lord's prayer in Gaelic. This she did eagerly, only too happy to oblige. To my surprise, she even winked at him as she began her recitation. Unfortunately, in her confusion she said: "Ar n-athair a bha air neamh" *Our Father who wert in heaven* using "bha", instead of "tha", *art*. I felt alarmed when I heard the murmur of disapproval from the spectators, for they all firmly believed that she was referring to the Devil – who had been cast out of heaven – as her Lord.

There followed an expectant hush from the hecklers as Captain Ross looked down at us from his high bench. His eyes were cold as the sea that had lapped at my feet. Speaking in a powerful voice, he read out the verdict. We had been found guilty of witchcraft, and sentenced to be burned the following day. I heard what he said but my mind refused to believe it. It was not until the guards came to take us away, that the full realisation of our fate took hold. I threw myself to the floor, pleading for mercy, whilst my confused mother stood by smiling apologetically for my behaviour. Whether it was my pitiful pleas or my tender years, I was later pardoned on the grounds of being an unwilling accomplice and an innocent party. But I did not go completely unpunished, for it was decreed by the Minister that I should be a witness to my mother's humiliation and burning.

Early the following morning under a grey, overcast sky, I stood hiding in the shadow of the Tolbooth, away from the unruly mob that had gathered outside. A cheer went up when the heavy studded door was finally opened. My mother, looking tired and baffled, hobbled out, escorted by her guards. Although she was too weak to struggle, they held her fast as she was stripped of her clothes - which were now reduced to rags - and painted her with warm pine tar. Handfuls of chicken feathers were stuck on, making her look grotesque. When they were satisfied, they put her in a barrel and loaded it onto a waiting cart so that she could be paraded around the town.

Nearly all the townsfolk turned out to see the witch. They lined the streets, pushing and jostling to catch a glimpse of her. I saw small children sitting on their parents' shoulders to see her better. Young boys ran alongside her, throwing stones. Although a few hit her escort, some found their target. Thin rivulets of blood could be seen trickling down her tarred face.

At last we arrived at a large open space near Little Town, where a huge bonfire was already burning fiercely, fanned by the sea breeze. My mother, cold and bewildered, cried out with delight on seeing the blaze. Not realising that it was meant for her, she held out her hands to warm them. Staring at the fire she said, "An teine beag!" *(the little fire)* I could feel the crowd listening closely, for they had expected her to say, "An teine mor" *(the fire of hell)* – which for her it was. Whilst warming her hands, my mother looked around at the jeering mob and, smiling at them all I heard her shout, "Oh, what a cheerful sight to see such good and fine neighbours gathered here," which caused a stir of laughter.

I felt the sudden surge of the crowd, fighting for a favourable place to watch, as two strong guards lifted her barrel. She had no idea what was about to happen right up to the moment when they threw her, still alive, on to the fire. I cried out in horror for she had not been strangled, a privilege given to those who had freely confessed. Her screams still haunt me to this day. They were inhuman. They stopped abruptly as the fire engulfed her. Her head burned a grisly black, her mouth opened wide in a silent scream. Then the stench of burning flesh, sweet and sickly. The thick, oily smoke made me retch as it got into my nose and throat. Disgust and horror overwhelmed me, and instinctively I wanted to run away, but I knew that I had to watch. I stayed throughout the night praying for her soul. It was the least I could do.

The dawn appeared red on the horizon, glowing like the fire that had reduced my mother to blackened bones and ash. I turned my back on it and limped home. I collected my few belongings, and taking one last look at our cottage, I pulled the door shut behind me. I didn't bother to lock it, for I knew I would never return.

South Side Selina
Len Hollywood

Steel tips of her thigh high boots
tap out a tune on wet pavement,
sending it to her head.
It echoes off the high walls.
Red hair stuck to her face,
makeup shiny from damp air
around the dockyards.
No ships in tonight.
Red knee-length skirt
held together with Velcro,
wrap-around blouse short coat,
small brown bag under her arm.
She heads back to her car,
condoms unused, no need
for air freshener tonight.
Driving through a near dead city,
no likely punters around tonight.
Heads home to her flat,
Once inside locking the door,
Hangs her coat, skirt and blouse in a wardrobe
till next weekend.
Heads for the bedroom, pulls the blinds,
mixes a drink,
sits at a dressing table, takes off the wig
Puts it on a wooden head.
Drink in hand she heads for a bath then bed.

Wakes up to the radio at seven thirty, a quick shower,
takes the empty glass through to the kitchen.
Sitting in a pink housecoat, has a
healthy breakfast, dresses in
pale blue bra and panties, blue
blouse, dark blue trousers, blue stockings,
flat black shoes.
Leaves the glass and bowl in the sink.
Picks up briefcase, glasses and coat,
locks up behind herself,
drives across the city.
It looks old and new in daylight.

They stand in a row as she crosses the car park.
As one they say "Good morning Margaret."
She unlocks the door as they move inside
and she looks down the aisles
with their rows of books.
Then heads for her office,
where she manages the libraries programme.

Just Passing Through

Catriona Tawse

The sad brown bird had lost his song. He flew in from a far country and perched on a great grey boulder near the top of a very high hill among other dark and unwelcoming hills. A big bird with black feathers and a tight orange beak glided down to inspect the stranger.

"What is this place?" asked the sad brown bird, "And what can I find to eat?"

"These are the Mountains of Gloom," answered the bird with the black feathers. "You will have to do as we do, climb up and up into the sky and swoop down on the small creatures which are our food. You must have strong claws and a beak that tears. Will you stay here with us?"

"No," said the sad brown bird. " I cannot find my song in this cruel place. I am just passing through."

The sad brown bird flew down to the tall trees and found a branch on which to land. On this side and on that leafy limbs waved and dipped, the sun did not shine through their denseness. A green-speckled bird with a twisted beak fluttered down to inspect the stranger.

"What is this place?" asked the sad brown bird. "And what can I find to eat?"

"This is the Forest of Dark," said the bird with the twisted beak. "You will have to do as we do, grasp the cones of these tall giants and prise them open for the seeds inside. Your beak must be a hook. Will you stay here with us?"

"No," said the sad brown bird. "I cannot find my song in this bleak place. I am just passing through."

The sad brown bird flew down to the wide moorland. He crouched among the heather and stretched his neck up high. A sturdy red-speckled bird with strange white feet scuttled over to inspect the stranger.

"What is this place?" asked the sad brown bird. "And what can I find to eat?"

"This is the Moor of Lost," said the red-speckled bird. "You will have to do as we do and nibble the stems and shoots of these tough plants. You must be able to hide from danger. Will you stay here with us?"

"No," said the sad brown bird. "I cannot find my song in this hard place. I am just passing through."

The sad brown bird flew down to the edge of the ocean. He dropped onto a rough rock and turned his head from the wind. A large strong-winged bird landed on the next rock to inspect the stranger.

"What is this place?" asked the sad brown bird. "And what can I find to eat?"

"This is the Sea of Storm," said the strong-winged bird. "You will have to do as we do and dive into the water to catch the fish. You must be able to float and swim. Will you stay here with us?"

"No," said the sad brown bird. "I cannot find my song in this watery place. I am just passing through."

The sad brown bird flew over streets and rooftops. He came to a grassy place with coloured flowers and sheltering hedges beside a small wooden house, and he rested on top of a wooden post. Another small brown bird with a lot of red feathers on its chest hopped onto the next post to inspect the stranger.

"What is this place?" asked the sad brown bird. "And what can I find to eat?"

"This is the Garden of Plenty," said the bird with the red feathered chest. "You will have to do as we do and sing your merriest song to earn the crumbs and seeds and all the other good things. Will you stay here with us?"

The sad brown bird opened his beak. He had found his song in this kind place and he trilled and chirped with all his might. He was no longer passing through, here he would stay. From out of the house came a smiling lady clasping the hand of a boy with no sight in his eyes. They scattered before them crumbs and seeds and pieces of fruit.

"I hear a new song in the garden today," said the boy.

Air an t-Slighe
Catriona Tawse

Bha an isean donn brònach air a ghuth a chall. Bha e air a thighinn à thall thairis, agus shuidh e air clach mhòr ghlas faisg air mullach beann àrd am measg beanntan eile dorch agus neo-fhialaidh. Thàinig isean mòr le itean dhubh agus gob orainds sìos a bhruidhinn ris an strainnsear.

"Dè an seorsa àite a tha seo?" dh'fhaighnich an isean donn brònach. "Agus dè a gheibh mi airson ith?"

"'S e Beanntan an Gruaim a tha seo," fhreagair an isean le na h-itean dhubh. Feumaidh tu deanamh mar a bhios sinne a' deanamh, dìrich suas dhan an àdhar agus thig sìos le ruathar air na beathaichean beaga a tha mar bhiadh dhuinn. Feumaidh spuirean agus gob gu math làidir a bhith ort. Am fuirich thu an seo còmhla ruinn?"

"Chan fhuirich," thuirt an isean donn brònach. "Cha tig mo ghuth air-ais thugam anns an àite borb seo. Tha mi a' dol a chumail orm a' siubhal."

Chaidh an isean donn brònach sìos air iteag chun na craobhan àrda agus fhuair e geug airson fois a ghabhail. Air gach taobh bha geugan duilleagach, cho tiugh 's nach fhaigheadh dearrsadh na grèine trompa. Thàinig isean le breacan uaine agus gob snìomhte sìos a bhruidhinn ris an strainnsear.

"De an seorsa àite a tha seo?" dh'fhaighnich an isean donn brònach. " Agus dè a gheibh mi airson ith?"

"'S e seo Coille an Dorchadas," thuirt an isean leis an gob snìomhte. "Feumaidh tu deanamh mar a bhios sinne a' deanamh, gabh grèim air na cònaichean àrda seo agus feuch rim fosgladh airson faighinn chun an t-sìol a tha nam broinn. Feumaidh do ghob a bhith mar dhubhan. Am fuirich thu an seo còmhla rinn?"

"Chan fhuirich," thuirt an isean donn brònach. "Cha tig mo ghuth air-ais thugam anns an àite gruamach seo. Tha mi a' dol a chumail orm a' siubhal."

Chaidh an isean donn brònach sìos air iteag chun a' mhòintich fharsaing. Chrom e sìos am measg an fhraoich ach chum e amhach os cionn an fhraoich. Thàinig isean tapaidh le breacan dearg agus casan geal a bhruidhinn ris an strainnsear.

"Dè an seorsa àite a tha seo?" dh'fhaighnich an isean donn brònach. "Agus dè a gheibh mi airson ith?"

"'S e seo Coille nan Call," thuirt an isean leis na breacan dearg. "Feumaidh tu deanamh mar a bhios sinne a' deanamh agus gasan agus cuiseagan na lusan seo ith. Feumaidh tu thu fhèin a chumail bho chunnart. Am fuirich thu an seo comhla rinn?"

"Chan fhuirich," fhreagair an isean donn brònach. "Cha tig mo ghuth air-ais thugam anns an àite chruaidh seo. Tha mi a' dol a chumail orm a' siubhal."

Chaidh an isean donn brònach sios gu oir a' chuain. Sheas e air creag gharbh agus chur e a chùlaibh ris a' ghaoith. Thàinig isean mòr sìos air a' chreag ri thaobh a bhruidhinn ris an strainnsear.

"Dè an seorsa àite a tha seo?" dh'fhaighnich an isean donn brònach. "Agus dè a gheibh mi airson ith?"

"'S e seo Cuan nan Stoirm," fhreagair an isean mòr. "Feumaidh tu deanamh mar a bhios sinne a' deanamh agus a dhol dhan a' bhùrn airson na h-èisg a ghlacadh. Feumaidh comas fleòdradh agus snàmh a bhith agad. Am fuirich thu an seo comhla rinn?"

"Chan fhuirich," thuirt an isean donn brònach. "Cha tig mo ghuth air-ais thugam anns an àite fliuch seo. Tha mi a' dol a chumail orm a' siubhal."

Chaidh an isean donn brònach air iteag os cionn sràidean agus taighean. Thàinig e gu àite feurach le flùraichean de dh'iomadh dath agus callaidean ri taobh taigh beag geal, agus sheas e air post fiodh. Thàinig isean donn eile le tòrr itean dearg air a bhroilleach chun a' phost ri thaobh a bhruidhinn ris an strainnnsear.

"Dè an seorsa àite a tha seo?" dh'fhaighnich an isean donn brònach. "Agus dè a gheibh mi airson ith?"

"'S e seo Garradh am Pailteas" fhreagair an isean leis am broilleach dearg. "Feumaidh tu deanamh mar a bhios sinne a' deanamh agus an òran as aighearaich a th'agad a sheinn airson criomagan agus sìol agus rudan math eile fhaighinn. Am fuirich thu an seo còmhla rinn?"

Dh' fhosgail an isean donn brònach a ghob. Bha e air a ghuth a lorg anns an àite choibhneil seo agus sheinn e gu àrd a ghuth. Cha robh e a' siubhal tuilleadh, bha e a' dol a dh'fhuireach an seo.

A-mach às an taigh thàinig boireannach còir agus grèim aice air làmh balach a bha dall. Chuir iad air an talamh na criomagan agus an t-siol agus pìosan measan.

"Cluinnidh mi òran ùr anns a' ghàrradh an diugh," thuirt am balach.

Shetland

Christina Macdonald

Sweet, mellow, drift the banks
Of sea-pink and wild thyme,
Mingling their fragrance on summer air.
Golden vetch and buttercups
Carpet the machair where brown ponies graze.

There once a croft house stood.
I trace the flat grey lichen-covered stones
Still resting gently one on other
Marking, like recumbent tombs,
The lives of those long gone.

Silence is constantly filled with sound.
Guillemots squabbling on spare rocky ledges
While silent and dove-like the fulmar wings,
effortless
Gliding on spiralling thermals of air.

A curlew calling from watery meadows
Rises up suddenly into the air.
The menacing brush of the wings of the bonxie
Casts shadows above me
Far out on the moor.
Always and ever the sound of the sea
And whispers of breezes soft off the land
Wafting sweet perfume of wild wayside flowers
A million golden mimulus nodding in the wind.

Steadily, slowly, the life pulse of Shetland
Beats beauty incessantly into my mind
The magic of islands where summer long lingers
Un-ending in lines of lightness and sound.

Sylvia

June Munro

My last act of friendship was to give a reading at Sylvia's funeral service. I was humbled and honoured to do so, closing forever that shared window on our past.

Sylvia was exactly a week younger than me and our grandparents and parents had been neighbours so it was almost pre-ordained that we would be friends. We were both only children and our early lives were lived in tandem.

As very small children I was the more hardy of the two and took the role of protector and general organiser of our games - not that I always got my own way, she was no pushover! I was a little taller than she was and she always retorted that I had had a week longer to grow. I was Princess Elizabeth and she was Princess Margaret Rose in our dressing-up games. She learned to play the piano so became 'Auntie Vi' when we played at 'Children's Hour': I was usually the Prince when we did a pantomime. On one occasion when the audience was sparse we lured one unsuspecting little boy in to watch, and locked the door so that he couldn't escape! In Sunday School concerts we were always paired and being slightly taller I was usually cast as the boy, or, in one instance, the back sails of a windmill when we sang 'By the Side of The Zuider Zee'.

Her father was a hero to us both and when Sylvia said 'My Daddy says' I knew I had to take note. He was the Oracle. Like all his family Mr Jones was musical. He played the violin and had a fine tenor voice. He sometimes made up silly words to songs.

'The girl that I marry will have to be, tall and slim and as nice as me'. I read somewhere recently that 'Her Benny' had been adapted for the stage and I was immediately five or six years old and listening to Mr Jones reading the book to us.

We both had vivid imaginations and told other children that we were cousins and that our full names were Sylvia Priscilla and June Allison. Tired of me boasting that when we went to Scotland each year we 'passed through' any place anyone else went to (even Cornwall) on one occasion Sylvia announced that she would be 'passing though' Scotland on her way to Lytham St Annes! She followed this by saying 'My Daddy says we will.' End of my protests!

I listened with envy when she came home from hospital having had her tonsils removed and saying she had had ice-cream for breakfast. I tried every trick to convince my mother that I needed mine removing too.

We grew up. Sylvia became a teacher and remained a gifted musician and I became a nurse. We had other friends but we remained important parts of each other's lives. We were bridesmaids to each other, our husbands became friends and we followed with interest the lives of each other's children and eventually grandchildren. She would ring me to check on something no-one else knew about; I would tell her about an incident and she would fully appreciate my feelings and reactions. My daughter's name is Fiona but all her life she has heard me address her as Sylvia on occasions.

Sylvia stoically coped with a long and painful illness and died four years ago, but her musical legacy has passed down through her daughters to her grand-daughters, one of whom has just won a music scholarship. My interest and contact with her family continues, but I miss my first friend.

Beautiful for a Day

Louise James

Roddy woke early. The rain had stopped sometime during the night, which was good. The pitch wouldn't be too muddy by the time the match started at noon. He turned over and saw Billy moving about in a light sleep before waking up properly.

"Billy!" he whispered loudly. "Billy. Are you awake?" He had persuaded – bribed – Billy to help him with his paper round that morning, so Roddy could get the shopping done for Mum and make sure Kirsten was ready for Gran to collect.

"Billy!" his stomach knotted. What if Billy changed his mind? He could be like that. He might say he wouldn't help after all and then Roddy would never get everything done before cycling to the park for the match. It took half an hour to get there and Coach said if you weren't there for half eleven you could forget about being in the starting line-up. It was the Under Fourteens Championship Match. Their opponents, the Muirbay Rovers, were favourites to win but Coach had said they didn't show the character the Wee Toonies did under pressure. And he should know about pressure! Coach used to play for County and he'd promised a County scarf to the boy who scored the winning goal.

Mum was already up. He had heard her putting the kettle on and calling the cat in for her breakfast a little while ago. Maybe she would be alright today. Maybe she would say the shopping could wait and why didn't he just see to Kirsten and then head off to his match in good time? He let out a big sigh and got up. He'd better not count on that happening.

"Billy!" Roddy's voice was more insistent this time and Billy murmured, gradually gaining awareness of his surroundings. He brought the anxious, peering face of his big brother into focus and their deal, made before they went to sleep, came back to him.

"If you help with my paper round in the morning, you can have the loan of my BMX for a whole week, I promise!" Roddy had pleaded.

After some thought, Billy had countered: "Two weeks and it's a deal!"

Roddy had saved up his paper round money to buy that bike. He'd told Billy that Mr. MacLennan was always looking for more kids to help with deliveries, and he'd put in a good word for Billy, but somehow Roddy knew that a paper round would be too much like hard work for his younger brother. He was happy to borrow a bike but not up to putting the effort in to buy one. Still, he had a deal and he just hoped Billy would honour it at seven o'clock the next morning.

Now, everything hinged on Billy's sense of fair play. An agonising full minute later, Billy reached his conclusion. He swung his legs out of bed and stretched.

"Are you gonna be in the first line-up Roddy? Betcha lose anyway. Muirbay's got a monster team, half of the guys are being scouted for the Scottish Premier, I heard anyway."

Roddy took this to mean that Billy was going to co-operate after all, and he smiled in relief. "Nah, they're rubbish. We'll play them offa the park."

The brothers wolfed down their jam pieces and mugs of tea. "Mum? How are ya?" asked Roddy, walking on eggshells, gauging the odds for an easy time of it.

"Hmm," his mother replied. "Didn't sleep hardly at all. Goin' to need a lot of help today. Thank God it's Saturday, I've got a list as long as your arm, stuff that needs doing."

"Mum, remember I've got my match today. Under Fourteens Championship. Mr. Shearer says he's gonna start me in the first line, long as I get there by half eleven."

"Half eleven! Half eleven! What kind of a time is that when you've got family responsibilities and a disabled sister? No, sorry Roddy, my head's killing me and Gran may not be able to take Kirsten today. So that's the end of it I'm afraid. It's only bloody football for god's sake. Jeez didn't I have that with your da' when he wasn't off at the bookies anyway."

Roddy froze. Not be allowed to go, not to play, today of all days. The Championship Match! Mum promised. She didn't remember, but she had promised. His eyes stung with tears.

He started to speak, but she'd already sat down and was well into her set piece. She buried her head in her hands and started to cry.

"I can't go on," she moaned. "How am I supposed to manage? I've only got the bairns, thank God for the kids. You're a wee angel, Roddy, so you are. Ma's helper, that's right."

Billy and Roddy rushed out the door to do the papers.

"Don't worry, Roddy, she'll come round." For once Billy was on his side and Roddy was grateful. For all that he resented the way so many things fell to him, he had a suspicion that Billy got overlooked, squashed between a big brother who worked hard and could play footie, and wee Kirsten who took up so much of everybody's time.

"It's not fair, Roddy," Billy continued. "She did promise, I heard her. She just wishes she hadn't now that it's Saturday. Maybe she'll be in a better mood when we get home."

They were both doubtful but raced round with the papers and hurried home to see if Mum's mood had lifted. And there was Gran! She'd remembered it was match day, she had absolutely not said she wouldn't have Kirsten today, and she was actually going to stay with Mum and Kirsten, to let both boys go to the match. So there!

The world was now sunny and everything was right. Billy rode pillion on Roddy's bike, clutching his brother's kit tightly as they cycled the four miles to Eastside Park where the match was to be played. They arrived in plenty of time, and Billy joined the small knot of parents and friends who'd come to cheer on the Wee Toonies.

Roddy was beside himself with excitement as they warmed up, but to his dismay Coach made a last minute change and opted to start with Frankie Morris on right wing.

"Sorry, Roddy, but Frankie's got a lot more mass than you and Muirbay are a big team. Can't believe their lads are all under fourteen but there you go. They eat more beef on the west side I reckon. See how the game goes. You're my first sub choice anyway. It's all about the team Roddy. Remember that."

Despite his disappointment Roddy took to the bench showing as little emotion as possible. He didn't want to be labelled a cry-baby and something told him that Frankie's temper might be his undoing. He might get a chance, he had to hope so.

The two teams were evenly matched for most of the first forty-five minutes. There had been plenty of chances all right and the subs on the bench were on their feet cheering till they were hoarse. Five minutes before the half time whistle, Muirbay scored against the run of play following an error by Frankie. Roddy could sense what would happen next; he knew Frankie well and sure enough his temper flared. Frankie tackled the goal scorer recklessly at the first opportunity, jabbing him in the leg with his studs, and was immediately red-carded. The Wee Toonies would have to finish the match with ten men, one goal down. It was a gloomy team huddle in the dugout at half time and Roddy's heart was in his mouth. How would Coach change the team formation now they had their backs to the wall?

"Roddy, I'm taking off the midfielder and putting you on. Good man, see what you can do," said Coach, as Frankie, red eyed and humiliated, left the technical area.

Out ran Roddy, rocket propelled. He seemed radio-controlled, passing and receiving the ball with precision. The Wee Toonies played like demons, and the driving force seemed to be the skinny wee ginger lad with legs like sticks. In the sixty-seventh minute, he provided a beautiful pass for Ritchie Wilson, and Ritchie fired it over the keeper's head to equalise. Roddy was in a state of elation he had never experienced before. Coach was waving his arms about in jubilation and Roddy stole a look at the small crowd to spy out his brother. There was Billy, cheering wildly, caught up in the embrace of a dark-haired man in a denim jacket. It was Dad. He'd come! Roddy had left a message on his mobile but never thought for a minute he'd bother. Dad hardly ever replied to his messages.

If he'd played well before the game-changing pass, now Roddy upped his game to new heights. Despite being one man down, despite Muirbay's superior strikers, Roddy and his team couldn't be contained. Then in the final minute of injury time, just as the prospect of a penalty shoot-out was looming, the impossible happened. Roddy broke through a gap in a sloppy defence, raced down the field, feigned a left kick and shot the ball over the keeper's shoulder and into the goal. The roar from the small crowd of onlookers, the ecstasy amongst the players and on the bench was amazing.

Dad and Billy ran onto the field and helped hoist Roddy up onto willing shoulders as he was declared Man of the Match and lapped the park. He had never been so happy; he had never known such joy. It was a beautiful game and a beautiful day.

Dead Love

Christina Macdonald

I once gazed with revulsion
On this decaying body of our love.
I looked with deep distress
Upon its slow and lingering demise.
But now, with passing time
I see only the bare skeleton,
Cleansed of clinging flesh
And therein lies a kind of sterile,
If macabre beauty
Which evokes merely a passing interest
Bereft of all emotion
Save that of curiosity.

The Summons
Christine Rolffe-Budd

Darkness had grown pale on the horizon. The sky was split with narrow bands of light tinged with shades of pink. Moonlight illuminated the memory of a forgotten path where an elderly woman was cautiously walking, her bare feet wet with dew. It led her to a large round stone, carved with mysterious symbols. They were no longer defined, but had been eroded by the wind and rain, their meaning lost and forgotten. She lay down naked upon its flat surface, her woollen cloak spread out beneath her, her long greying hair draped over sagging breasts. Her pale blue eyes focused on the full moon sinking low in the sky. Soon it would become transparent, like a phantom of its former self. A light breeze swept over her as if to chase her away, but she remained motionless and, closing her eyes, she began her invocation. The words floated above her, uniting with the retreating night. She repeated the citation over and over again only stopping when she felt the first tendrils of sun caressing her body.

Pulling herself up, she sat and gazed at the rising sun as it dissolved the last remnants of the night. Its warm rays painted her gold as she waited patiently, listening to the wind whispering through trees, like gossipy old women. They were interrupted by the flurry of birds as they dashed in and out of their branches twittering excitedly to herald a new arrival. Smiling, the woman turned her head towards the sound of a light footfall approaching carefully over the overgrown path. The summons had worked.

He had come, looking just as she remembered him: tall and upright, dressed all in black that defined the contours of his broad shoulders and narrow hips. His dark brown eyes were filled with tenderness and desire as they embraced and kissed. They were in no hurry. They had the whole day to rediscover each other. Like two young lovers they made love under the clear blue sky, their bodies once more united in passion. As the day grew on, they bathed in a nearby burn, splashing and giggling like children. Neither of them spoke of the past or the future but enjoyed the moment and the urgency of need. Their day was filled with excitement and pleasure.

They sat clasped in each other's arms, as they watched the setting sun. Its mantle of red and gold filled the sky. They lay together until the light faded and darkness took over. It was time for him to go. She made her way home, back along the path, the moonlight following at her heels. The night was chilly but the memories of the day and the knowledge that they would soon meet again kept her warm. Reaching the churchyard, she whispered: "Until the next time my love," as she placed a small bunch of wild flowers upon his grave.

Frooti

Reg Holder

A tide of humanity ebbs and flows on the platform. This is India. Porters rush suitcases to the train, piled high on their heads and their bow legs carrying impossible loads. The *chai wallah* sends his cry through the throng, small cups dangling from the yoke around his neck as he dispenses hot sweet tea with dexterity. We push our way through the crowd and manage to find our carriage. Every seat is booked against a name and assiduously checked by the conductor; Sanjay and I are in 2 *Tier AC,* which means we are accommodated amongst our fellow passengers but have some privacy with curtains and a long bunk seat for when we need to stretch out and rest. Whistles blow and a flourish of the guard's flag signals the start of our journey. Baruch to Mumbai will take six to seven hours and we have time to get to know our fellow passengers.

A smartly dressed business manager sits opposite, wearing a blue and yellow striped tie to complement a dark blue suit that on closer examination shows some shiny patches on the collar. He pulls a newspaper from his brief case and I notice that there is little in it but for that and a few forms. Mrs Gupta, as we come to know her, sits cross legged against the corner Wrapping her dupatta around her face, she settles herself comfortably and is soon snoring gently.

Sanjay and I engage in desultory conversation, discussing the project and how our client will manage the operation after it commences. Soon he climbs onto the top bunk, his briefcase for a pillow, (one never loses sight of one's possessions) while

78

I half-heartedly read my book and watch the passing countryside. Fields of cotton, mighty rivers that we thunder across on bridges built long ago, the Western Ghats rising up in the distance–all part of a country that is emerging with frightening speed and yet remains timeless.

"Fascinating is it not?" I look up at our fellow passenger, his earnest face leaning forward.

"I am always looking at countryside and I wonder sometimes how the 'Little Master' managed to walk this whole country. You, you are British?" He speaks tentatively, as though frightened to offend me.

"Yes," I reply and return to my book–a clear hint, not taken.

"Yes the British, they did so much for India, this railway for instance, every bridge we go over, built all those years ago. But you had to leave in the end and now we are masters of our own destiny. But sir, tell me, are we better off?"

We pull into a station and I am saved from answering. Another passenger gets in and the two are soon in conversation. I immerse myself in my book again. After a while Sanjay swings down from the upper bunk. Mrs Gupta has also awoken and is enjoying a quiet lunch from her *chatti tin*.

We join in with the others. Mrs Gupta is visiting her daughter and son-in-law, who live in Mumbai.

"He is General Manager of an export-import firm that specialises in marine equipment. It's a very good job," she tells us with evident pride.

The man in the blue suit says that he has an important job down in Narriman Point. He is careful not to tell us what he does and Sanjay and I exchange glances. He is obviously down on his luck and we do not want destroy what little confidence he may have. The other man does not join in much. The steward passes and takes orders for lunch. We order *chapattis*, I have chicken and Sanjay opts for veg.

Mrs Gupta wants to know where I am from and how many children do I have and when do I expect the next grandchild. The man in the suit, following on from our previous discussion, is curious about my business and what I am doing in India. Again we are engaged in the aftermath of the Raj and the progress that has been made since independence. Mrs Gupta says that she is only interested in the present and future and anyway she has family in a place called Leicester and that one day she will visit and maybe even stay there. I explain that this may not be possible and why would she want to leave if she is happy in her present life. She reaches into her capacious bag and pulls out a "Frooti" – a carton juice drink – and offers it to Blue Suit who thanks her, drives the little straw into the carton, and drinks. We are still eating and have *chai* to follow. Later, when we have finished our lunch she delves into her bag again and offers a Frooti to each of us and another to Blue Suit who declines politely but urges us to have one. We take them. That is the last thing we remember.

I slowly come out of deep sleep and wonder why the train has stopped. There's no sound. A white-coated man leans over me, lifts my eyelid and through the blur I see a torch shining into my eyes. I hear him saying something but can't make it out and then relapse back into blackness. My head is hurting and pain pounds at the back of my eyes. Waves of nausea crash through and I am violently ill over the side of the bed. Something awful has happened and I have no idea where I am. A vision of Mrs Gupta looms, a huge fist grasping a carton races up to me, her face and bottom lip twisted into a grotesque leering mass. "Have a Frooti, have a Frooti." I am powerless to resist but dimly hear my voice shouting 'No! No!' Then, nothing.

I come to again with no idea of the time or where I am. My head still pounds but this time I am conscious and can see properly. Across the room I see Sanjay. He does not move, and is in deep sleep. I call for someone to come. I need to know what has happened, what I am doing in this room. A nurse appears at my bedside and gently tells me she will fetch the doctor.

"He will explain all. You have been very sick," she adds, "and for now you must rest."

I fall back, exhausted.

Later that day, I wake again and see that Sanjay is also conscious and sitting up. We exchange a weak lifting of hands, in acknowledgement of the fact that we have survived.

We spend the next few days slowly getting better. We are in Mumbai. We learn that, thankfully, on our arrival at the station, the train conductor noticed we were still asleep. He couldn't wake us. He called an ambulance and we were taken to the hospital, just in time. We have to deal with the aftermath of losing our money, cards and in my case, passport. The police are helpful but do not hold much hope of recovering anything. This sort of crime is common, the inspector tells us, and we should never have relaxed our guard. The Frooti had been laced with opium, and we were lucky to survive such a heavy dose.

Having recovered, I continue work on the contract in the Mumbai office for a while and then move back to Baruch for the start-up of the project. Sanjay has gone on ahead and I travel alone from the station in Borowali.

I am in *2 Tier AC* again. The conductor helps me to find my seat and says he will be along later to see that all is well. I put my case under the bunk and settle down for the journey.

Opposite, sits Mrs Gupta, cross legged in the corner, bag resting on her lap.

Emancipation

Terry Williams

Why don't you join us, become suffragette?
What, tied to the railings, force feeding? You bet!
They're holding a census, we don't have the vote.
Answer their questions? it sticks in the throat.

"Are you blind, are you deaf, lunatic,imbecile?"
Refuse and they fine you five pounds – that's for real.
"Enumeration has to be done."
Tell Enumerator we won't be at home

"Registrar James MacDougall says he must insist."
But you can't count a person who doesn't exist.
I'm joining my sisters out on the street.
To hell with your census, I'll vote with my feet.

In Cheltenham, Manchester, Cardiff, Dundee,
There was Davison, Bowker, Pankhurst…and me.
Edinburgh restaurants, Trafalgar Square,
So long as it wasn't called home, we were there.

We gathered in cafes, walked out on the moors,
Anything rather than staying indoors.
Police searched in broom cupboards, bike sheds, and tents.
Against Enumeration there was no defence.

Did you answer their questions this census just past?
And in their elections, was your vote cast?
For you are a person who counts, don't forget,
Thanks to my time as a suffragette.

It's Not What It Seems
Len Hollywood

Jack Mackay sits in the corner of the bar downstairs, never without a drink in front of him as he tries to get lost in it. He listens to the songs as they come through the speakers from upstairs, it's Brenda singing the blues with a sparkle of jazz in it. She's still pulling them in upstairs, with her band.

Jack moves his fingers over the ivories, only it's just a beer-stained table. Someone sometimes might see a tear roll down his face as he hears the notes he should be playing. Then he holds his drink up to Brenda upstairs; only four songs to go. It's time to fill up again, two doubles in one glass, for the road. He takes it back without spilling a drop. Stands the empty glass on the bar while the last song comes down to him.

It's one of his. She's letting him know she's still got it and he should know it. All he had wanted for so long was to help make her a star, the real star she had wanted to be – the golden albums, the shows around the world. They had finished her eighteenth album in twenty-two years on the road. The twins were in Findhorn with her family, but they joined up every school holiday, wherever they might be. Then that night in El Salvador, when she was let down by someone he'd never known about, and Brenda knocked him over and his left arm went through a glass coffee table, leaving him with only sixty per cent use of it. Still she kept him around for the kids and then just in case he came up with something new for her. Which he did once or twice a year, just to keep his hand in, she thought.

Now here she comes down the stairs, Queen Brenda with some new toy boy on her arm. Seeing Jack, she waves him away yet again as she gets into her car, and the boy shuts the door. She smiles at him as the radio comes on. The DJ's voice comes through saying that he's going to play songs from the first CD by Joanne MacKay. All the songs are written by Joanne and her father Jack MacKay, so it looks as if she's going to follow in her mother's footsteps. As it comes on, Brenda grabs the steering wheel, and screams and screams, all the way through the song. The boy jumps out of the car and runs for it, back into the bar. People going by look in at her as she pulls away with a screech of tyres, trying to pull herself together. Not quite two miles from home her car stops dead, as Joanne comes back on with the last song of the radio show.

Grabbing her bag from the back seat, Brenda finds her phone. It's dead. Turning, looking out of the car at the night, yanking the keys from the dash, she opens the door. As she gets out, her high heel catches in the door frame and breaks off. Locking the car, she takes off her shoes and heads home through the grass as the rain starts. She tries to hold up the hem of her dress, after all it cost her around four hundred dollars in Monterey last year. With each step she feels as if she has been cheated by them both. Something runs across her foot. She lashes out at it, landing on her arse. She staggers up, turning into their drive, key ready, goes in, slams the door behind her.

Looking in the main room, she sees Jack sitting at a baby grand piano playing her favourite song.

"Bastard, you bastard," she yells at him as her stocking feet squelch up the wooden stairs, into the bathroom. She struggles out of her wet things, dropping them on the marble floor. Brenda looks in the full length mirror, remembers when it was put in, with her standing in a white towel advertising it for a magazine, so long ago – as her hand goes to the tap she remembers all her past attempts to look younger. She turns the handle. Cold water left in the pipe comes from the overhead shower – as it hits her it's the last straw, and her knees buckle. Sliding down the wall, sitting, she cuddles her knees as tears come while the room fills with steam. Suddenly she feels her age, not young not old just somewhere in between, stands up, finds a bottle of Jardins Du Monde Moroccan Orange Blossom and Jasmine shower gel. She takes her time in the shower, drying off, hair wrapped in a soft white towel, and comes down dressed in a rich plum negligee.

Going into the kitchen, she dumps all the clothes in the bin, comes into the front room. Jack's sitting on a sofa – in front of him on a coffee table is a large vodka and tonic next to his whisky – sprawled over the table are photo albums, he's looking at photos from the first time they played and she sang with a six-piece band, on the cruise ship *Maybellene*.

Brenda picks up her drink, watching Jack as he looks at her.

"The *Maybellene's* on her last run. She's heading for the breaker's yard. One more cruise to go – we are on it, one more trip with the old band."

"Why, Jack, why?"

Jack moves across the room to stand by the big window. As he turns to look at her, lightning flashes, thunder crashes, rolls away. Trying to keep his voice low and level, he says:

"Because that's what you do when you love someone."

"Jack, Jack…"

"No Brenda, no more surgery or fake tans. It's me now. This cruise is our last chance. Joanne's finishing your club dates. I've arranged a house sitter till we get back."

With that he goes back to the baby grand piano and starts to play something new.

The River
Sandra Bain

The spluttering engine died. We looked at each other and at Richard, the boat owner. What now? We were still two hours from our destination where we hoped to catch a plane. Now the small boat was stranded in mid stream...

"Don't worry, girls, we'll get it fixed." Richard seemed oblivious to our sense of dismay as he organised his tools and began work on the offending piece of the motor. We were slowly drifting back downstream.

For the previous week Karen, Louise and I had been staying with Richard and his wife in a small jungle village – which bore the name San Francisco – on the banks of the Ucayali River in Peru. Having travelled there for twenty-eight hours on a cargo boat, our plan had been to hire a plane to take us on the return trip. It had all seemed straightforward.

Then we had listened in disbelief to the disembodied voice on Richard's short wave radio: "The plane can accommodate two people and luggage." There were three of us.

The commercial airline would not touch down at San Francisco because the loading pontoon on the river was unsuitable. The alternative was to go by boat to Contamana, about four hours away, where a plane could load safely.

And so Richard worked on the engine. The longer he took, the further from our destination we were. Then the unthinkable happened. He dropped the piece of engine into the water. It sank. As I watched the ripples spreading, a feeling of hopelessness crept in.

"What are we going to do now?" Louise had arranged this trip to visit her friends and she felt responsible. We had to be back in Lima for work and here we were on the wrong side of the Andes mountains, on a jungle river, in a broken down boat.

There was some hope in this disastrous situation; there was a paddle. Had Richard expected engine-failure, or had the paddle been loaded as a precaution? It was needed now ... but one paddle made little impression. Then Karen had an idea. We pulled our flip-flops from our luggage and put them into action. There we were – one paddle, three flip-flops and a gentle flow making for a speed of about one hundred metres per hour as we headed back downstream.

The equatorial sun was beating down on us, its rays bouncing off the water. The air was full of the sounds of the jungle – crickets croaking, parrots screeching and monkeys calling. It was an indisputable fact that the river was infested with piranha, and there were alligators. We were far from civilisation. Snakes and who-knew-what-else lurked in the jungle vegetation. There was no possibility of landing. But Louise just had to go ashore. How running water aggravates the problem of a full bladder!

"What does she want to get out for?" Karen was troubled.

"She'll be going to pick flowers," was Richard's observation, perhaps to lighten the mood, as we somehow steered the vessel in to the bank where there was a trace of beach. Louise swiftly hopped out of the boat and disappeared behind some vegetation – brave girl. We said nothing about the fresh alligator tracks until she was safely back on board.

Time was passing; the sun was sinking fast – no long bright summer nights there. The darkness wrapped round us, warm and humid, bringing closer the smell of rotting vegetation (and occasionally rotting animal). The blackness was punctuated by lightning which flashed over the jungle trees. We heard no thunder, which was reassuring. The flashes were distant. But the thought of spending the night on the river in darkness was disturbing. No one knew where we were. Richard's wife would be thinking we were on our flight and that he would be on his way back down river – nearly home.

"We better not use the torch too much. You never know when we might need it." I would like to have ensured that the alligators kept away but could see Richard's logic.

We might reach San Francisco by morning but we were no nearer getting back to Lima on schedule and there was no way of letting the people there know that we were delayed. That was a concern.

Richard was matter-of-fact about it. We suspected this was a frequent occurrence with a boat as unreliable as his. He pointed out interesting features – the change in sounds as the nocturnal creatures came to life; the Pole Star just visible low on the horizon - though we had our doubts about that and were glad he wasn't navigating by the stars.

Somewhere ahead of us this river flowed into the mighty Amazon. Not too far to the east of us this jungle became part of Brazil. We were a long way from where we needed to be – Lima on the Pacific Ocean.

We each had our own thoughts and I'm sure, like me, the others were praying for some solution. Our shoulders and arms were sore with paddling. Where could relief come from? There was no sign of habitation. We longed to see even a tiny peep of light indicating the presence of another human being, but there was just blackness.

Karen started to sing and we all joined in:

"Row, row, row your boat gently down the stream!" This made us laugh, and we relaxed a little.

Above the jungle noises and our voices there came another sound – faint. *Peki -peki, peki-peki, peki-peki.*

"Listen." There was a smile in Richard's voice. The sound was now unmistakeable. We were hearing the engine of the large dugout canoe used extensively in the jungle, and known as a *peki-peki* because of its sound.

Richard flashed the torch and we yelled loudly. A light flashed back. The crew had seen or heard us.

It's strange how relative feelings of danger are. We had no idea who might be in the *peki-peki* and imaginations went to work. Maybe it would be preferable to spend the night on the river. We couldn't understand what they were calling. Richard spoke to them – he seemed to know a little of their language. We trusted his judgement and his considerable knowledge of the jungle inhabitants.

As their light approached us we knew we could do nothing but wait. We were at their mercy whether they were pirates or bandits or friendly. There were still tribesmen who were antagonistic to white people and although they sounded friendly we could not be sure. As they loomed out of the darkness, a few yards from our little boat they looked quite fearsome.

"Fishermen. Taking their catch to San Francisco. I've bought from them before." It was some relief to hear Richard's explanation. "They're going to throw us a rope and tow us down river." Would they be true to their word? Would they think we were easy pickings? There was a belief that all foreigners were rich. If they only knew how little we had between us.

The *peki-peki* skimmed through the water in spite of the extra weight of our little boat being dragged along behind.

The immediate problem seemed to be resolved, as we saw the lights of San Francisco. The fishermen had been true to their word. They were rewarded and there was much handshaking and goodbyes.

"Good morning, girls." Richard and his wife greeted us the following day when we appeared for breakfast.

"Just come and have a look at this." He beckoned us to the window. There on the river was a completed pontoon. "They started building yesterday after we left. When news spread last night that we didn't reach Contamana they agreed to be at the river early this morning to finish it. I was down helping them."

"Do you think the plane will land today?"

"I've been on the radio and they're going to come in for you. It'll be about an hour."

It was a long hour as we sat near the river surrounded by our luggage, wondering. Then the plane came, like a large white bird skimming the water and gliding in to the edge of the new construction.

The Seaweed Gatherer
Catriona Tawse

It was when the coach was halted in the flow of traffic that I caught sight of the rusty red roof. There would be ample time before dinner to come back for a closer look at the old house once we had been decanted at the hotel at the end of our tour of the Trotternish Peninsula. The new bridge was a wonderful feat of construction and a great saver of travel time.

Even if my arthritic knee would have allowed me to climb over the dry stone wall, a jungle of whins and bracken posed a further deterrent. Not that there was much to look at: pale yellowing walls beneath faded sheets of corrugated iron, the missing windows staring blankly and part of the old front door hanging by a hinge. Skylights open to wind and weather, one chimney fallen in on what would once have been a welcoming hearth and on either side of the low building, ridges and hollows a reminder of time-old attempts at cultivation.

"I wonder who once lived here?" I turned from my leaning position on the dyke.

"That was Femmin's house," a voice answered. I must have spoken out loud.

I saw a very old man, buttoned up in an ancient khaki greatcoat, his clear blue eyes steadily meeting my startled gaze. On the end of a rope was a small brown dog of indeterminate breed, who looked to be easily his master's equivalent in canine years.

"Femmin stayed here for many years after the war and then he just disappeared. He was never heard of again. Some say the fairies took him." He spat on the ground. "There were some strange goings-on."

My writer's curiosity prevailed over the notion that the old guy was a little wandered in his mind.

"Tell me more about Femmin," I began, wondering if he'd been a bit 'you know'.

"Femmin was a very manly fellow and a great athlete in his day." The old man must have heard doubts cast before.

"He used to gather seaweed along the shore. The Gaelic word for seaweed is Feamainn. 'There's treasure in seaweed,' was what he always said. He was a great man to have at a ceilidh, he gave us all the old songs. There was quite a few of the girls had an eye for him but he was a bit shy for that sort of thing."

We walked companionably to a wooden bench where he sat down and seemed to expect me to do the same. The little dog flopped on to the grass with a sigh.

I told the old man my name and my reason for being in the area.

"Pleased to meet you," he said. 'I'm Murdochan, son of Iain, son of Seumas." A piece of some Runrig song sprang to my mind.

"When he came home from the war Femmin – the name he was blessed with, was Finlay, Fionnlagh in the mother tongue – he was a changed man. As were many others, though I was but a boy myself. One side of his face had been badly burned and his eye was slanting down, there was no sight in it. There was only tufts of hair left on his head so he always had on a bonnet. You seldom saw him out of the house unless for the shop or to the church, but he stopped going to it as well. People stared and children called cruel names and the young girls all turned their heads away. He was spending his time along the shore picking up bits of anything and filling his barrow with seaweed, you would hear the squeak of its wheel at all hours. And sometimes he would be wailing at the turn of the tide, usually when the moon was coming to its fullest. It was the saddest sound you ever heard."

"You'll know yourself," he turned to me, "that the ground is better off for a bit of seaweed, but Lord alone knows what Fionnlagh wanted with it all. He kept a cow and a few sheep and hens and planted bits of crop and enough potatoes to do."

I offered him a pastille from the packet in my bag, thinking he'd be dry from all the talking but he said no thanks he was fine.

"Then one day when Dougal the post went to Femmin's door, he saw a woman putting washing across the wire of the fence. A small woman in a long green dress down to her feet. Her eyes were the blackest he had ever seen and her skin as dark as a gypsy. A curly tangle of brown hair grew almost to her waist.

"'Nach e latha breagha a th'ann,' she said as Femmin appeared in the doorway. He thanked the postman for what he had brought then after a minute he explained that the woman was called Freyann, she'd come to him across from Skye in a boat. Dougal finished his round at top speed to get back to the village with the news.

"After time had passed, the remarkable situation became accepted, people left them alone to get on with life. Femmin and Freyann seemed content together. There was even word of a child coming. Femmin still gathered his seaweed and he took to going out in the boat with Gimlet, an old fisherman, trawling hand lines for mackerel and coleys. Freyann had taken an appetite for fish, in the way women become needy when they are with child.

"Gimlet told folk he would never forget returning to the shore at the fading of the day only to see Femmin's barrow tipped on its side close to the outgoing tide, the seaweed spilling over onto the shingle. He made his way up the brae to Femmin's house as fast as his old legs would take him. There was not a soul to be seen. The front room was neatly tidied and a fire still burned. The paraffin lamp sat silently on the dresser. Gimlet pulled open the door of the other room but he couldn't get in, the place was packed with seaweed from the floor to the low ceiling. There was a bit of a tunnel going into it as if some creature had burrowed in and out. A terrible fear came on Gimlet and his breath went in gasps with the smell, the awful smell."

Murdochan gave his nose a blow. I worried that the telling was becoming too much for him.

"The policeman and two of the roadmen went back the next day with graips and a couple of terriers in case there was rats ran out. I'm not sure if I should tell you what they did find, they all lost their breakfasts with the sight of it. Well, anyway, right in the middle of the seaweed den they found a small body, a child's body long in size and with a skin covering part of its face. There was no proper feet on it and the wee arms were like the bent wings of a penguin. Someone of high authority had to be called from Inverness."

I tried not to dwell on such a gruesome end for any living being. Murdochan got up and announced that he would walk the rest of the way back with me. I promised him a very large dram once we'd got there and thanked him for such a fascinating tale. Not that I believed it for a minute.

A tour bus rumbled past, reminding me that I'd need to put a step in it if I wanted to make myself presentable for dinner.

"But that's not all," Murdochan tugged on the dog's rope.

"Gimlet had another queer thing happened next time he went out in the boat. Two big grey seals bobbed up and swam alongside him as he pulled on the oars. One of them had a patch of white scarring down the side of its head and Gimlet reckoned it was blind in one eye."

Observation Car

Janet Macdonald

The train judders out of the station and clanks its way across the points on its well-worn route to the south. Meanwhile, its passengers arrange themselves for the journey, checking seat reservations, waving to relatives, stowing luggage, choosing the most advantageous places for better leg room, draught-free space, a quick exit, or perhaps even congenial company.

The people in the seats opposite are an elderly couple who chortle happily as they settle, and rustle amongst their belongings to unearth a bag of snacks for their journey.

"We mustn't forget the nosebag!"

Confident in their shared memories, they are brimming with long rehearsed witticisms. The topic this morning is Great Aunt Maude the Spinster, and how frightfully difficult it was to persuade her to co-operate when one wanted to have a jolly trip together with her. Inexplicably, she seemed to prefer to travel alone.

The couple are returning from a coach tour to Loch Ness, travelling with their not-so-young daughter. Strangely dependent, she is tolerated in a somewhat restrained way. A fellow traveller from their tour joins them for a while, and gets out a board game. She takes pains to explain the rules (rather loudly) to the dependent daughter. The daughter seems to have little problem in understanding what she has to do. But the parents are delighted with their friend's tolerance and perseverance.

She lets the daughter win of course, and heaps her with extravagant praise.

Sitting beside me is a young lad with a twitchy left leg, which he bounces continually. Is he impatient to see his girlfriend, or did he forget to buy a ticket? It's difficult to say. He unplugs himself from his iPod, which continues to play tinnily to the rest of the coach, then he rings his mum, and inevitably we all hear his story.

"Maam?"

I recognise that tone of voice and so does the man opposite. We smile knowingly at each other. We twinkle. We almost wink.

"I've no cash, I've had no breakfast, I've got no lunch, and I'm staarving."

He seems to be living off a bottle of Irn Bru. Why didn't he buy a sandwich instead? Well, no doubt she will rescue him. It's what mums do.

Now here is a lady who has arrived late. She is nicely dressed in matching navy cardigan and skirt, with just a little gold brooch to set it off. She tries to persuade the man opposite to move seats.

"Do you *mind* sitting by the window, or what do you prefer..?"

He is not moving seats but, sighing heavily, he stands to allow her in. She is not sitting down yet, but struggles rather plaintively down the train to rescue her bags, while he gives the odd horsey snort, jingling the coins and keys in his pocket, waiting with barely contained impatience for her return. It takes her some time, but it would be uncharitable to imagine that this was intentional. She successfully recruits him to put her bags on the overhead shelf.

"Would you mind terribly? Thank you *so* much."

She won that round, then.

Finally, just behind my head, a couple are sharing plans for their daughter's wedding, with two fellow travellers. Apparently the wedding has resurrected many long-held grievances between members of the family, and the negotiations over who should attend have dissolved into outright acrimony.

"Six bridesmaids and one bride tha's just ridiculous. I feel sorry for 'er, really I do. I'm sure they could've met each other 'alfway. All of a sudden the granddad who 'asn't seen 'er for years wants to come and see 'er. Well Chloe just said no, I'm not giving 'im any second chances. Some of 'er aunties 'ave started Facebooking 'er. Really it 'as to be all or nuffink. D'you know what I mean by that? You know what I mean?"

The two fellow travellers nod sagely. They are wondering what is left in the fridge for tea.

In the centre of this activity is a somewhat sombrely-dressed woman, heading for the office. Clearly she has Important Matters on her mind. She therefore has no intention of speaking to anyone in the carriage unless it is absolutely essential. Her glasses slide to the end of her nose as she frowns at her laptop; but she occasionally melts with a wry smile. She taps the odd key, stares out of the window and then types frenetically for a while:

"When will they all SHUT UP is what I want to know. This is a Quiet Coach and instead of getting my work done I find myself writing about them."

Heron

Christina Macdonald

Tall, motionless he stands
In the reeds by the sea.
Neat, sober-clad
Regarding with disdainful detachment
The busy-body flock of sanderlings
Scuttling across mud flats
In search of food.

He stands aloof, hunch-backed,
The elder by the church door,
Observing the chattering classes passing by,
The worldly bird-throng.
Sober-suited, grey back hunched,
He looks out, complacent, over a calm sea.

Soon he will rise, swoop and fly
On long slow wings
Beat, beat, beat,
Long legs stretched out behind
Beak, a beacon,
Heading for the meal he hopes
Awaits him on the far grey shore.

Nowhere to Hide
Louise James

It was dark under the table, but this added to its attraction. Here Mikey could play with his yellow JCB, given to him by Uncle Norm, and not get in Mummy's way. Today he was going to dig up the road again. It was hard work and he had to keep rolling over to make sure he got round all the parked cars and didn't bump into the wheelie bins and broken shopping trolleys that had fallen into the road. He rolled closer and closer to the back wall and hummed very quietly to himself as he finished off one side of the road and prepared to reverse into the side street. It was a tricky move, and the tracks of the digger caught on the cable running down from the portable telly that was balanced on the table. Mummy had the volume up high and he heard voices talking about the price of a lovely necklace. The noise was good; Mummy couldn't hear him, and the telly muffled the sounds of Mummy talking to herself as she slammed around the kitchen, back and forth to the door of the flat, looking out into the hall, back again.

CRASH! The telly fell to the floor. Mummy yanked the long oilcloth back, and her hand with the sharp red nails grabbed him by the arm. He felt himself being dragged across the kitchen floor.

"You Little Monster! YOU LITTLE MONSTER!"

Each monster got louder and louder as Mummy bore down on him. WHACK. That was her hand across his arm. SMACK. That was her hand across his face. Slap. Slap again, and she threw him against the wall where he landed with a sickening thud.

Cowering, Mikey brought his arms up to his head, the taste of blood filling his mouth. His eye hurt where Mummy's sharp nail had run across his face. She was crying, she was screaming, she kept running to the door and looking out, then back again.

"You broke the bloody telly, you little monster." But now she was moaning, not shouting, and she sank down on the floor beside him, shaking. She put her arms out and tried to pull him to her. He drew away, whimpering.

"I'm your MUMMY!" she shouted. "I LOVE YOU! You'd better get up and do as you're bloody told. Now go to your room or I'll throw you there."

Before she could carry out this threat, the door opened and in strode Uncle Norm.

"Jeez, Donna, what've you done to the kid? Jeez, he's bleeding all over the place."

"Shut up about Mikey. Did you get the stuff? Gimme, gimme, Norm, I'm sick, I thought you were never coming."

She reached shaking, sweating hands out to him, lunging for his pockets, tugging at his sleeves.

"Okay, okay, relax babe. I got it, I got it. It's good stuff. I met Dave."

Donna was barely listening; she was sorting out her gear and tearing open the little packet he'd thrown on the table. She sat down, crying, as she struggled with the tourniquet. It wasn't until she felt the wave of euphoria creeping over her that she slumped forward and rested her head on her arms.

Norm put the kettle on and lifted a limp and whimpering Mikey onto the settee where he tucked a blanket over him.

"Com'on babe." He bent over Donna, stroking her head. "I'll run you a bath. You'll feel better."

She moaned in thanks, a smile creeping over her tear stained face.

"See to Mikey, will you? The telly fell on 'im when he pulled it off the table."

Norm didn't answer but glanced over at the boy, who was now lying quietly. He reassured Donna and helped her to the bath. She sank down, buried in bubbles, the world a brighter place now. Norm took two mugs of tea through, slammed the door shut behind him and sat on the toilet lid, lighting reefers for them both. Soon they were giggling and talking loudly.

Mikey thought dimly that Mummy would leave him alone now for a while. Later Norm would go out to the chippie. He needed the toilet, he thought through a haze, but Mummy and Norm were in the bathroom and the door was closed. When he could hold back no longer he stopped trying and warmth filled his trousers. He knew Mummy would be angry later, but for now he could only think of the thumping in his head and the pain in his arm. He couldn't move it without crying.

The sound of Mummy and Norm in the bedroom, the smell of fish and chips that filled the flat – nothing wakened Mikey from his slumber. Later Norm picked him up in his blanket, not noticing the wetness or the smell, and deposited him on his bed. During the night Mikey drifted between sleep and a dim semi-consciousness, aware only of loud blasts of music from the stereo. No one disturbed him. Someone opened the door once to look in, but his eyes were closed and they went away.

"Open up! Open up!"

There was pounding on the flat door and whoever it was wasn't going to go away.

"Open up Donna! It's Muriel. Donna! You must open up."

Muriel wasn't fooled by the unnatural silence and banged again. She kept pounding, persistently. It was her fourth visit in as many days and this time she had backup. Donna and Norm roused themselves from stuporous sleep, and Donna staggered to the door, opening it a crack. A man's foot instantly wedged it open. He was burly and authoritative; Donna recognised him from the last Family Panel meeting and fear gripped her throat.

"We know Mikey's here, Donna. He's not at your mother's, we've just been there. Open up, now Donna." His voice was sympathetic, but unyielding. Suddenly all the energy seeped out of her, and tears rolled down her cheeks. She stood back and let them enter.

"He's asleep, please don't wake him," Donna wept, as they looked around for him. Muriel opened his bedroom door and rushed in.

"Jesus Christ!" She choked out, frantically feeling for signs of life. "Oh my God, Donna, oh my God."

Norm had to hold Donna back when the ambulance arrived; she was in no fit state to accompany the body to the hospital. And anyway the police were there now. During those awful hours there was no chance to top up. By the time they led her to the waiting van, the shaking and sweating had begun again.

The Visit

Christine Rolffe-Budd

I tapped gently on his door and with a composed smile I entered his room. I noticed he was dressed and was getting up out of his chair to embrace me. Then he sat down and picked up the opened book on the bed. I asked if he gave everyone the same welcome. Laughing, he replied that he knew it was me by my gentle knock and the slight pause before entering. The others usually barged in, knocking loudly.

I busied myself hanging up his clean shirts that I had ironed carefully, the smalls in the top drawer of the dresser and neatly-folded pyjamas in the second. I picked up his dirty washing, waiting for me in a neat pile on top of his bed, and stuffed it in my bag, remembering to give him the books he had asked for. All the while I felt his eyes following me around the room, as he talked about the staff, the other patients and what he had for lunch. He beckoned me to sit beside him and to tell him all my news - what I had been doing, work, the children - and had I missed him?

"Of course," I said, laughing.

All too soon it was time for me to go. He walked me to the main door of the hospital, firmly holding my hand. I remembered his kiss, and waved as I got into my car. I could still see him in my rear mirror. He stood watching as I drove away. As I turned out of the gates, I noticed he had gone.

On my next visit, I didn't tap on the door or smile, for I knew he wouldn't be there. Instead, I took a deep breath, and with only the slightest hesitation, I walked in. The wardrobe doors were slightly ajar and I saw that it was bare, his locker and the drawers in his dresser empty. The bed had been stripped and cleaned and freshly made ready for the next occupant. I stood at the window for a while, looking at the view that he must have gazed upon. I noticed his arm chair - the cushion still had a faint memory of his imprint. I sat down and stared around the room. The plain magnolia walls, the Highland landscape, and the blue patterned curtains. Wiping the tears from my eyes, I picked up the black plastic bag containing his belongings and left, closing the door quietly behind me.

Old Timers

Catriona Tawse

Remembrance Day

Farquhar watches the programme every year from the cosy comfort of his Pensioner's Apartment. He feels he could almost recite the commentary himself after following it so many times. The day is occasionally wet; it's sometimes bright and dry; it always looks cold. The pattern is unchanging, which is as it should be. Such courage and sacrifice and fearful endurance must never be forgotten. Military band music muffles the intrusive sound of traffic, the flags move imperceptibly against the Cenotaph wall, everyone waits for the royal party and other dignitaries to file into their places. After praise and prayers there comes the poignant reverence of the two minute silence. Farquhar closes his eyes briefly, thoughts of fallen comrades drift ghost-like at the back of his mind. Big Ben strikes, guns fire a salute. Then, as Her Majesty the Queen steps forward to place the first symbolic wreath of red poppies, the old man struggles to his feet, his shaking hand clutching for the edge of the mantelpiece. A half empty teacup shatters on the hearth. Chiding himself for his clumsiness he sinks back into his chair. Other royal family members, political leaders, ambassadors and representatives from Commonwealth countries all make solemn moves to lay their tributes, stepping back and bowing their heads. It is not long before the steps are a sea of bright red and the participants have left the area, possibly returning to indoor warmth and hospitable refreshments and, Farquhar shouldn't wonder, in pressing search of a loo; it's been a chilly morning.

Then comes the part Farquhar enjoys best, the actual March Past with its perfectly-selected pieces of music.

Members of the Armed Forces, Navy, Merchant Navy, H.M. Coastguard, the narrator reads out the lists, adding occasional comments on individual acts of courage. St John Ambulance, Nursing Corps, Land Army, WRVS, no-one is overlooked. Then come the Veterans, proudly representing whichever service to which they had given unflinching loyalty, colourful medals gleaming on sunken chests and heads held high as they file past and the salute is taken.

Ageing remnants of a once vigorous life-force, some are pushed in wheelchairs, legs covered with rugs against the cold, others self-propelling in the more recently introduced mobility scooters. The scene never fails to bring a tear to the old man's eyes.

If you asked him, Farquhar couldn't remember which year, but he had once actually been part of the parade, himself and Dougie Macgregor and Donnie Red and The Kipper and others of his regiment whose names he now found it hard to recall. The terrors and obscenities which they had witnessed were seldom spoken of, but regularly resurfaced in the stillness of a night without sleep: ducking from sudden bursts of gunfire, trudging on exhausted legs over unknown terrain, giving hopeless comfort to what was left of a comrade. And a lone piper's rallying skirl all too often silenced by an enemy bullet.

So few of his comrades are left. Donnie Red spending his failing years at St Dunstans; the Kipper drowned in a boating accident; of Dougie's fate he has no knowledge, he married a Danish girl and possibly moved abroad. All the old timers, he muses, departing this earth one by one. It would soon be his turn. Farquhar inhales a deep breath and zaps the TV to a Sports channel. Time to lift the gloom and yell at some hapless referee.

Fisherman

An old man doing an old job, proud tired back bending to the unending task, the untangled lines slowly curving to fill the willow creel. Frayed at the collar, his faded blue gansey shimmers with the scales of unnumbered catches, his canvas cap tipped down to avert the sun's low morning rays. Callused and arthritic, his fingers spear each shelled mussel onto a hook's cruel barb. His hands are scored with the marks of many years' toil, half a finger lost, the nails split with age. Seagulls scream from a furtive sky. He shrinks inside himself, reaching in his mind to the slipped-past days when he was strong and able, pushing the boat into the sea's frothing margin, salt spray knifing the skin, the tide's mighty force defied by the plunging oars. No time to dwell, he shifts his mind away from the drowned sons and the grief-dead Mother's stricken face. The part he plays now may be small but it is for him a joining to the old way of life and is the provision he must make for a crippled daughter. Fancying there's a call from within the shack behind whose wall he shelters, he makes to rise from his wooden seat, a broken barrel which came swept ashore to him after a night of storm. He is ever fearful that Martha-Ann will come to some harm with the lifting of pot or kettle. The sound comes nearer; it is only the cat. With a smile he throws down a mussel morsel, watching as the animal licks daintily. His morning's task done, the old man lifts the creel to the door; there might be tea brewed. Hoisting its tail the cat follows at his heels.

Pulling Together

Alf Mustoe clambered onto the edge of the cart, huddled himself under the damp jute sack which sheltered his shoulders and flicked the reins lightly over the horse's back.

"Gee up there Dobby, that's a good chap, soon be home now. Cup of tea and a Woodbine for me, nice bag of oats for yourself. Ooooh, it'll be good to get out of this perishing wind."

Patiently the old brown horse leaned into the worn straps to pull the cart forward, his neck chafing where some padding had broken out of the stiff collar. A combination of age and the bitter weather made his tired bones ache as he plodded up the cobbled street, where many chimneys still reeked plumes of grey smoke. The last but one call was on old Mrs Grimmer, who always took her time answering the coalman's knock. Sharp faced with a tongue to match, she was impossible to please. She wouldn't spend a shilling if a tanner would do. The few moments he spent waiting, as she searched laboriously through the contents of a bulging leather purse, were enough to make him glad he was on his own. Flighty Lil, his one-time better half, had gone off with a fat man who sold pies from a stall at a Clapham Common Carnival, and Alf had never felt the need to replace her. He and old Dobby had soldiered along together. Both of us fit for the knacker's yard any time now, Alf would remark with a wheezy laugh.

A blue Bedford lorry from William Millburn Coal Merchants drove past, Alf giving the driver a cheery wave. They would likely meet in the Feathers later, for a pint and a bit of good-natured teasing about how he had never moved with the times. Alf always said one horse power was good enough for him and the old brute was more of a companion than a smelly diesel truck.

Over in Rainers Wynd, Ethel Murphy opened the back door to Alf with her usual friendly smile.

"I heard the coal rattlin' in, thanks Alf, you must be frozen to the marrow on a day like this. Come in for a drop of tea."

"No ta, look at the state of me Ethel luv, I'd make a right mess of your nice lobby. Better get the old nag home anyway, he's due for a break, Gawd bless him, I don't know what I'd do without him."

"Take this then," Ethel held out a brown paper parcel. "Just a wee bit cod our Rosie took home from her work, the boss is a decent sort."

"Cheers Ethel, you're a gem. Be just the thing with a few boiled spuds. There's your two bob change. See you next week then, thanks again."

Alf winced as he climbed back onto the cart. A pain in his shoulder had nagged him for weeks. Never one to make a fuss he'd shrugged it off as a bit of rheumatism, common at his age. The doc would only tell him to take things easy and not be out in all weathers humping heavy sacks. He clicked his tongue at Dobby who seemed to be slowing down a bit on the last lap, feeling his age as well Alf reckoned, as he struggled to recall what that might be. About ninety in human years he guessed. There wasn't much traffic on the side street where Alf had his yard and the two rooms above a rickety stable. Dobby seemed to know his work was done for the day; he harrumphed noisily as Alf began unhitching him from the empty flat cart.

"Whoa, hold still old pal, I'll get this side unhooked." He struggled to reach the leather trace, fighting against the pain in his arm. Perhaps it was time to see the doc, he'd make an appointment on Monday.

"That's it Dobby, soon have this lot off you, steady up there a minute". There was a gurgling sound from the old horse as his front legs buckled and his body drooped in the shafts. Alf strained desperately on the strap to release the bulky cart. He knew something was very wrong. His hobnailed boots scraped on the stone floor. A pail clattered over in the darkness. There was no other sound.

PC Ronald Whittaker was conscientiously doing his rounds at a quarter to midnight. He thought it strange that Old Man Mustoe hadn't closed up the stable as he usually did. Shining his torch, he made his way inside, disturbing a ginger tomcat from its feast of whatever had been in the torn brown paper. Fish by the smell of it, thought the young Constable, wrinkling his nose as he followed the thin beam of light.

An Eye for an Eye
Sandra Bain

Betsy placed five eggs in the pot of boiling water and glanced at the clock. Five minutes and the supper would be ready. She speared a piece of bread with the toasting fork and knelt at the hearth, holding the bread in front of the glowing coals as she waited for the eggs to cook.

Davie and the two boys were already at the table, and she noticed that a piece of oatcake had been surreptitiously moved on to a plate. Betsy always insisted that no one began eating until everyone was seated at the table and the grace had been said. However, her irritation went deeper. With all the girls away from home, one of the boys could be making the toast. But no! All the work of the house was left to her. Davie's job didn't bring in much money and if she weren't so resourceful, they would have problems making ends meet.

She listened to the boys telling their father tales about their day at school and felt thankful that for once Davie was on time for his supper. Sometimes he went to the pub after work, and forgot to come home.

She had turned the piece of bread over to toast the second side when Davie hissed:

"Here's Jocky!" Their old neighbour, drunk again, was staggering up the drive.

"What's he wanting now?" Betsy was exasperated. But she didn't need to ask. Jocky, when he was drunk, always turned up at mealtimes.

He and Davie often used to drink together until it became apparent that Jocky was what they called a "mooch". He had a knack of letting others buy his drink and seldom put his hand in his pocket. Now he had developed the habit of arriving at the house when food was being served.

"Well, Davie, he'll have to have one of your eggs!"

"Will he heck! Lock the door, laddie." And the boy leapt up. They heard the "clunk" as the lock slid into place.

"Take out the key."

Seconds later, as Betsy began quietly lifting the eggs out of the boiling water, the rap came on the door.

They sat still, although the boys were having difficulty suppressing their laughter. There was the rap again, insistent. Then the hammering started. Davie was concerned that he might yet have to give up one of his eggs to Jocky...

"I know you're in there." Then they heard the click as Jocky tried the door. "Open the door, Davie. Let a friend in."

"And give you my supper. Certainly not," Davie muttered.

Betsy was thankful that they had a good strong door as the thumping became fiercer. Then Jocky began to curse and swear...such language! Not for the boys' ears! And not the sort they'd ever heard from Jocky before. He ranted and raved until Betsy felt she would have to go out and remonstrate with him.

Suddenly everything went quiet. Betsy motioned to the boys with a finger to her lips, but they struggled to control their sniggers.

It seemed he had finally gone. They waited.

"I'll have a look." One of the boys darted through to the door before his mother could stop him.

"Don't let him see you," she whispered

"Not likely, Mam."

He bent down and put his eye to the keyhole. All he could see was an eye looking back at him.

Windblown

Terry Williams

Wind plays catch-me-if-you-can
Among trees that change the game
Into pass-the-parcel,
From beech to oak to willow to birch.
Unwrapped gusts
Chase me laughing – tag, you're "it" –
Through the hide-and-seek woods.

The Contributors

Sandra Bain is a native of the Black Isle but has worked in Perthshire and Peru. She has had non-fiction articles published and is Editor of the quarterly magazine of the Scottish Fellowship of Christian Writers. In 2005 her book on the history of Tore School was published.

Reg Holder grew up in East Africa, coming to the UK to train for the Merchant Navy. He is a Master Mariner–after sailing on cargo ships and tankers, he came ashore as a pilot, working in oil terminals. He is now a marine consultant and he and his wife Pat have lived in Ross-shire since 2001.

Len Hollywood has been a member of Ross-shire Writers since its inception. He lives in Nairn.

Louise James has lived in Scotland since 2003. She tries to 'grow where she is planted', drawing on her Canadian roots, as well as her twenty years in Yorkshire, to inspire her writing.

Christina (Taylor) Macdonald enjoyed the privilege of being born in Stornoway and educated at the Nicolson Institute and beyond. After half a life-time teaching young children, she now enjoys writing in the company of her friends in Ross-shire Writers.

Janet Macdonald has lived in Strathpeffer since 1987, with frequent absences for work, which necessitated extensive travel. Having cut her writer's teeth on worthy textbooks, she is now branching out into creative writing with friendly support from Ross-Shire Writers.

June Munro lives at the tropical end of the Struie and needs a forty-hour day and a ten-day week to keep up with everything. She values the friendships and guidance from Ross-shire Writers very highly.

Christine Rolffe-Budd was born in Lancashire, but despite living in the south for many years, has always thought of herself as a 'Lancashire Lass'. Her husband's work took her to Scotland in 1981. When he died, her daughter encouraged her to write and enrolled her with the Ross-shire Writers as a Christmas present!

Catriona Tawse (MacRitchie) has family connections with the Isle of Lewis, Dingwall and Aberdeenshire. She has spent several enjoyable years with Ross-shire Writers, at present working on a series of stories featuring assorted characters in a fictitious Island village. She is much involved with music and the Gaelic language.

Terry Williams describes herself as a travelling writer. When not out on the Highland roads in search of stories, she works in a garret with rooks and an eight-hundred-year-old elm tree peering in the window.